IMAGES
of America

COVINGTON

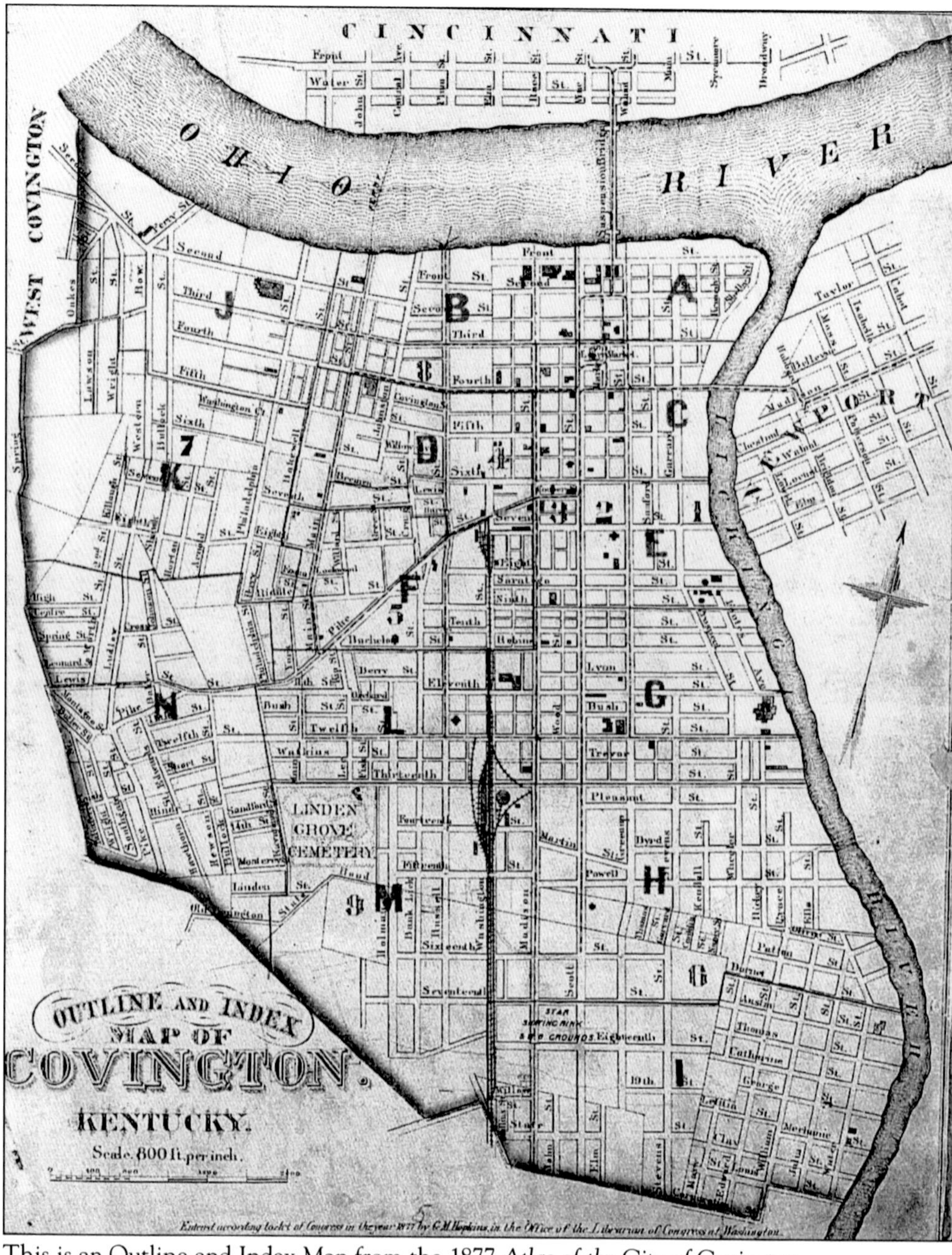

This is an Outline and Index Map from the 1877 *Atlas of the City of Covington*.

IMAGES
of America

COVINGTON

Kenton County Public Library

ARCADIA
PUBLISHING

ISBN 978-0-7385-1543-4

Published by Arcadia Publishing
Charleston, South Carolina

Printed in the United States of America

Library of Congress Catalog Card Number: 2003106428

For all general information contact Arcadia Publishing at:
Telephone 843-853-2070
Fax 843-853-0044
E-mail sales@arcadiapublishing.com
For customer service and orders:
Toll-Free 1-888-313-2665

Visit us on the Internet at www.arcadiapublishing.com

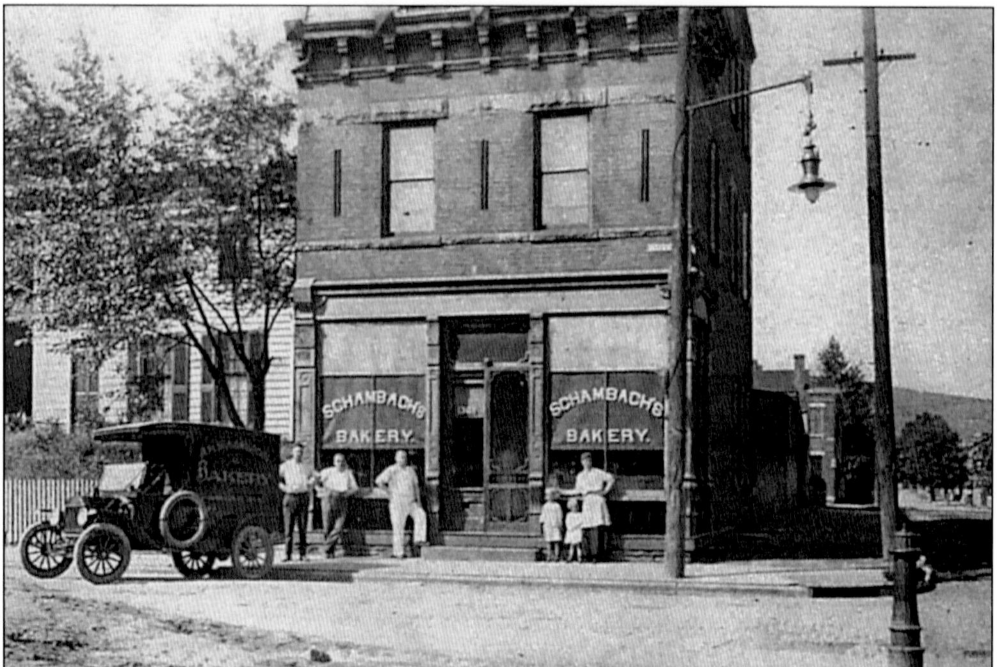

Schambach's Bakery, located on the corner of Banklick and West Thirteenth Streets, became a local landmark during its more than 30 years in business. Corner stores were ubiquitous throughout Covington and provided not only a service but a gathering place. Owned and operated by Philip Schambach, the bakery was photographed in 1912, six years after he opened the shop. The building still stands today.

Contents

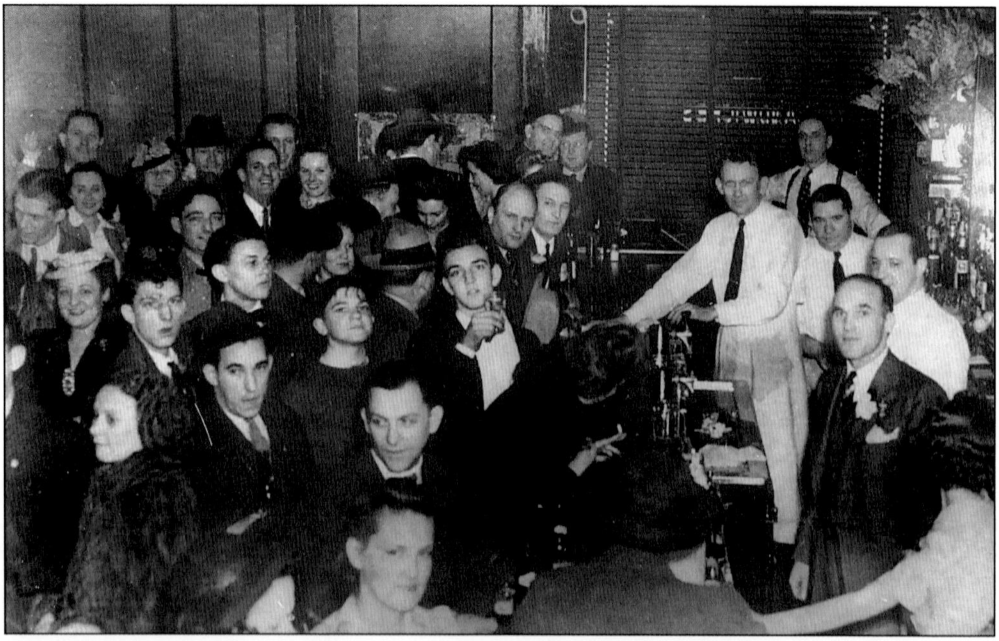

These people are celebrating the opening of the Press Club at 709 Scott Street in 1938. Jim Averdick and Joe Metz were the proprietors. The Press Club remained in business under subsequent owners until 1960.

Acknowledgments

The compilation of this book is the result of the efforts of a volunteer committee composed of Kate Carothers, historic preservation specialist for the City of Covington; Judith Boyers Gee, attorney; Charles D. King, the former local history librarian at the Kenton County Public Library; David E. Schroeder, the current local history librarian at the Kenton County Public Library; and Alexandra Kornilowicz-Weldon, historic preservation consultant.

All of the images in this volume are courtesy of the Kenton County Public Library, unless otherwise noted.

The photo collection of the library, consisting of thousands of images donated by individuals and institutions, is accessible to the public. It includes family photographs, professional photographs, postcards, and letters. Without the past generosity of the community to the library's collection, this book would not have been possible.

We would like to encourage anyone with access to historic images of Kenton County to consider donating or copying them to add to the library collection. Not only would they be available for researchers and students of local history, those images, combined with others already in the collection, could become the genesis for another publication such as this. In addition we would like to thank the following people for sharing their photographs, their memories, and their time: Dr. Joseph Gastright, Lisa Gillham, and Karl Lietzenmayer.

INTRODUCTION

Located at the confluence of the Ohio and Licking Rivers, Covington, Northern Kentucky's largest city, lies directly across the Ohio River from Cincinnati, Ohio. Founded in 1815, the history of Covington often parallels that of Cincinnati, both culturally and economically. After 1820, the success of the steamboat generated much growth and prosperity in the region, attracting a large influx of immigrants, primarily German and Irish, by the mid-19th century. These hardworking immigrants were to make a permanent home in what was often referred to as "America's Rhine Valley," bringing with them their religion, their customs, and their food. For the next century, meatpackers, breweries, and distilleries, alongside the city's many churches and saloons, were to dominate much of the urban landscape of Covington.

After a quick succession of several owners between 1780 and 1801, the 200 acres which were to eventually become the city of Covington were sold to Thomas Kennedy for $750. Kennedy lived near what is now the approach to the Suspension Bridge, where he ran a tavern and a river ferry. In 1814, he sold 150 acres of his land to John S. Gano, Richard M. Gano, and Thomas Carneal. These three men laid out the original plat of the city, which they named for Leonard Covington, a fallen general of the War of 1812. The boundaries of the original plat were the Ohio River to the north, the Licking River to the east, Sixth Street to the south, and Madison Street to the west. The town of Covington was officially established on February 8, 1815 by an act of the Kentucky legislature. In 1834 Covington received its charter as a city.

Growth of the community was slow until the 1830s when early industrial concerns started. The city more than doubled in size with the annexation of the lands subdivided by the Western Baptist Theological Institute, located south of Eighth Street. The enormous numbers of immigrants who arrived in the ensuing decades helped make Covington the state's second-largest city by 1850. The city continued to grow southward and westward. By 1890, State (now Twentieth) Street was the southern corporation line, and Lewisburg, along the curve of the Lexington Turnpike (now Pike Street), had also become part of Covington. By that time, the city had a power and light plant and single trolley electric streetcars. The early 20th century saw continued progress with a wider variety of industries developing and more annexations. Central Covington, Latonia, and West Covington were incorporated into the city of Covington in 1906, 1909, and 1916, respectively. Growth, both in population and area, began to slow down by the 1920s. The Depression, World War II, and the suburbanization of postwar America further curtailed the city's progress during most of the 20th century. Several areas south of Latonia along Madison Pike, however, were annexed in the 1960s and 1970s. These areas became what is now known as South Covington and have experienced tremendous growth and development in recent decades.

The city's population has remained fairly stable, and today the historic areas of Covington are beginning to experience a renaissance. The large amount of solid older housing stock is being appreciated for its architectural integrity and beauty, and the city's convenient location to transportation networks and downtown Cincinnati is making it once again a desirable alternative as a place to live, to work, and to shop.

The images presented in this volume present some of the people, places, and events, which together have woven the unique history of Covington. These maps, sketches, and photographs span almost 150 years, telling Covington's story as words alone could never do.

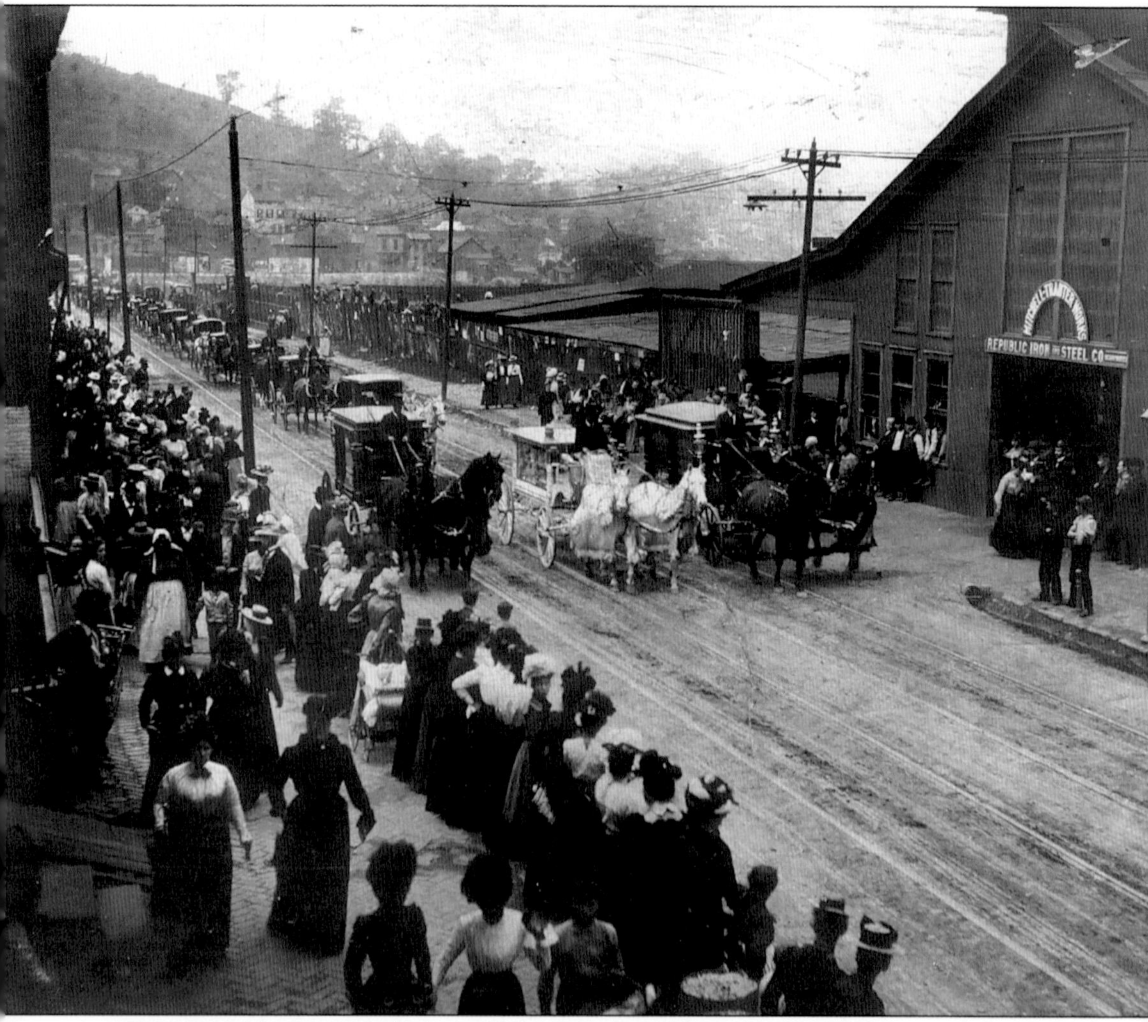

This turn-of-the-century photograph depicts a funeral procession marching eastwardly along Third Street in front of the Mitchell and Tranter Rolling Mill, located at the foot of Philadelphia Street. The mill was opened in March of 1873 by John Mitchell and James Tranter. This funeral is supposedly that of a man, his wife, and their child after he killed them and himself. A white horse and wagon were the tradition for children's funerals.

One

The Public Realm

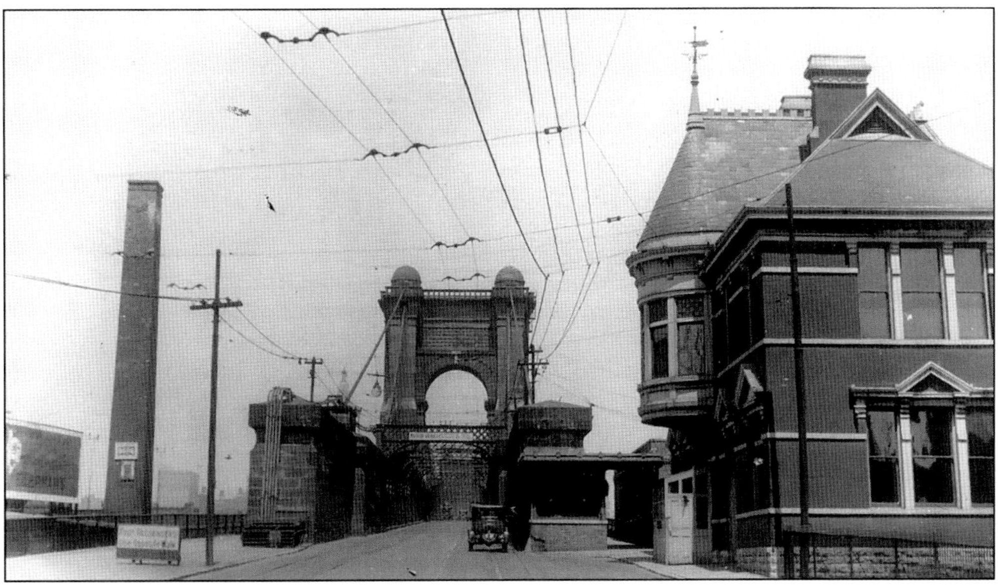

The construction of the John A. Roebling Suspension Bridge was begun in 1856 and completed in 1867. The construction of the bridge took 11 years to complete, due to work stoppages from lack of money and the Civil War. The bridge served as the first gateway into Covington from Cincinnati, and was funded by the Covington-Cincinnati Bridge Company, whose headquarters were located in the building to the right. The bridge, listed on the National Register of Historic Places as a National Historic Landmark, is considered a marvel of engineering. The bridge was the world's longest when it was completed in 1867, having a river span of 1,057 feet. This view is from Covington looking over towards Cincinnati, c. 1925–1930.

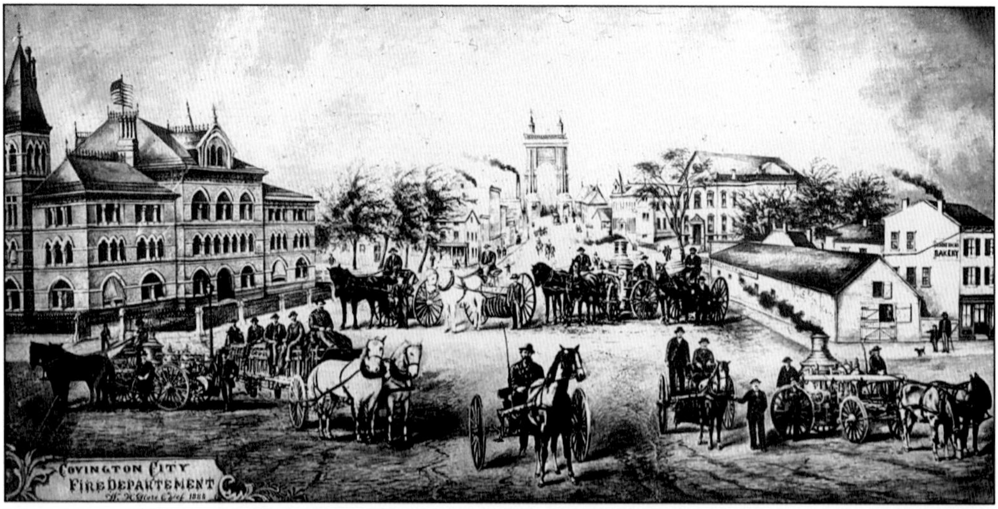

This is an 1885 view of the Covington City Fire Department, with Fire Chief W.H. Glore in his horse-drawn buggy at the center of the photo. The fire companies are assembled alongside the Federal Building on Court Street. The courthouse and Suspension Bridge are visible in the background.

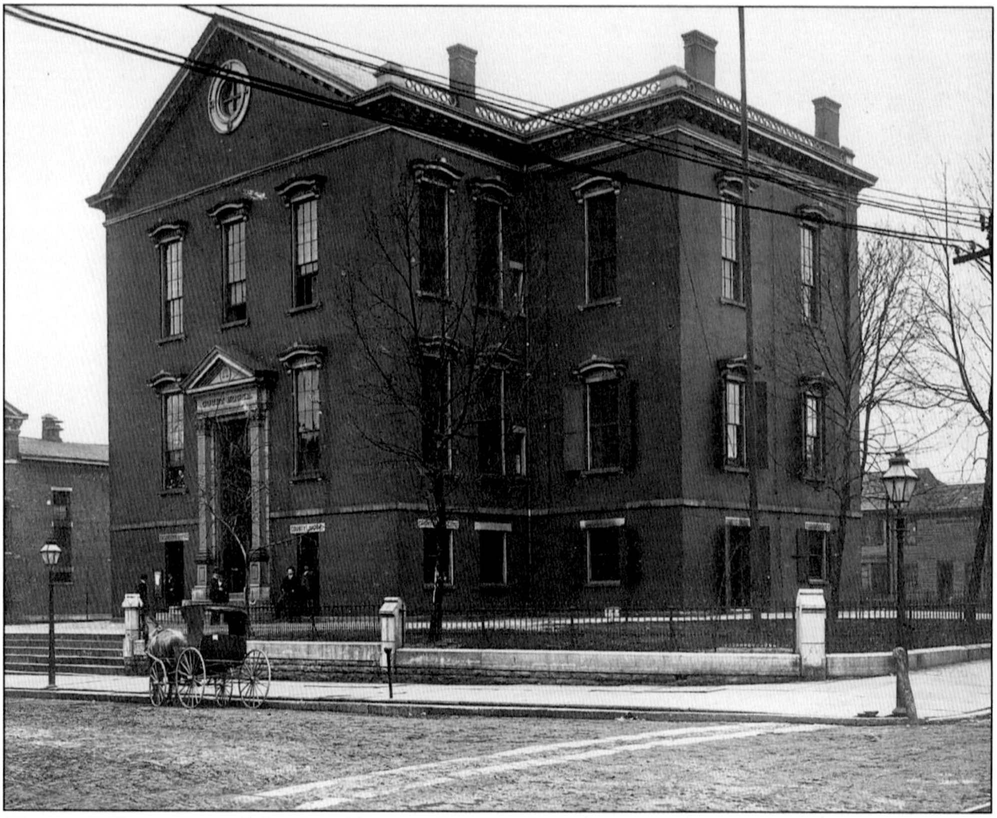

This *c.* 1885 image is of the first Kenton County Courthouse at the northeast corner of Third and Court Streets. This building was renovated in the 1860s to the Italianate style, but was torn down by 1900 for a new courthouse.

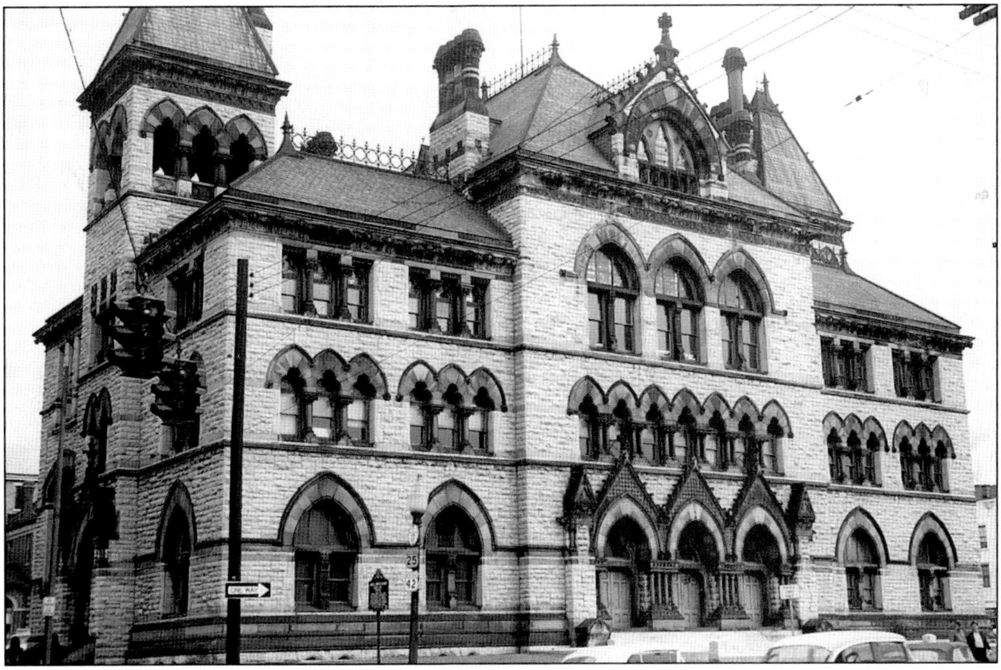

The Federal Building was located at Scott and Third Streets on the site of the current Kenton County Administration Building. This four-story stone, Romanesque style building was constructed in 1867, and served as the main post office and custom house until the federal government moved to its new location in 1938. After that time, the building functioned as a vocational school and then as a storage facility for Kenton County before being demolished in 1967.

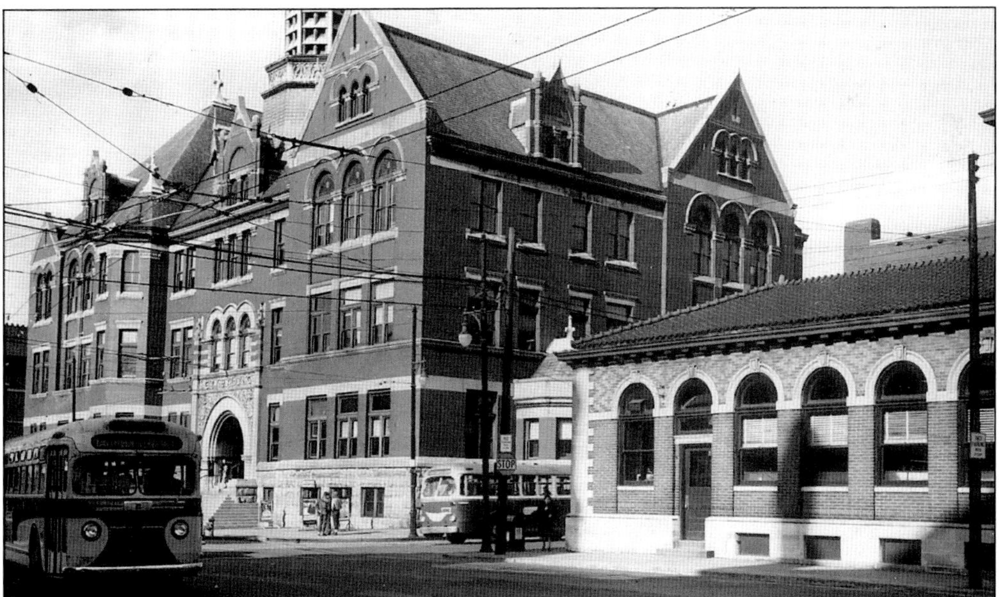

The second Kenton County Courthouse was constructed in 1900. This building was located at the northeast corner of Third and Court Streets. The building also functioned as Covington's City Hall and Kenton County offices until it was demolished in 1970.

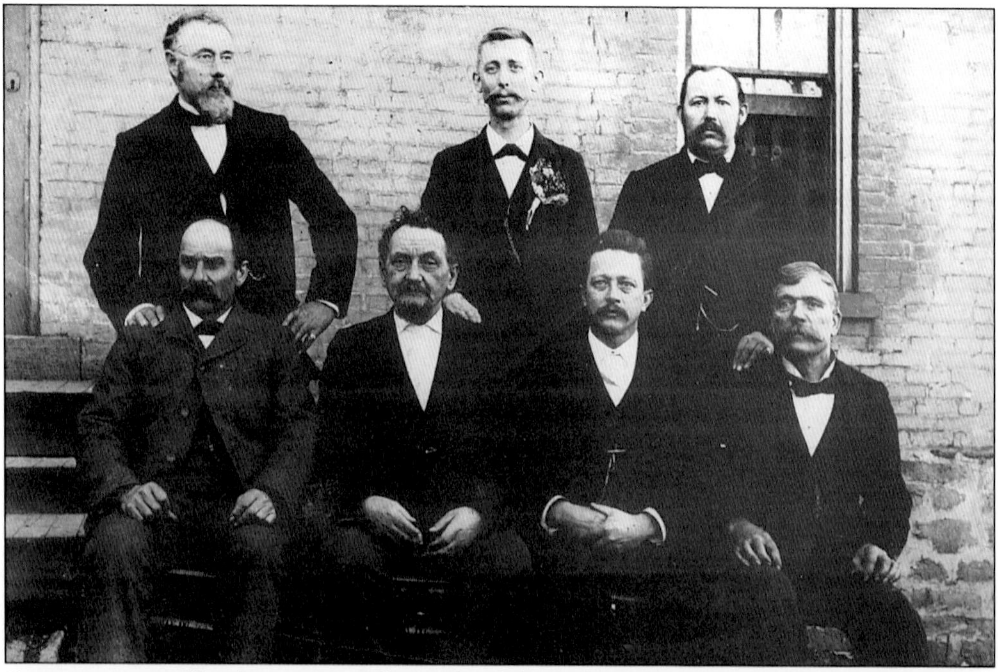

Covington city officials are pictured outside of the Independence Jail, *c.* 1898. Pictured from left to right are (front row) Mike Messingschlager, John Dorsel, Joe Rush, and Charles Avery; (back row) Henry Niemeyer, Tony Nienaber, and H.B. Heulefeld. The officials were put in jail for disobeying a court order.

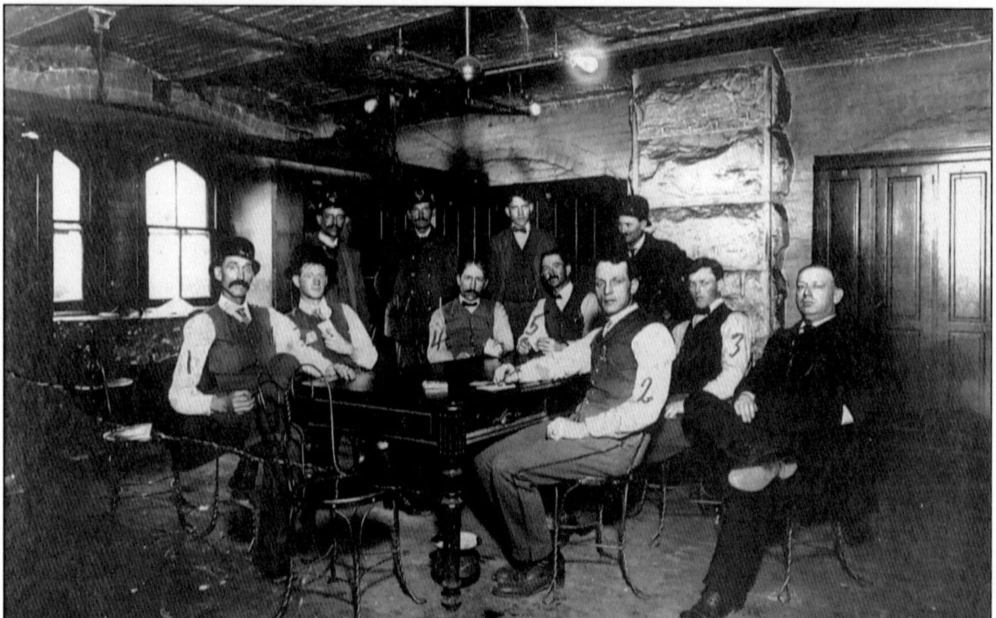

Pictured from left to right (sitting) are George Seiler, Maney Armstrong, Charles Meyers, Bill Piercy, and Ulysses Turner, along with several unidentified men, enjoying a break from work in the basement of the Federal Building, *c.* 1908.

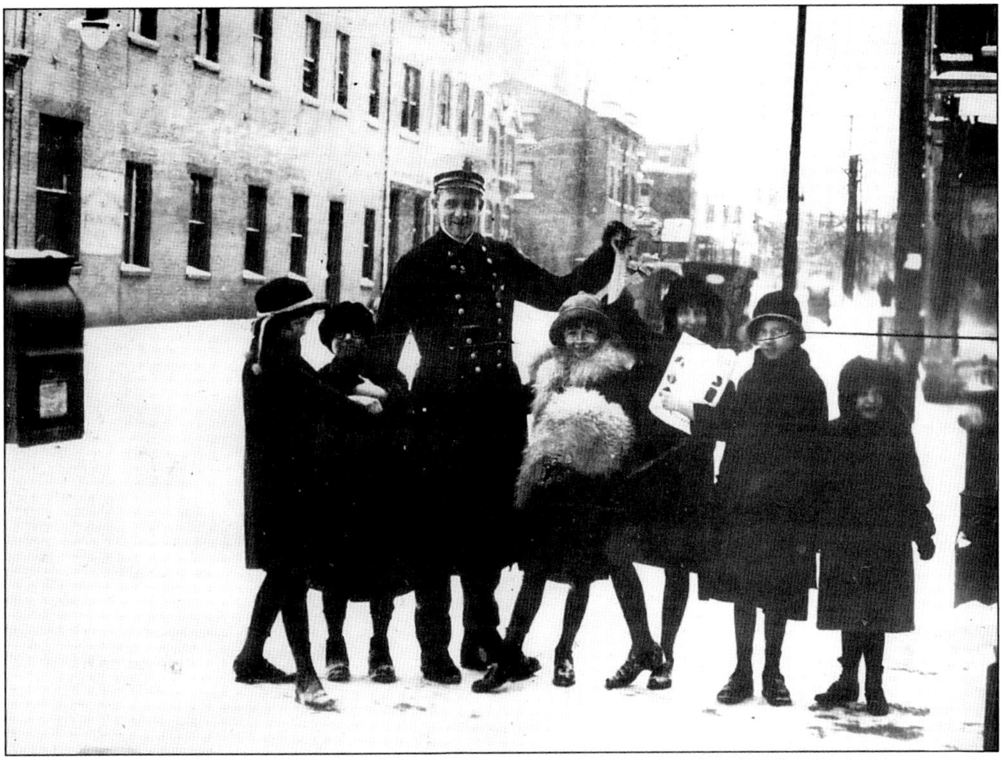

Police officer Tommy Harris was a beloved crossing guard for local school children at the southwest corner of Fifth and Scott Streets from 1912 to 1926. After his death, local schoolchildren saved pennies and nickels to buy a plaque in his memory. The plaque was dedicated on June 1, 1927 and installed in the sidewalk. The plaque is now located on the wall of the Mid-Town parking garage at "Tommy's Corner" on Fifth and Scott Streets.

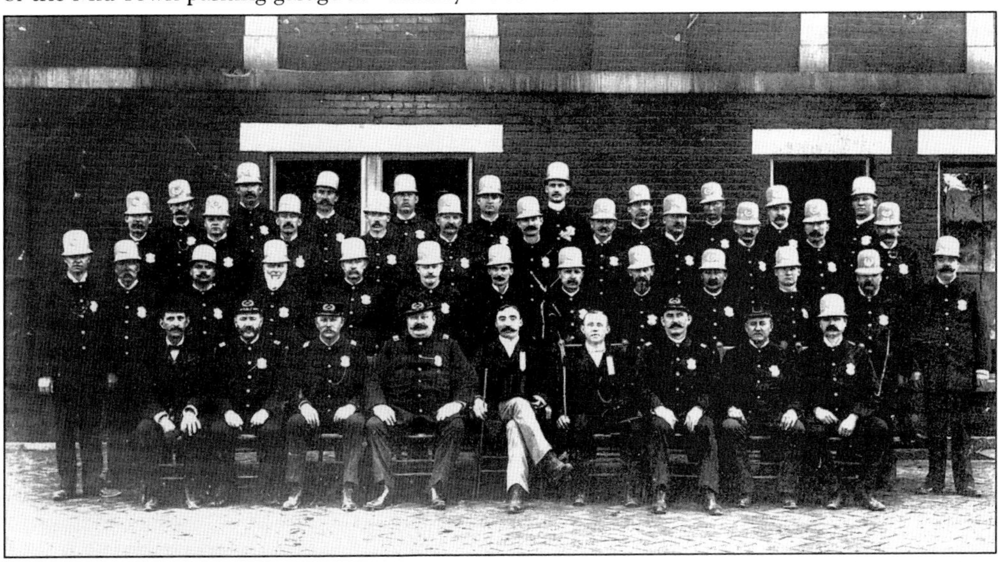

The Covington Police Department is pictured c. 1898. Hon. Joseph Lafayette Rhinock (the mayor) is seated in the front center, with Police Chief Joe Pugh to his left and Alderman Edward Doc Pieck to his right. (Rombach and Groene, photographers.)

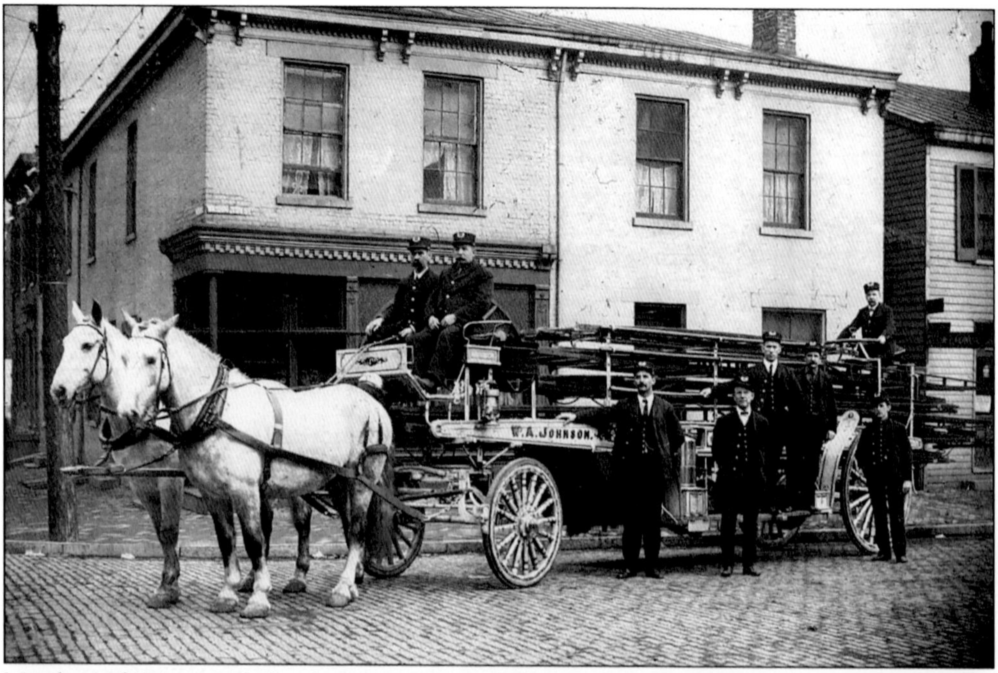

Members of Covington's fire department pose with their horse and ladder wagon, c. 1900. The firemen are on Washington Street. Note all of the different ladders stacked on the wagon and the brick-paved street.

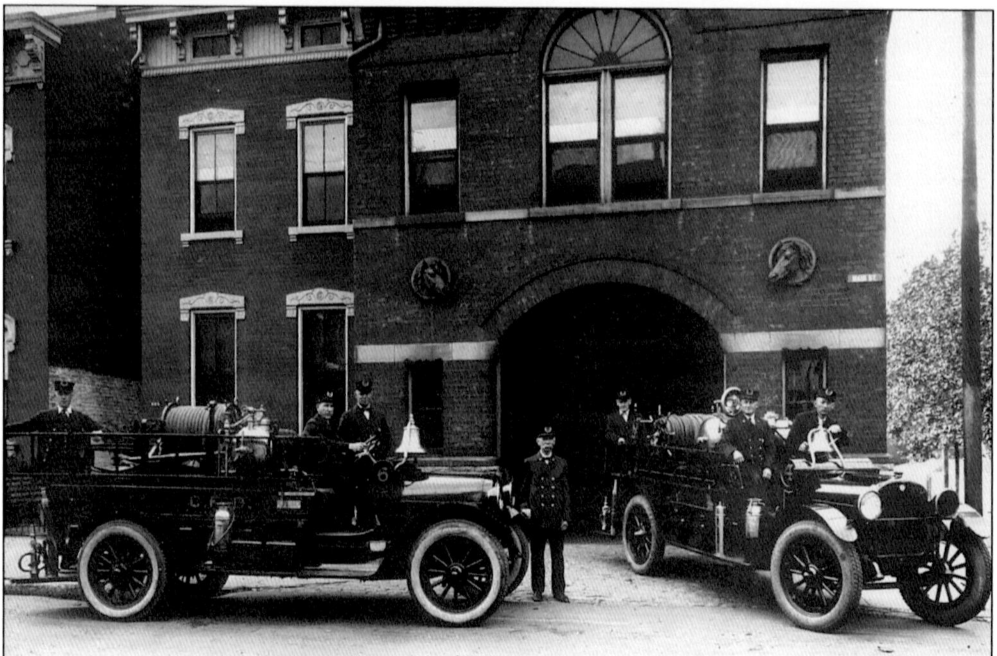

Members of Fire Engine Company No. 4 pictured outside their fire house at the southwest corner of Main and Emma Streets, c. 1920. The firefighters are showing off their new fire trucks. The horses' head sculptures were part of the fire house when it was constructed in 1885, but have since been removed. Today the building is a private residence.

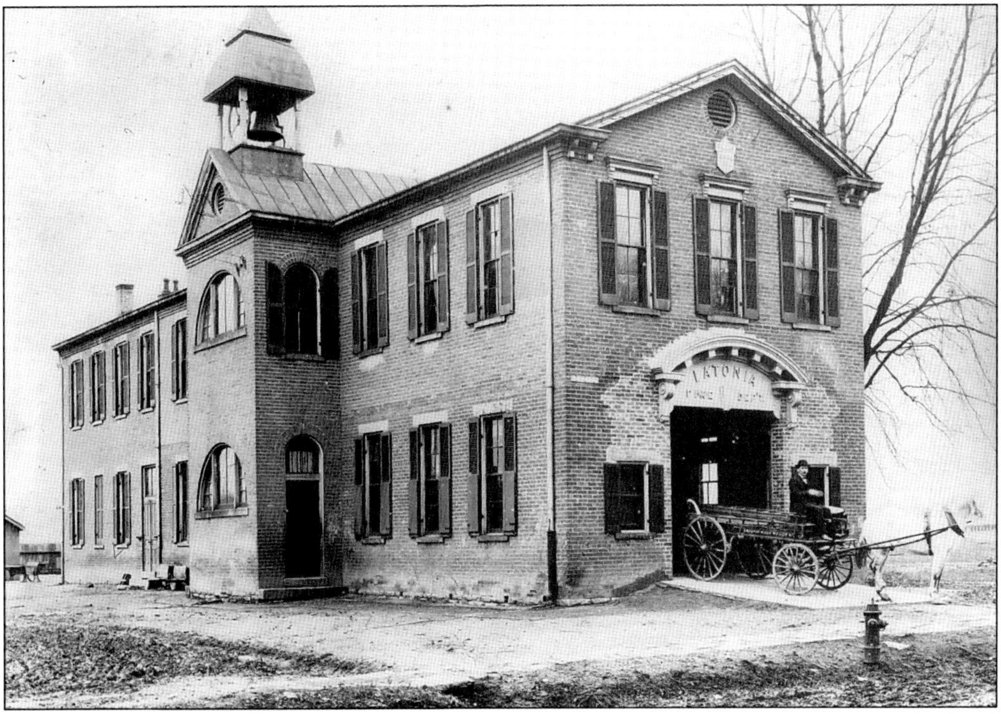

Pictured above is the Latonia Firehouse, c. 1900. The firehouse was in a converted school building. Latonia was its own city with separate services until it was annexed by the City of Covington in 1909.

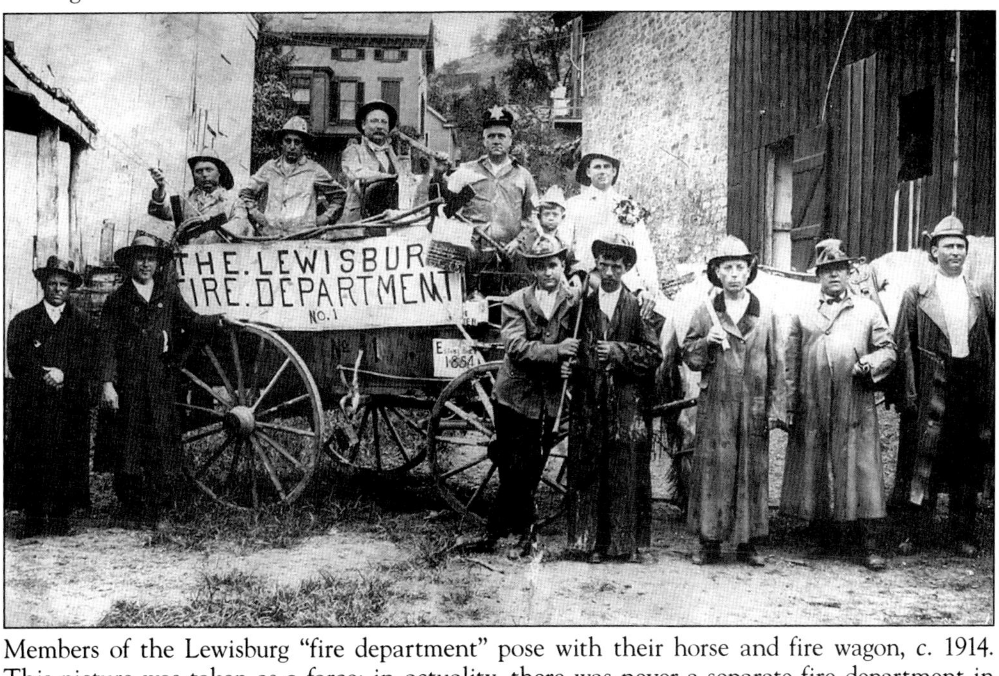

Members of the Lewisburg "fire department" pose with their horse and fire wagon, c. 1914. This picture was taken as a farce; in actuality, there was never a separate fire department in Lewisburg, although the neighborhood clamored for their own station. The men pictured in the photograph are unidentified.

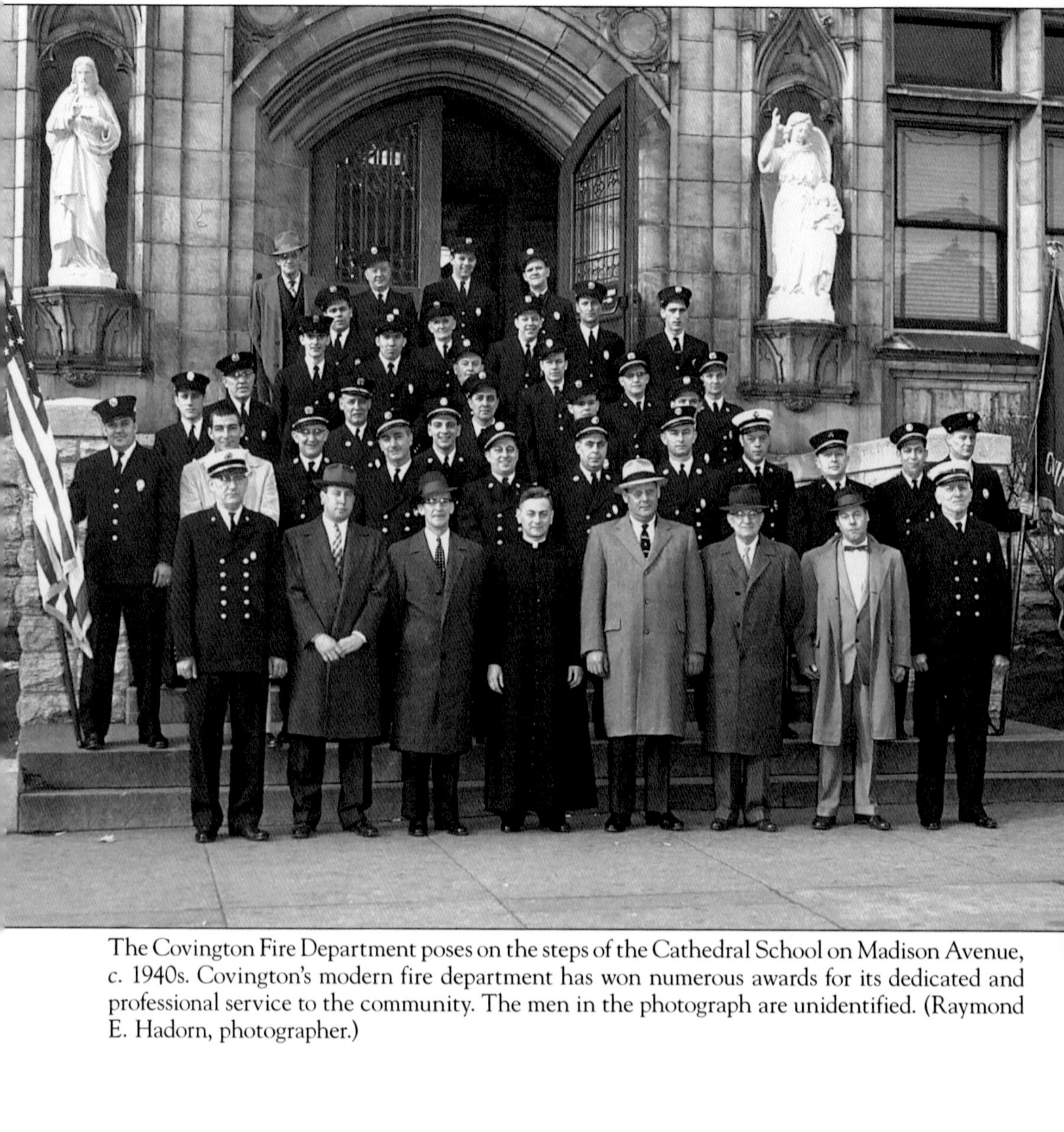

The Covington Fire Department poses on the steps of the Cathedral School on Madison Avenue, c. 1940s. Covington's modern fire department has won numerous awards for its dedicated and professional service to the community. The men in the photograph are unidentified. (Raymond E. Hadorn, photographer.)

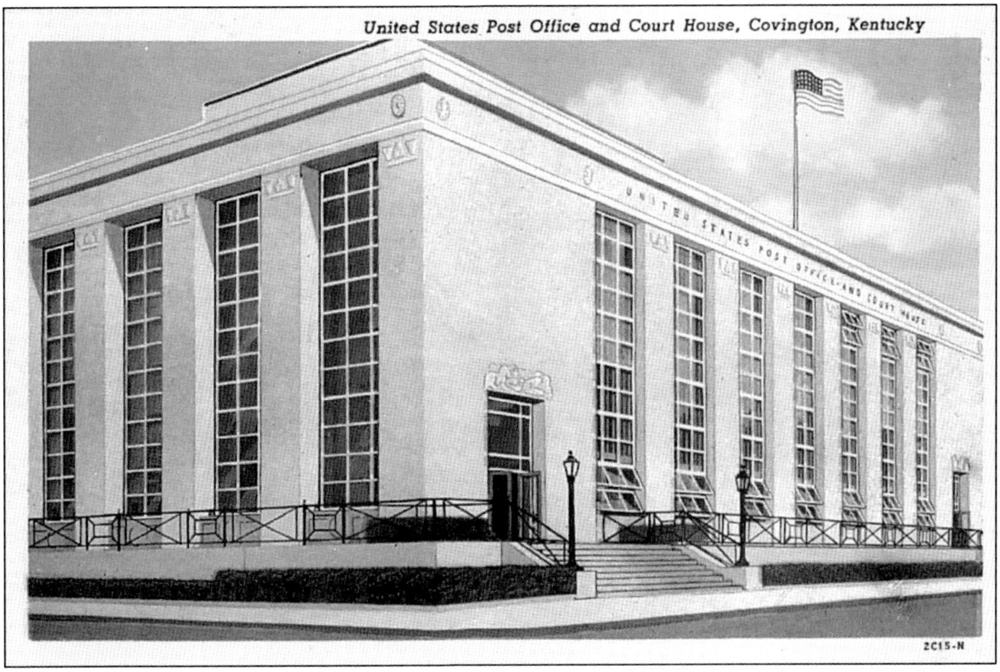

Covington's current post office was constructed in 1938 and is located at the corner of Seventh and Scott Streets. This building was designed by New York architect Thomas Harlan Ellett after he won a United States Treasury sponsored design competition for the building. Ellett's design was chosen from among roughly 650 submittals. The building replaced the Temple Israel Synagogue, among other buildings.

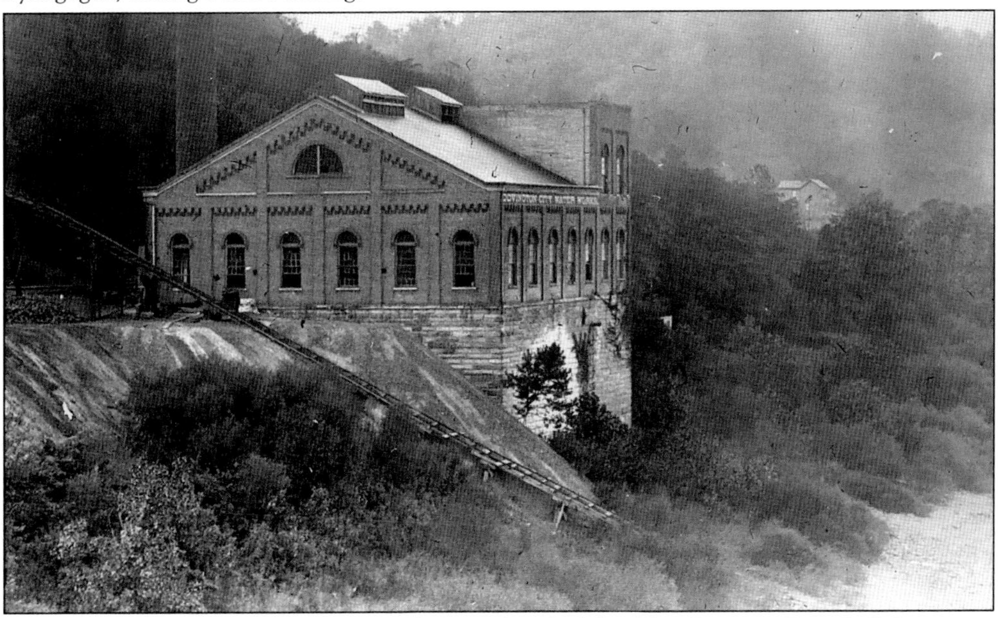

Covington's water works plant, located before a bend of the Ohio River in Campbell County, is pictured c. 1910–1920. Although the plant was built to service Covington and Kenton County, the best location for the plant was in the adjacent county due to Kenton County's limited waterfront along the Ohio River.

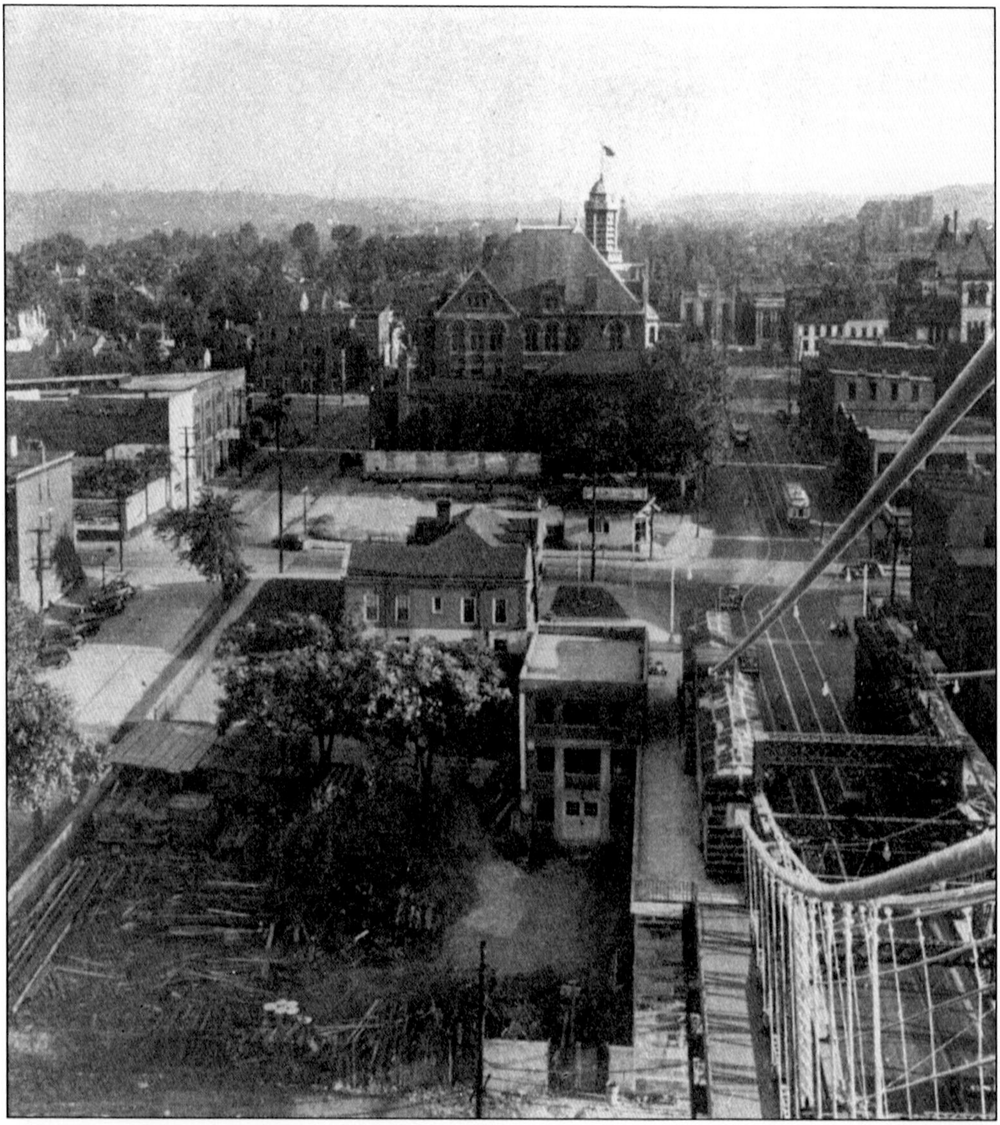

This is a view of downtown Covington, looking from atop the Covington and Cincinnati Suspension Bridge c. 1940. Pictured in this photo is Covington's stately City Hall in the center of the photo, the Federal Building to the far right, and the Cathedral Basilica of the Assumption in the distance in the very far right corner. Notice the trolley car lines and trolleys visible on Court Street.

Two

TRANSPORTATION

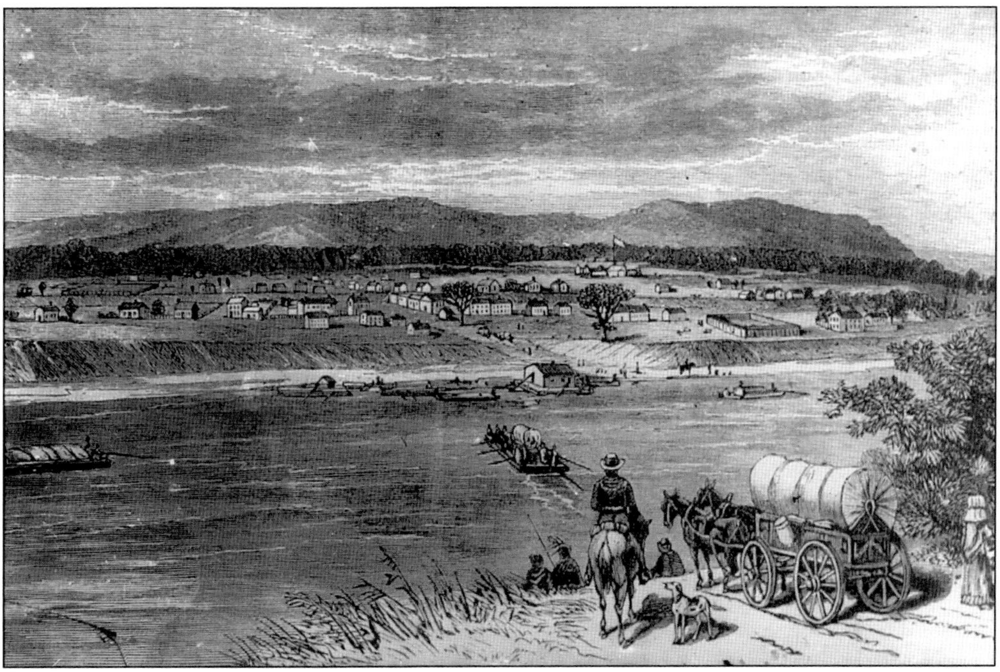

This artist's sketch shows one of the first ferry boats from Covington to Cincinnati, c. 1792. At this time Covington had not even been settled, and Cincinnati was little more than a village.

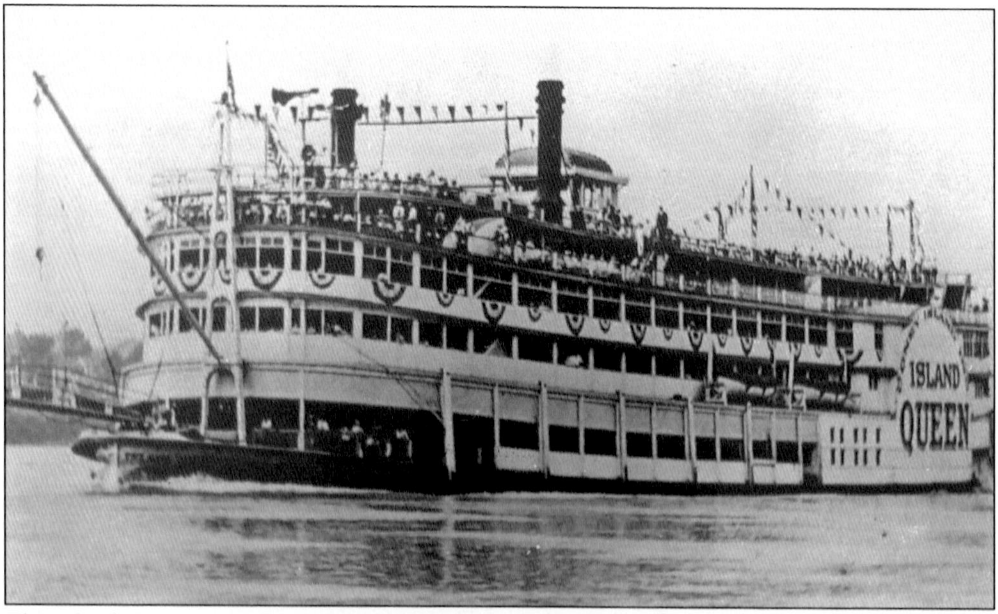

The *Island Queen* was the region's premier excursion boat for many years. One of its most popular cruises was to Coney Island Amusement Park in Cincinnati. The *Island Queen* burned in Pittsburgh in 1947, taking 20 lives.

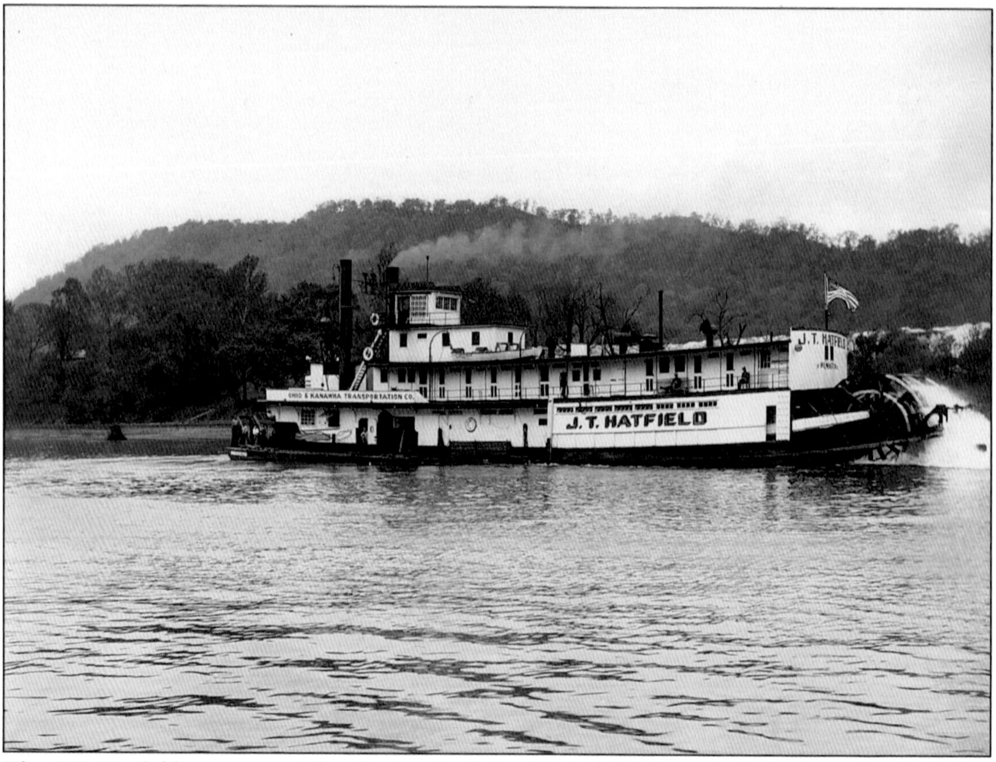

The *J.T. Hatfield* was named for the head of the Hatfield Coal Company, James T. Hatfield, a successful businessman and a leading citizen of Covington. The Hatfield residence was on Wallace Avenue.

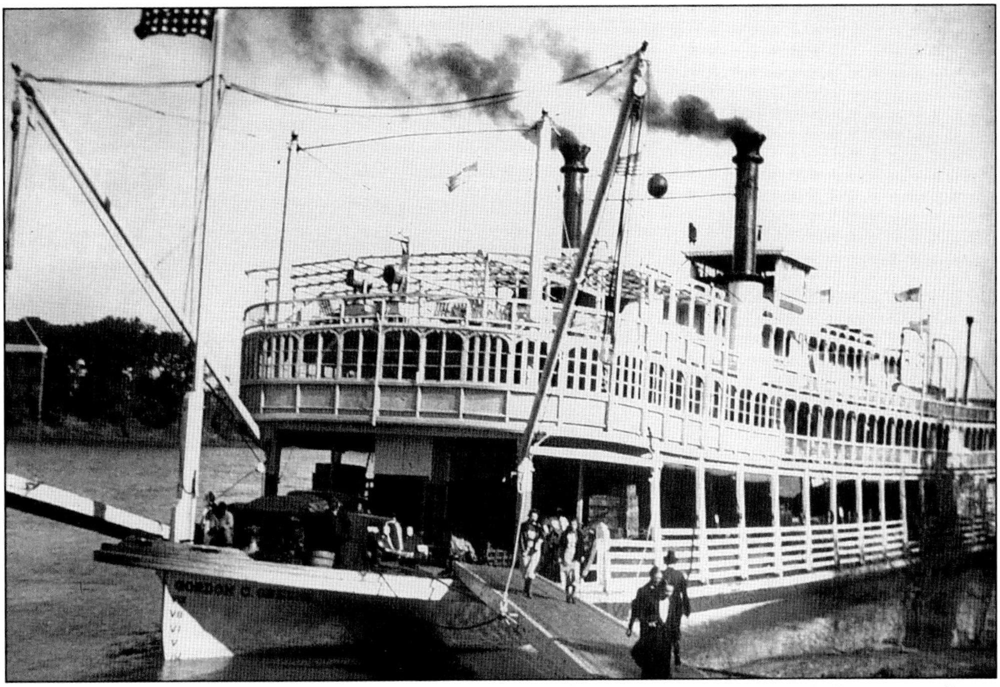

This *c.* 1930 photograph shows the steamboat *Gordon C. Greene*, one of the many ships, including the *Delta Queen*, owned by the Greeneline Steamer Co. After Gordon Greene died in 1927, his widow, Mary took over the company and became one of the few women river pilots. A statue of Mary B. Greene stands in George Rogers Clark Park.

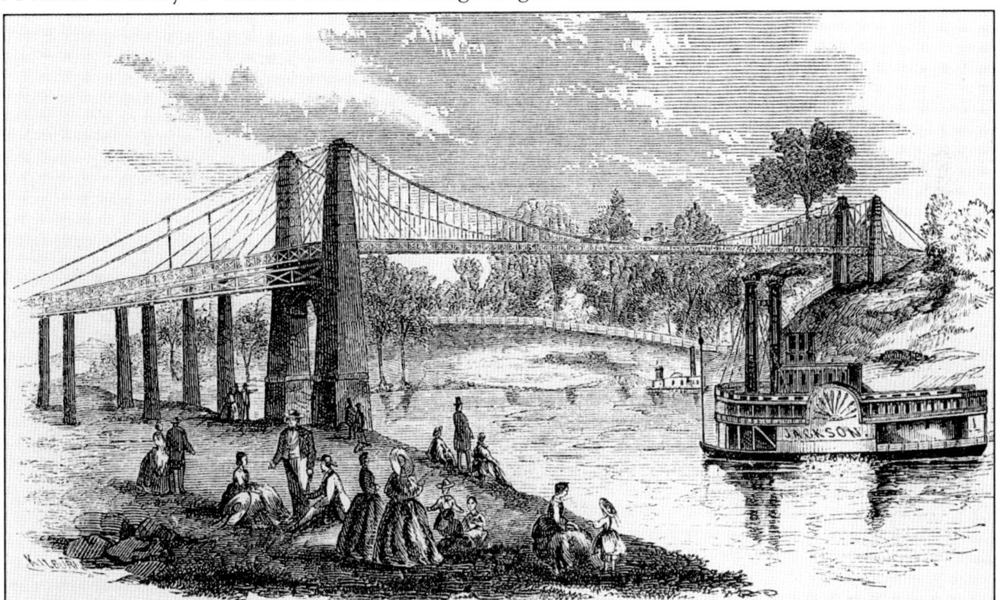

SUSPENSION BRIDGE OVER THE LICKING RIVER.

This *c.* 1850 engraving of the original suspension bridge from Covington to Newport spanning the Licking River appeared in *Harper's Weekly*, a national publication. The bridge collapsed shortly after construction.

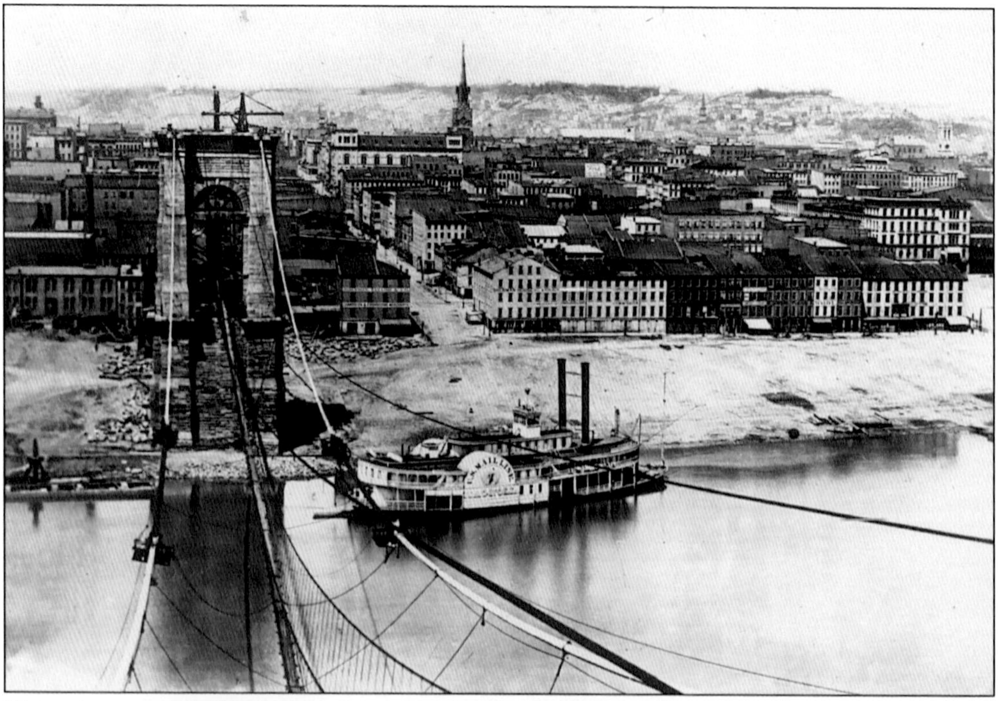

This view toward Cincinnati from Covington was taken during the construction of the Covington and Cincinnati Suspension Bridge in 1867. Designed by John Roebling, the bridge was a model for the Brooklyn Bridge and was also the first suspension bridge to cross the entire Ohio River. The steamboat *Magnolia* was a United States Mail packet.

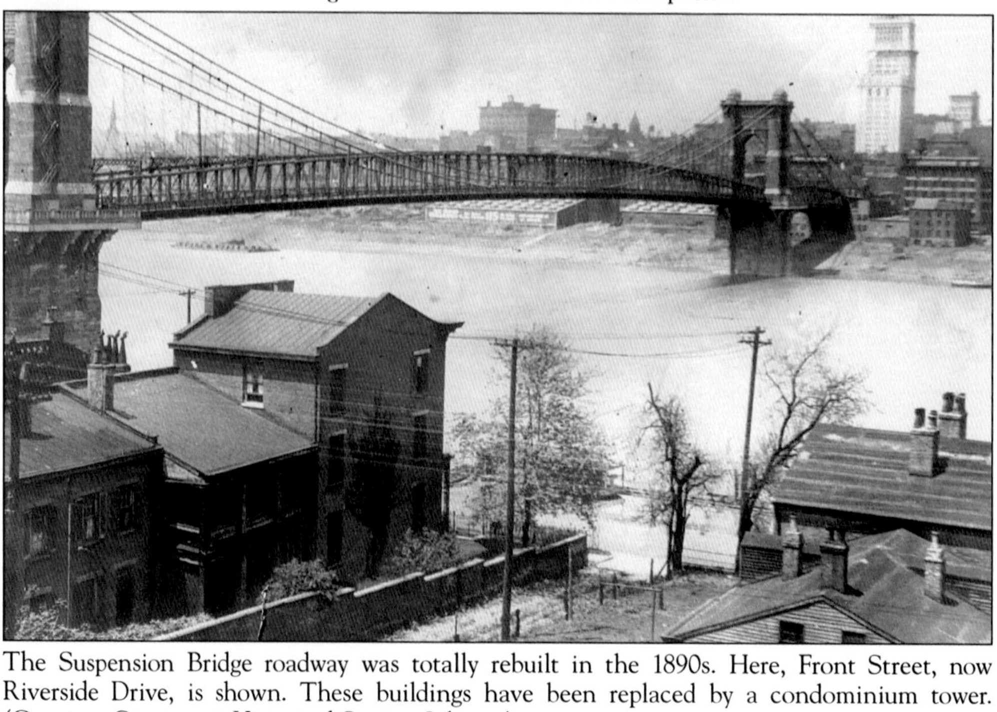

The Suspension Bridge roadway was totally rebuilt in the 1890s. Here, Front Street, now Riverside Drive, is shown. These buildings have been replaced by a condominium tower. (Courtesy Cincinnati Historical Society Library.)

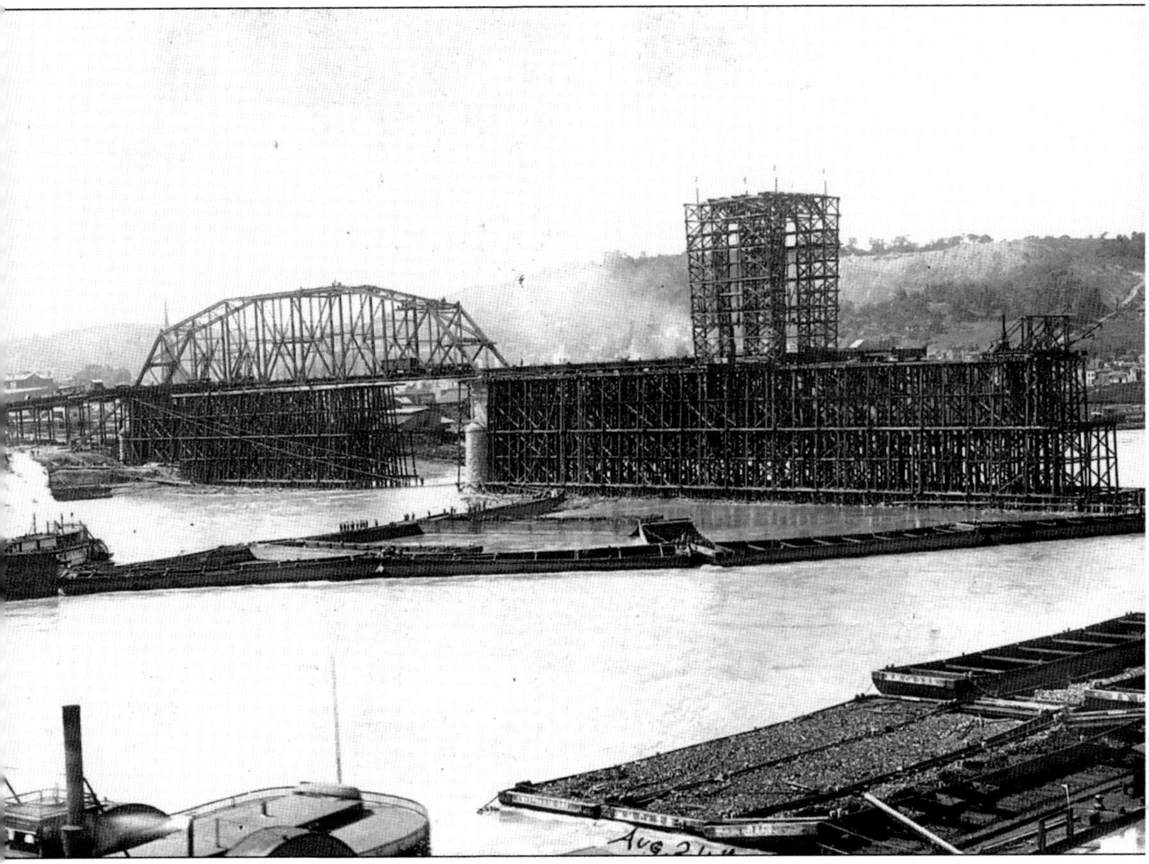

This 1888 photograph shows the construction of the Chesapeake and Ohio Railroad Bridge from Covington to Cincinnati, the first railroad bridge to Cincinnati. The bridge expanded Kentucky's transportation network and opened up a new market for goods coming from the Bluegrass. The construction of this bridge caused the closing of the Craig Street Cemetery; most of the graves were relocated to Highland or Linden Grove Cemetery. (Courtesy Cincinnati Historical Society Library.)

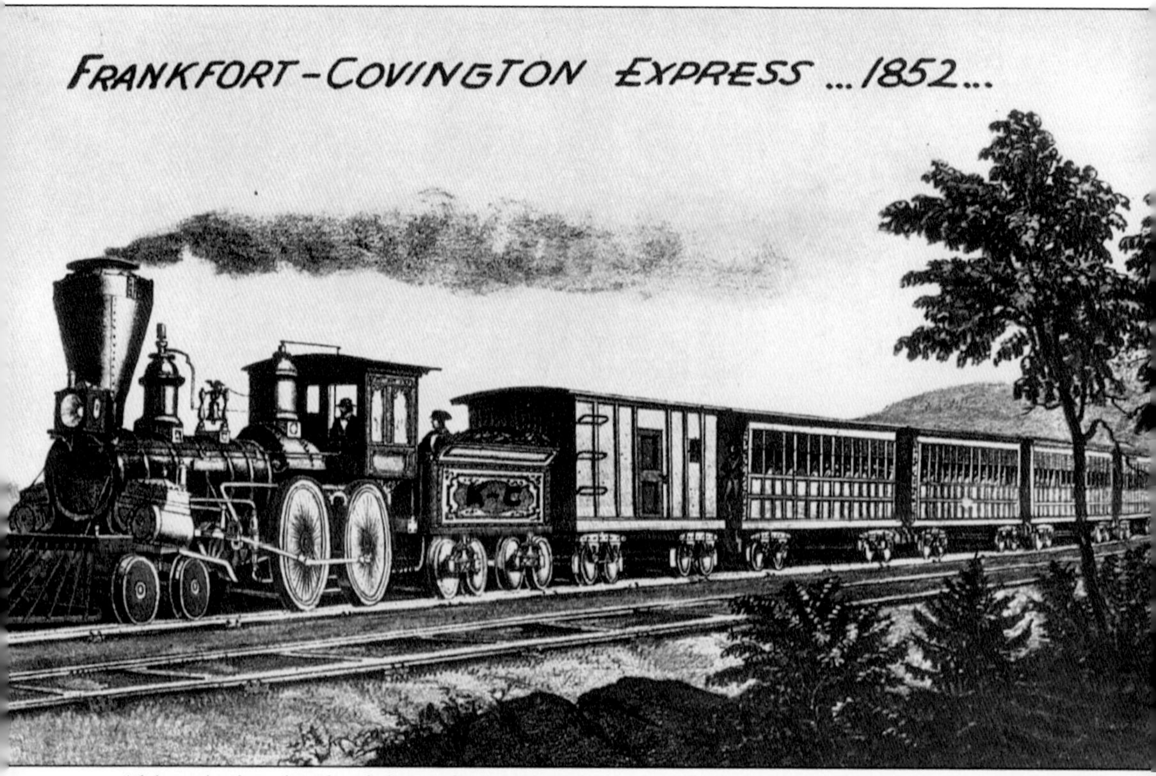

Although this sketch of the earliest railroad coming to Covington describes it as a Frankfort to Covington line, the route actually ran to Lexington. The completion of the railroad to Covington in 1853 created a building boom at Pike and Madison because of the area's proximity to the station. This quickly became the economic center of town, moving commerce away from the river.

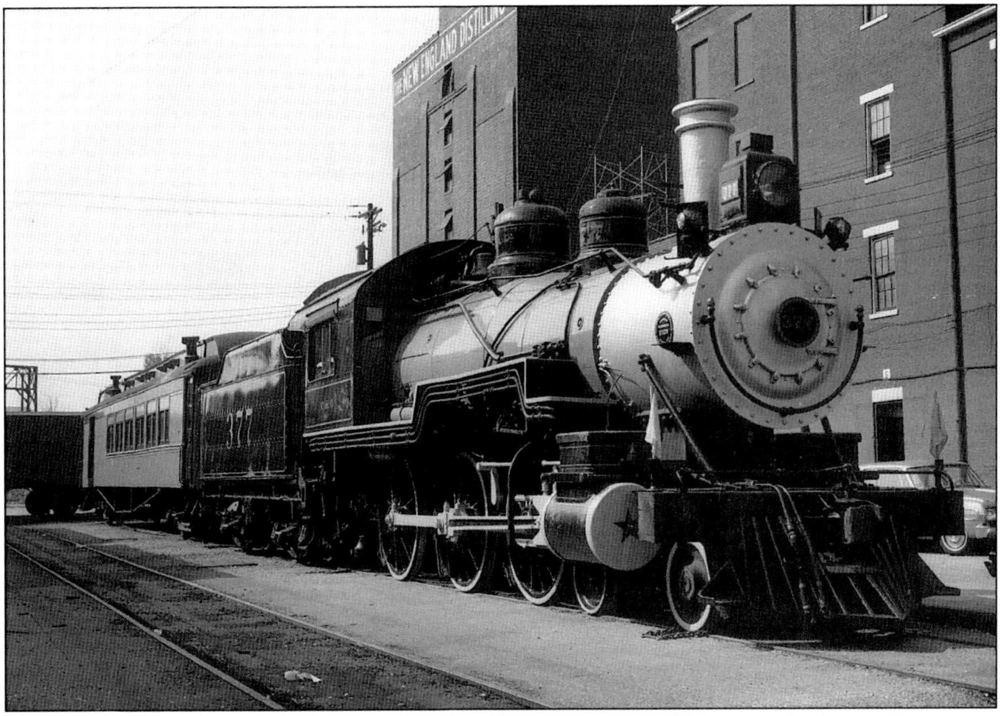

The Chesapeake and Ohio Engine No. 277, used from 1888 to 1925, was on display in Covington in 1965. In the background is the New England Distillery building on Washington at Ninth Street. (Raymond E. Hadorn, photographer.)

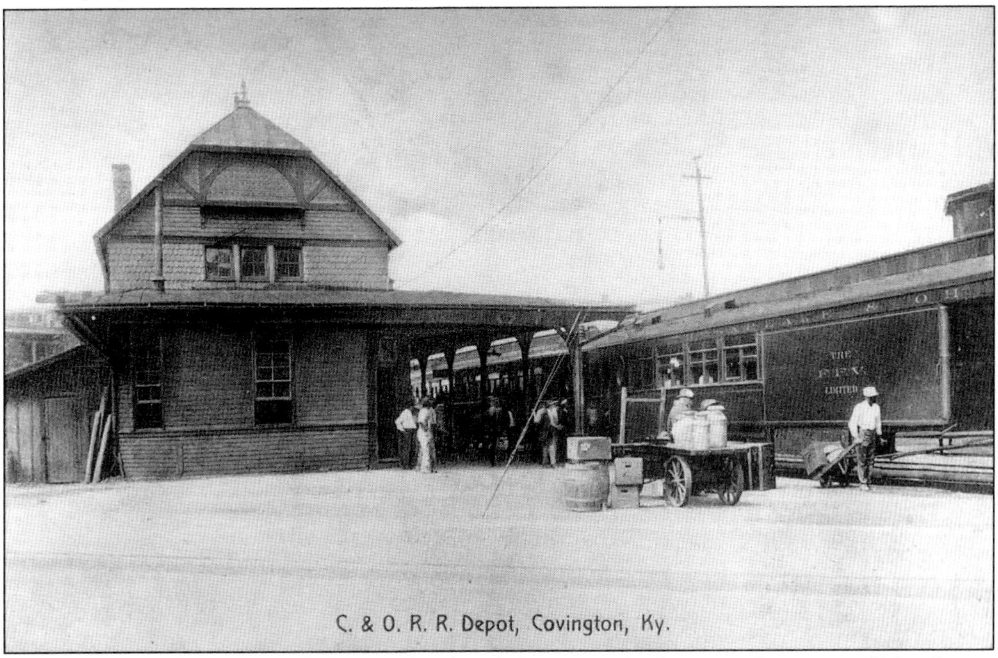

This *c.* 1920 photograph shows the old railroad depot on Washington Street near Pike Street. The city led a long and successful fight to replace this building with a new station during the 1920s. The new station is still in use today as an office building.

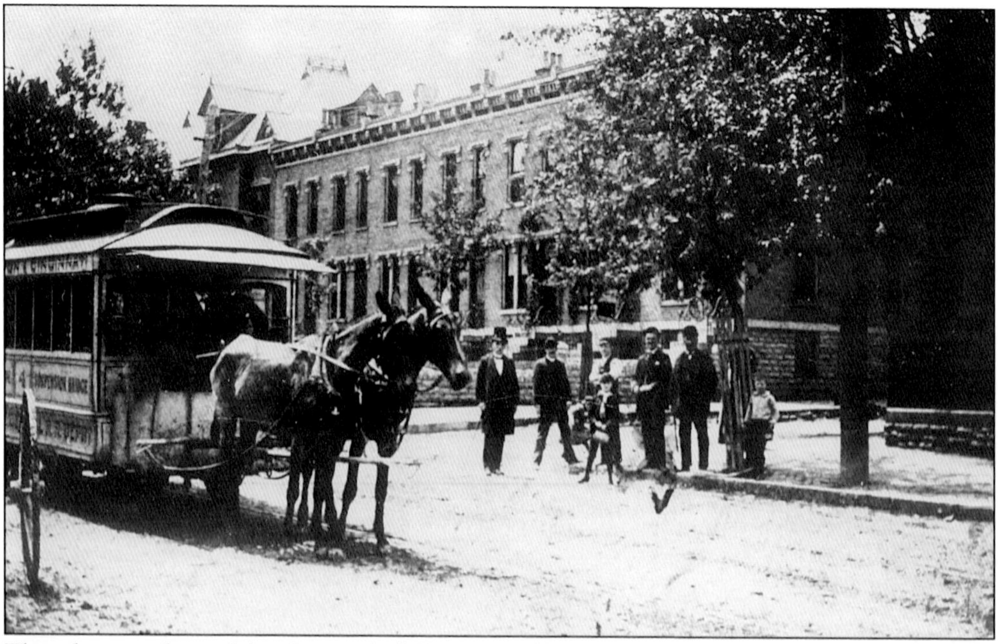

This photograph is of the Cannonball Express trolley ready to leave from the end of the line at Fifteenth and Madison on its way to Cincinnati. Note the man with the stovepipe hat. The Motch Flats and the Stewart house are seen in the rear, both of which still stand today. (Cincinnati Historical Society Library.)

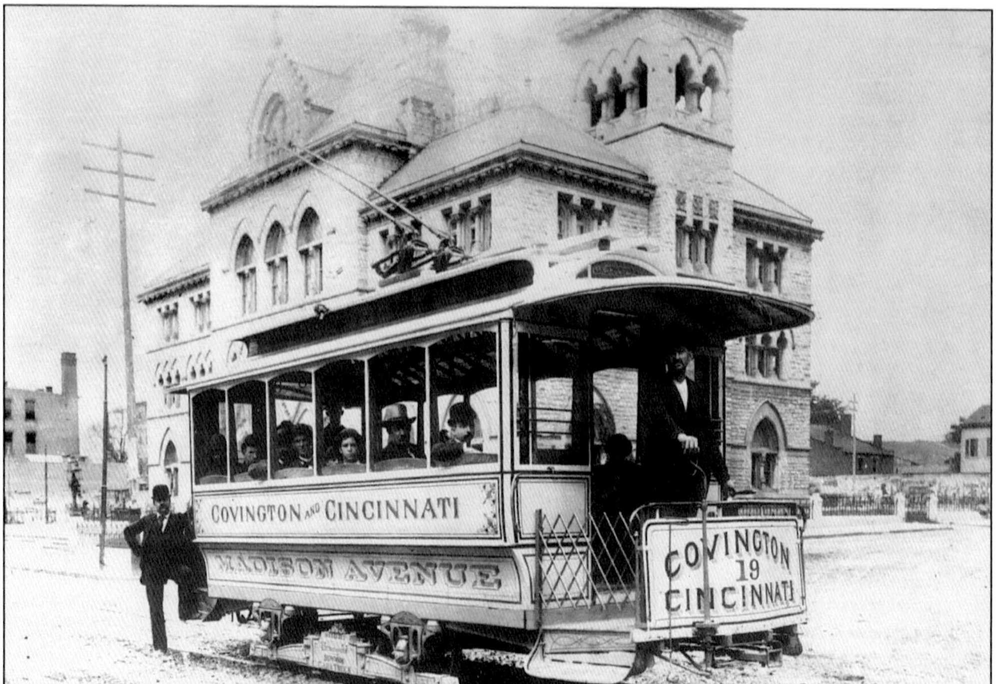

The Covington and Cincinnati trolley stops in front of the Federal Building at Court and Park. The Federal Building was built in the 1860s shortly after Jesse Grant, father of President Ulysses Grant, was postmaster.

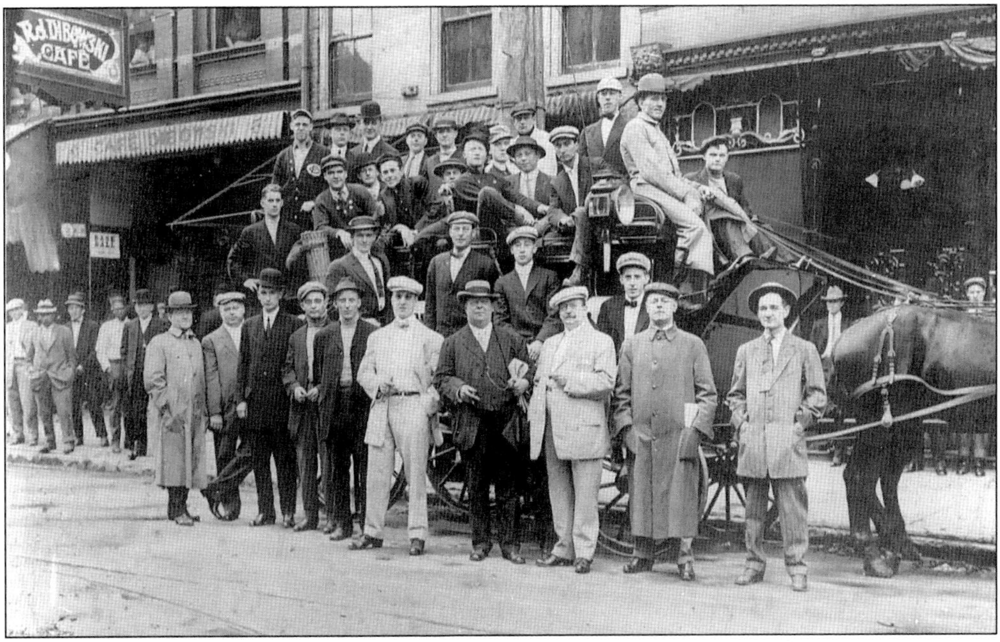

This group of Covington businessmen was leaving for a Cincinnati Reds game, c. 1909, on a rented omnibus. The trip was organized by R.J. Dibowski, whose Pike Street café is in the background. A native of Cincinnati, Dibowski also served on several local boards, including the Latonia Race Track, and was a local Boy Scout leader. There is an urn dedicated to him at the Eleventh Street Park.

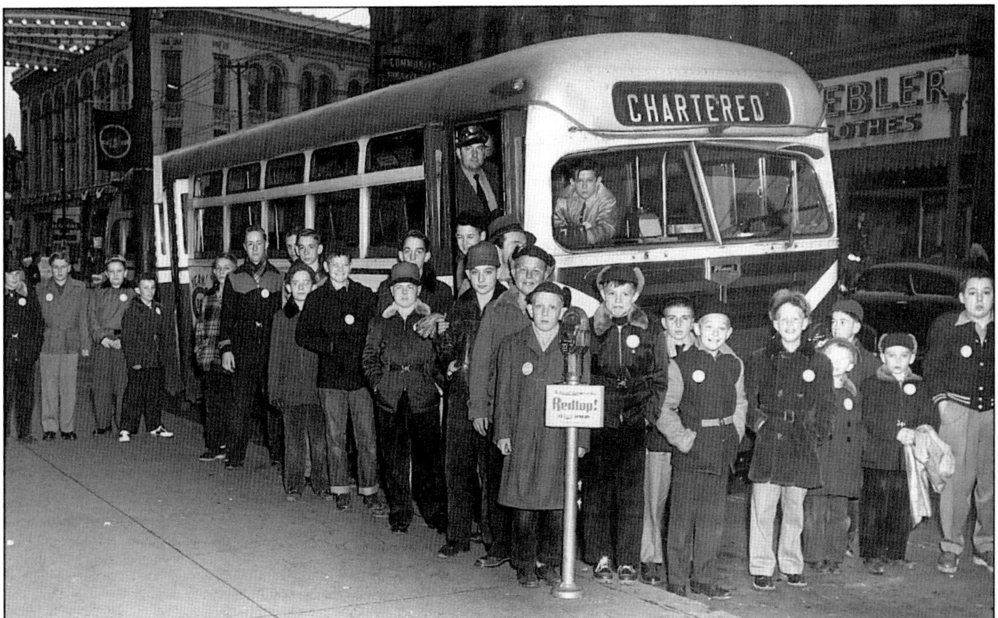

This chartered bus from Eilermen's Men's Store was taking a group of children to a Cincinnati Reds game during the 1950s. The Covington Mutual Insurance Company building in the background still stands today. Eilermen's was the primary men's clothier in Covington and Newport for many decades. (Russell Manuel, photographer.)

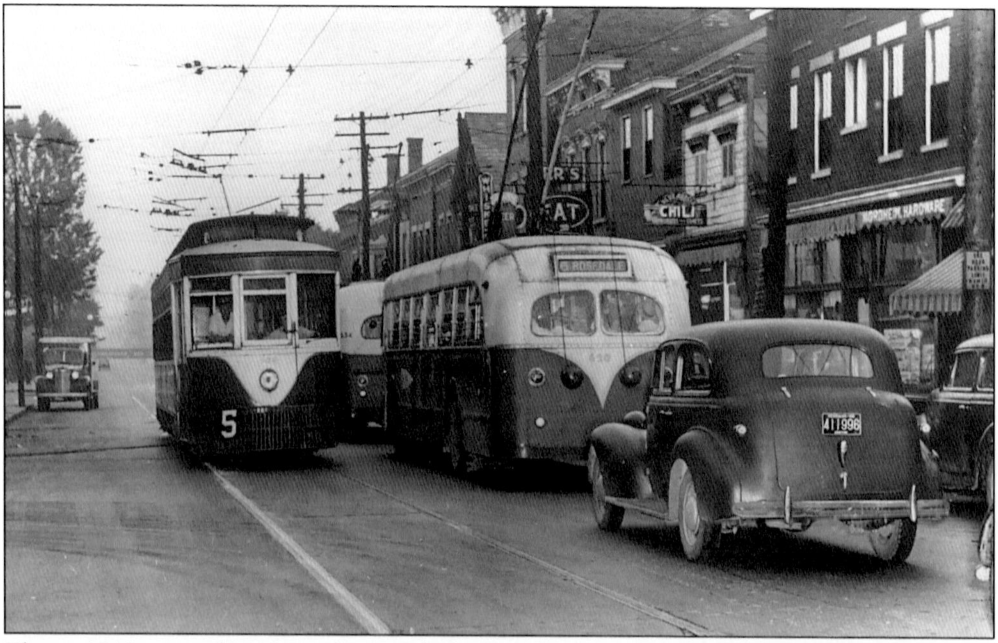

This *c.* 1946 view of Madison Avenue looking north from Twentieth Street shows what was then the commercial hub of the Austinburg neighborhood. Although most of the buildings are still extant, many are vacant today. Rouse Station, a tiny local post office, is around the corner. It is named for Congressman Arthur Rouse, who was able to get the funding through Congress for the post office.

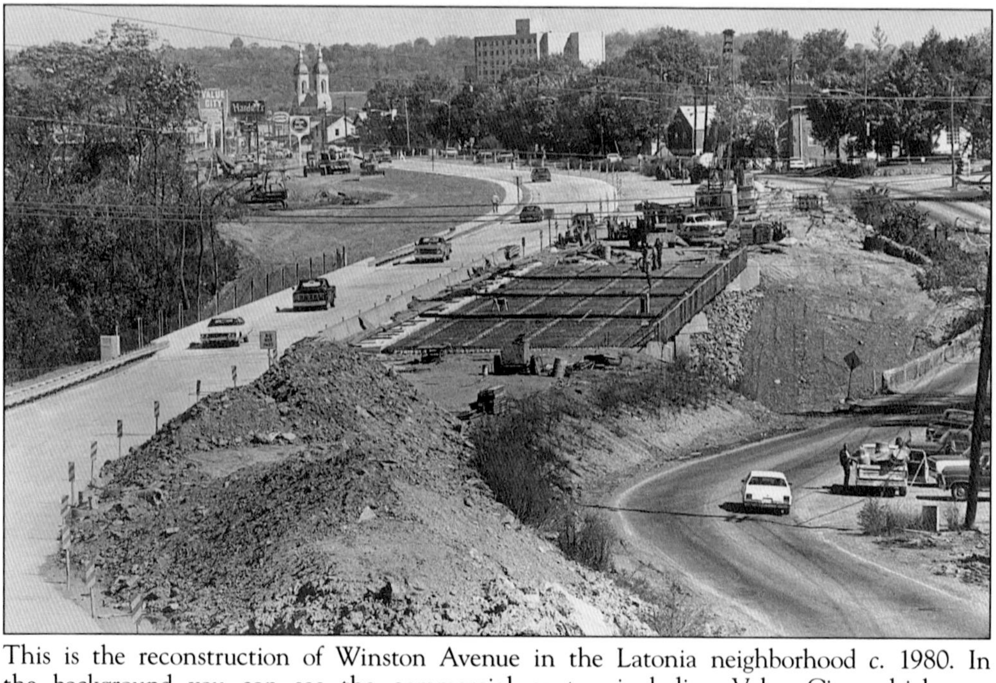

This is the reconstruction of Winston Avenue in the Latonia neighborhood *c.* 1980. In the background you can see the commercial center, including Value City, which was constructed on the site of the former Latonia Race Track. In the distance are the spires of Holy Cross Church.

Three

COMMERCE

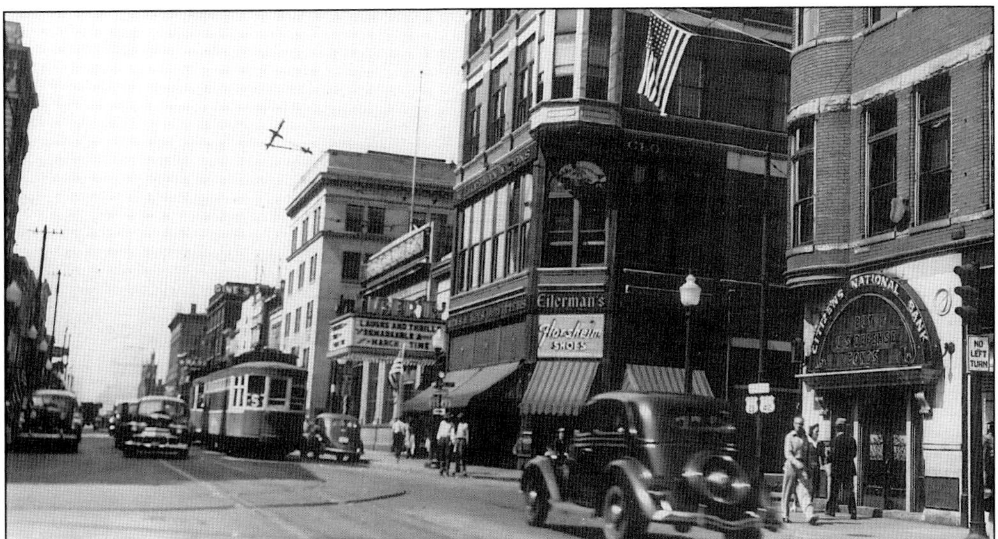

This is a view of downtown Covington, looking north on Madison Avenue toward Pike Street in the early 1940s. Visible on the right side of the street are several prominent downtown businesses, including the Citizens National Bank with its altered art deco entryway, H. Eilerman and Sons, the Liberty Theater, Covington Bank and Trust building, and Dines furniture store. Note the automobiles and trolley car sharing the street in this photo, and the marquee on the Citizens Bank building, exhorting customers to buy defense bonds during the World War II era.

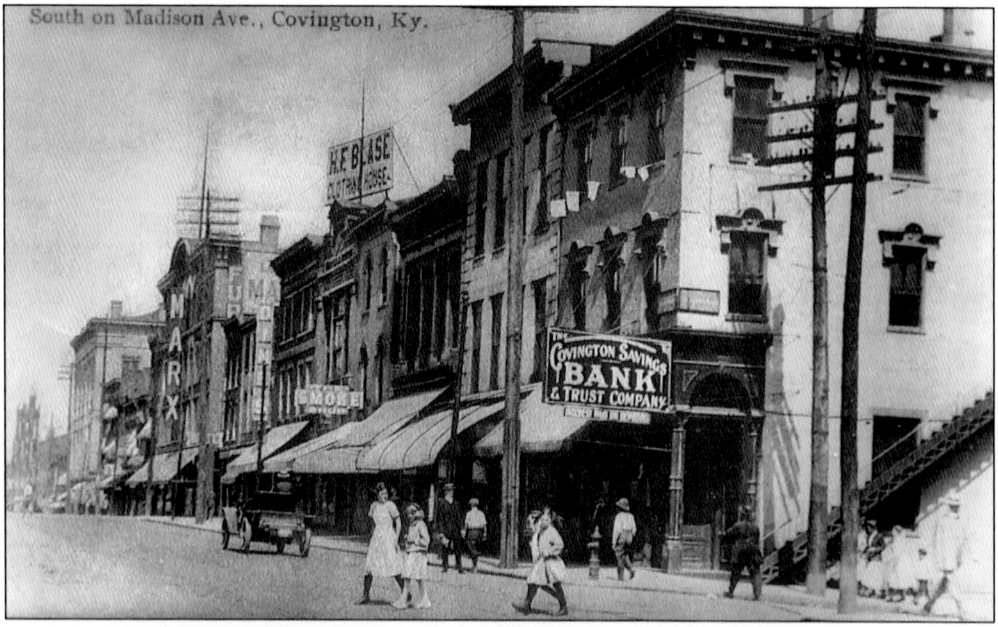

Another view of downtown Covington, this one—contrary to the postcard caption—is looking north on Madison Avenue from Sixth Street, c. 1910s. Some of the businesses shown are Marx Furniture, Blase Clothing Store, and Dines Furniture Store, The Smoke Shop, and Covington Savings Bank. The Odd Fellows Hall and Trinity Episcopal Church are visible at the far end of the street.

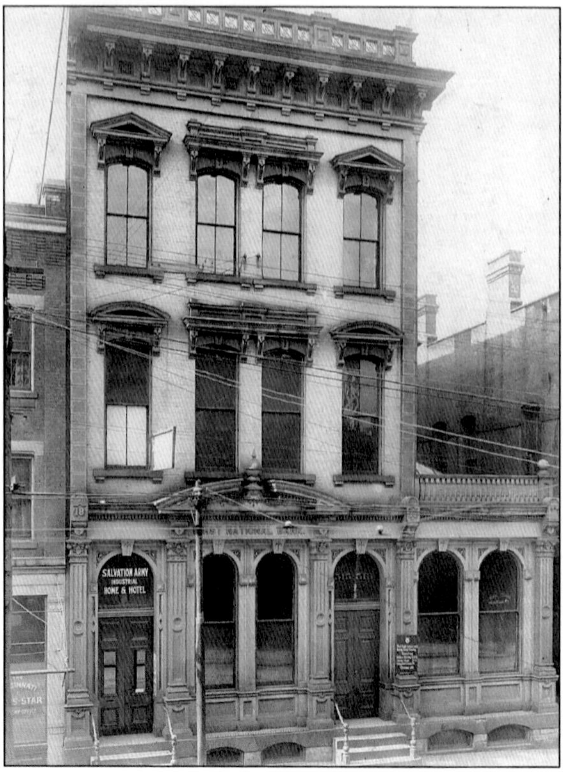

The First National Bank building at 513–515 Madison Avenue was constructed in 1875. This building later served as the Salvation Army Industrial Home and Hotel, which was its use when this photograph was taken, c. 1920. Amos Shinkle owned the bank, which moved to the northwest corner of Sixth and Madison at the turn of the century after consolidating with the Farmers' and Traders' Bank. The building was demolished in the late 1920s.

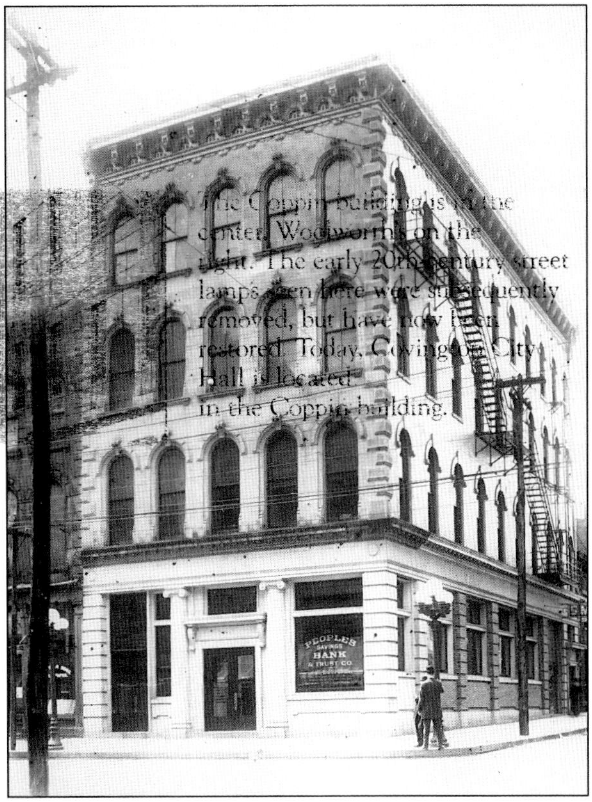

This is the People's Savings Bank and Trust Company building at the corner of Sixth and Madison, *c.* 1930s. This building was constructed in the 1870s, and was originally known as the Walker Building, named for dry goods merchant James R. Walker, the original occupant of the building. The building is attributed to architects Anton and Louis Pickett. (Courtesy Cincinnati Historical Society Library.)

This view of Madison Avenue is looking south from Sixth Street, *c.* 1941–1945. On the left side of the street is the People's Liberty Bank and Trust building, the Liberty Theater (now demolished), and H. Eilerman and Sons Clothiers. Visible in the next block are the Citizen's National Bank, the YMCA building, and the John R. Coppin Company building. Note the 1940s Pontiac automobiles in the photograph.

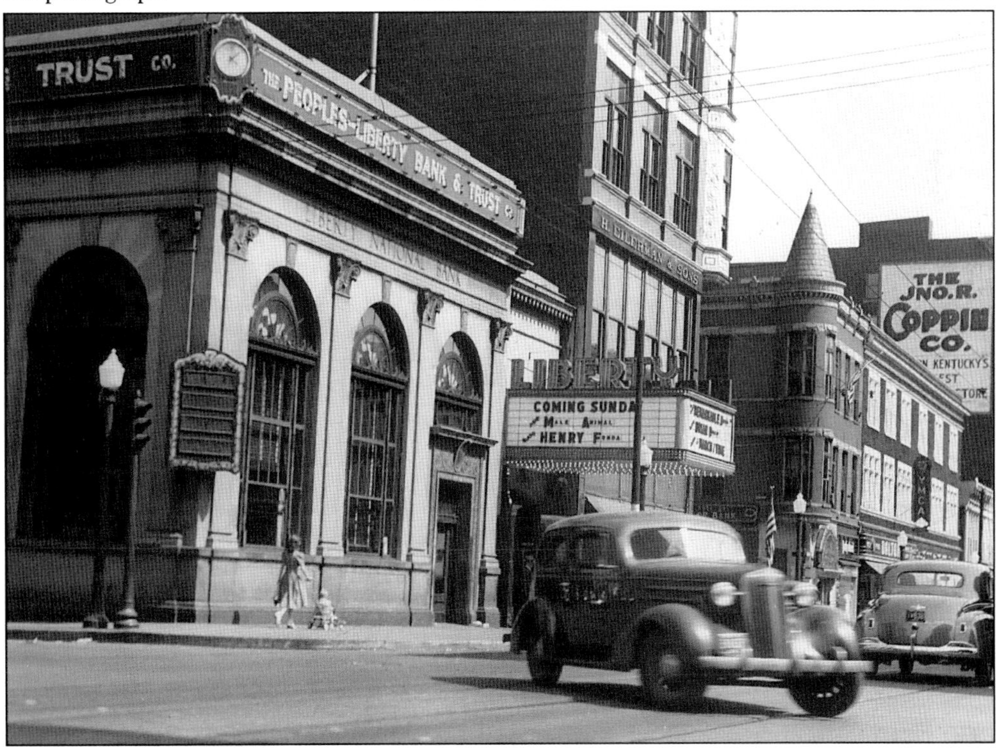

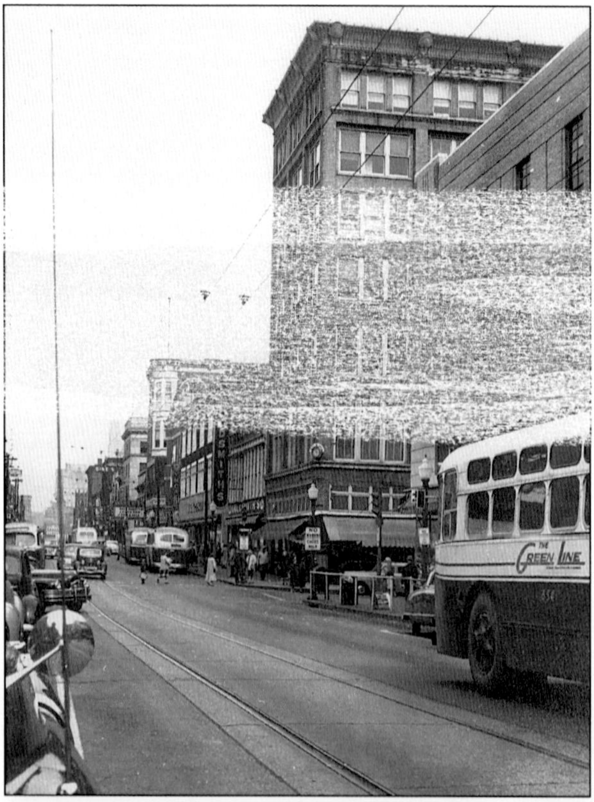

A still thriving downtown Covington is seen in this photo of Madison and Seventh, looking north, c. 1950. Note the railings along the street to prevent pedestrians from crossing traffic. The Coppin building is in the center, Woolworth's on the right. The early 20th century street lamps seen here were subsequently removed, but have now been restored. Today, Covington City Hall is located in the Coppin building.

Women are seen shopping on the first floor of Coppin's Department Store in the 1940s. Women's lingerie, jewelry, hosiery, and hat departments are visible in this photo, while men's accessories are located in the far right hand corner. Coppin's was the major department store in the Northern Kentucky area for several decades.

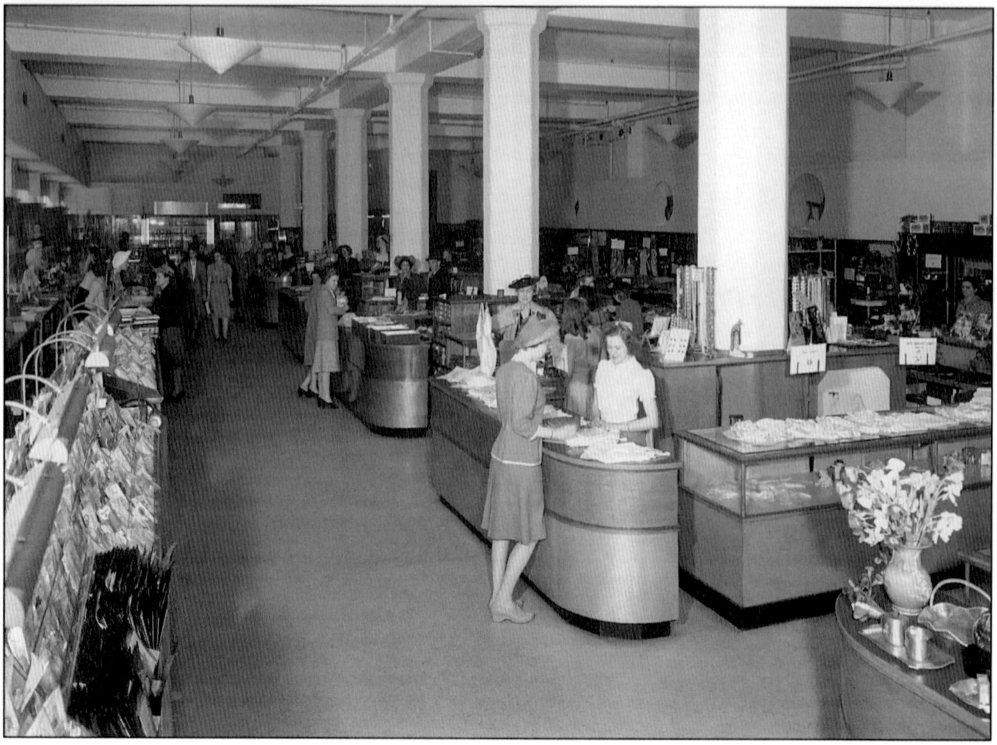

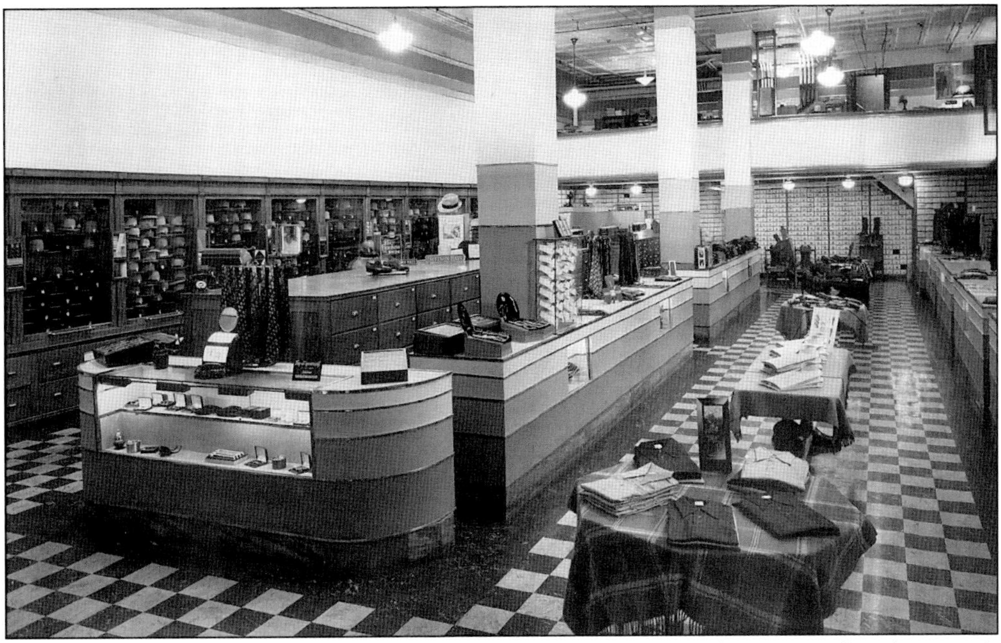

This is the interior of H. Eilerman and Sons, Clothiers, in the mid-20th century. This photograph shows the first floor of Eilerman's where the men's shirt, ties, hat, and shoe departments were located. The balcony office is visible at the rear of this photograph. Note the pressed tin ceiling. (Frederick A. Schmidt, photographer.)

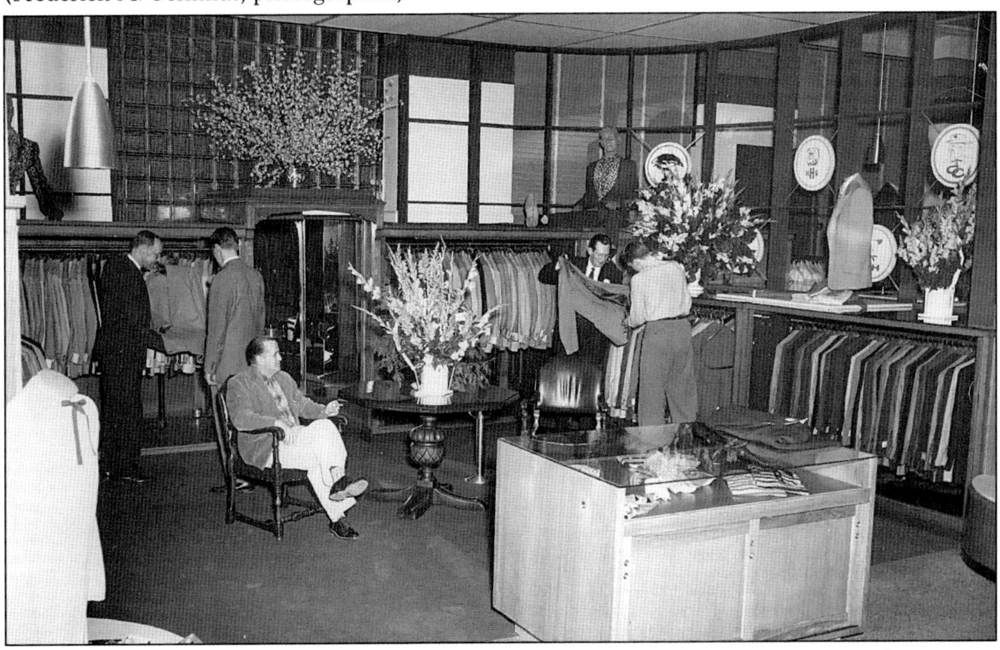

The third floor of Eilerman's, *c.* 1955, was the young men's department. Note the antique table, chairs, and casework in sharp contrast to the bullet light fixtures, glass block, white bucks, and leopard print suits on display. John Menne relaxes and enjoys a smoke break while younger clients peruse the merchandise. Local school logos adorn the walls. (Russell Manuel, photographer.)

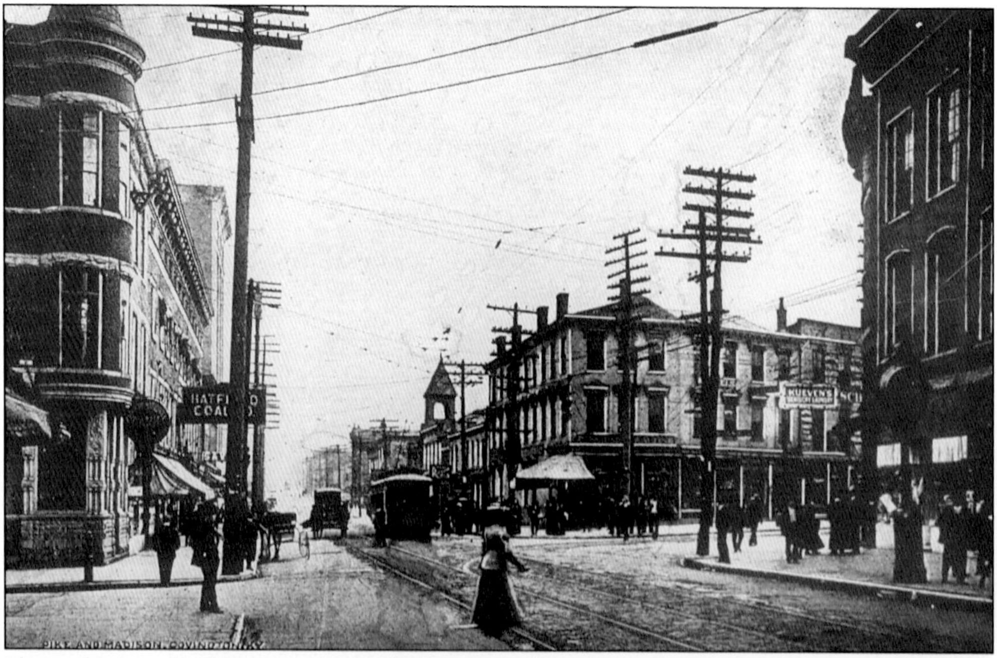

Shown here is the busy corner of Pike Street and Madison Avenue, the heart of downtown, looking south, c. 1886. Note the tower of the Seventh Street market house in the background and the Hatfield Coal Company's sign on the left side of the street. Horse-and-buggies and trolley cars share the road in this picture.

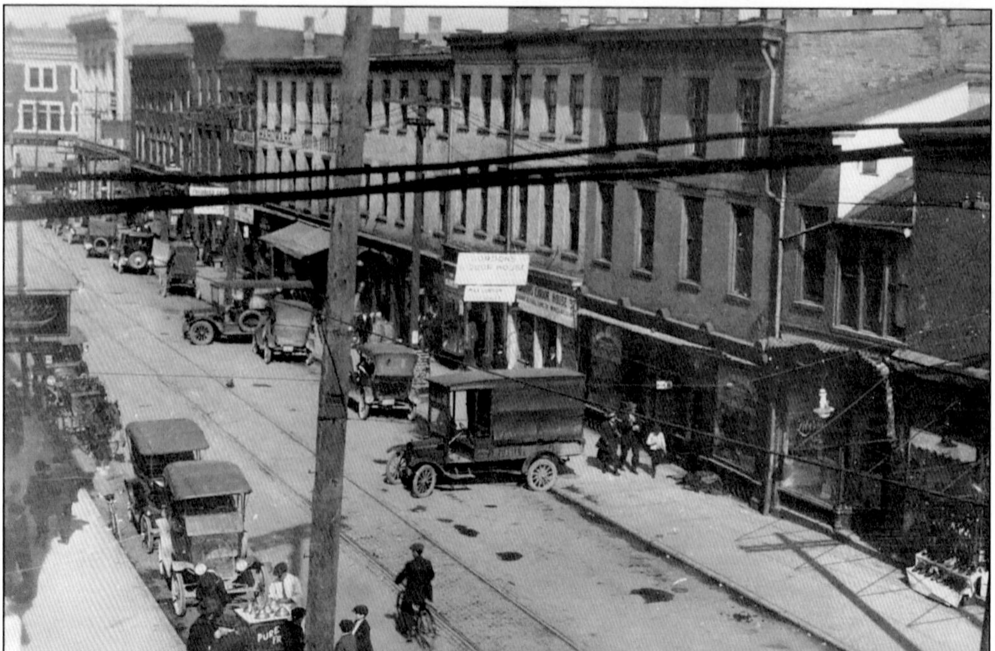

This photograph shows a busy day on Pike Street, c. 1918. Although many of these local businesses are no longer here, the YMCA and George Hill's business survived until recently. Note the young street vendor at the left selling his products to a group of youngsters.

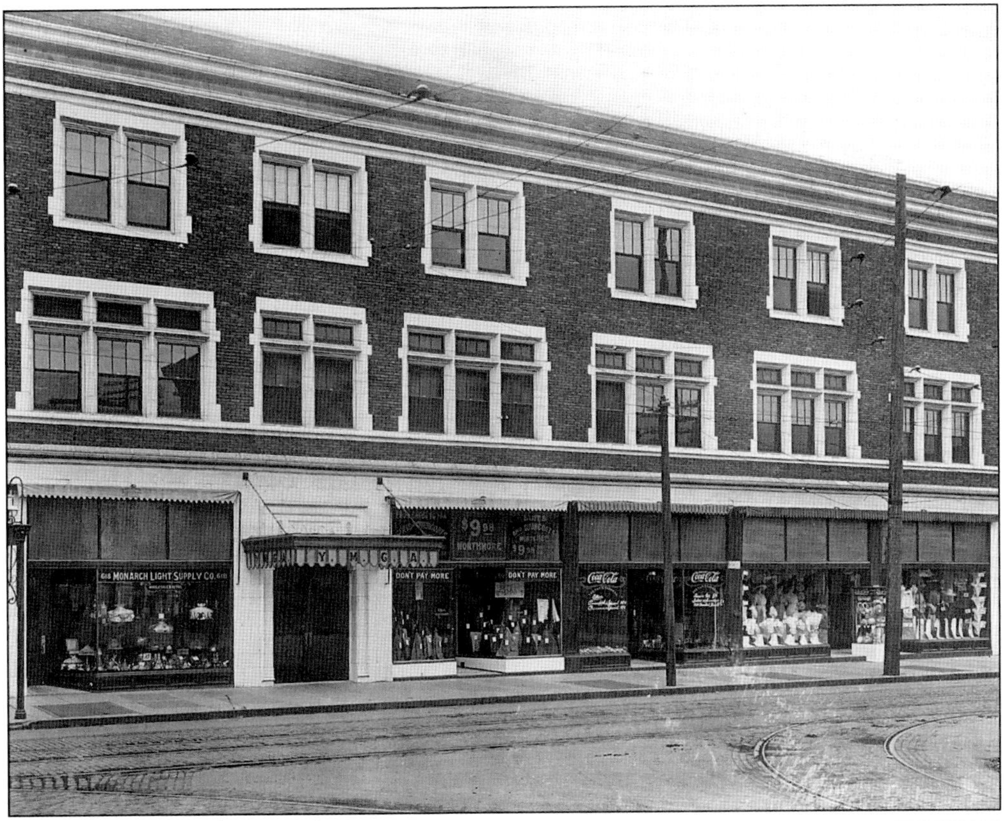

The Young Men's Christian Association (YMCA) building on Madison Avenue was constructed in 1914 to provide a place for young men to socialize, exercise, and live on a short-term basis. The YMCA was organized in Covington in 1888 by John D. Hearne, who served as president. When the YMCA was completed, it included a gymnasium, running track, social rooms, dormitory, library, and a swimming pool in the basement! (Courtesy Cincinnati Historical Society Library.)

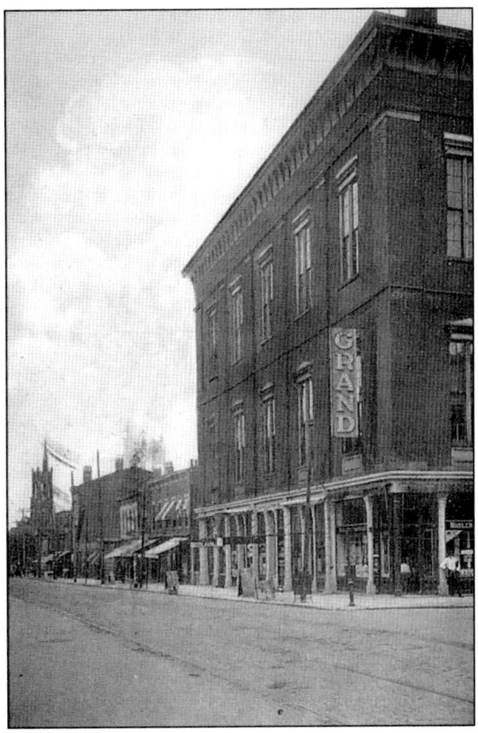

The 1856 Odd Fellows Hall, a three-story brick building located at the corner of Fifth and Madison Avenue in downtown. The Odd Fellows Hall has elements of both the Greek Revival and Italianate styles of architecture, and features cast-iron storefronts, a decorative cornice, and colossal brick pilasters. This building served as both a commercial and social hub for the city in the 19th and 20th centuries. A May 2002 fire caused severe damage to the building; the exterior is currently being restored.

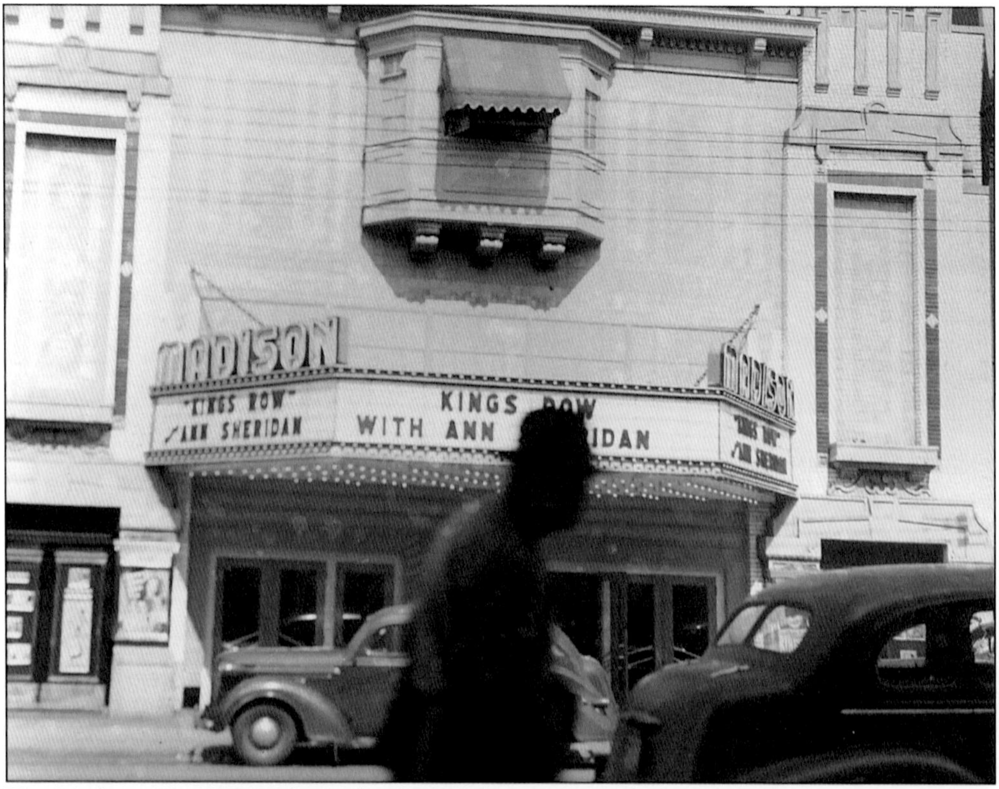

The Madison Theater was located at 728 Madison Avenue before the 1945 fire and before the building's subsequent remodeling to its current art moderne facade. The theater is in use again today as a music and entertainment venue.

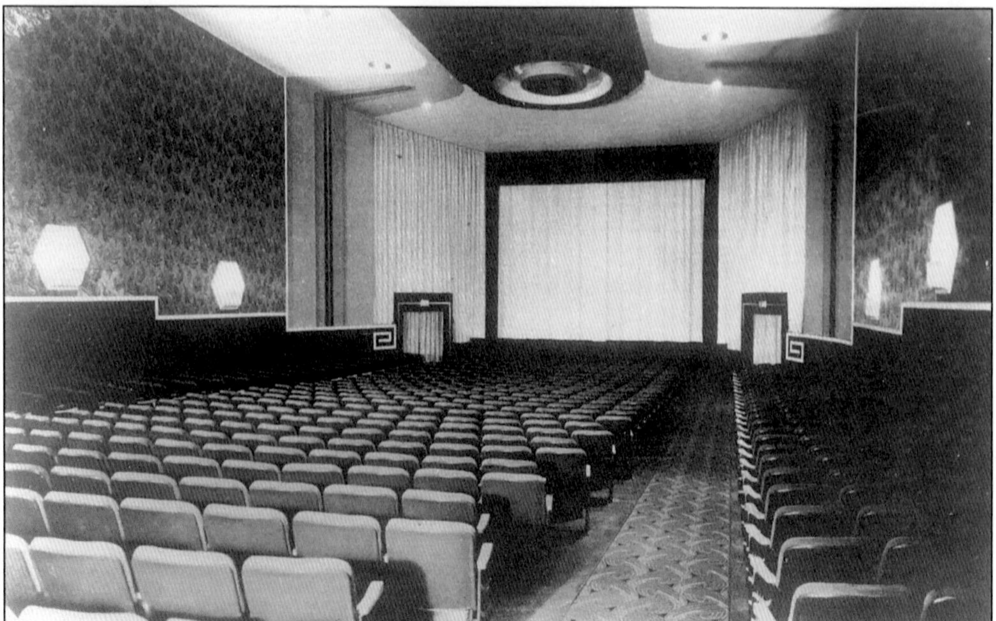

The newly remodeled art moderne interior of the Madison Theater is seen c. 1947.

This *c.* 1870 building was intact and thriving in this 1930 photograph. At that time the mixed-use building housed a confectionery, a barber shop, and a paint and hardware store on the lower level. The upper floors served as apartments. It is easily recognizable today at the southeast corner of Fourth Street and Madison Avenue. (Courtesy Cincinnati Historical Society Library.)

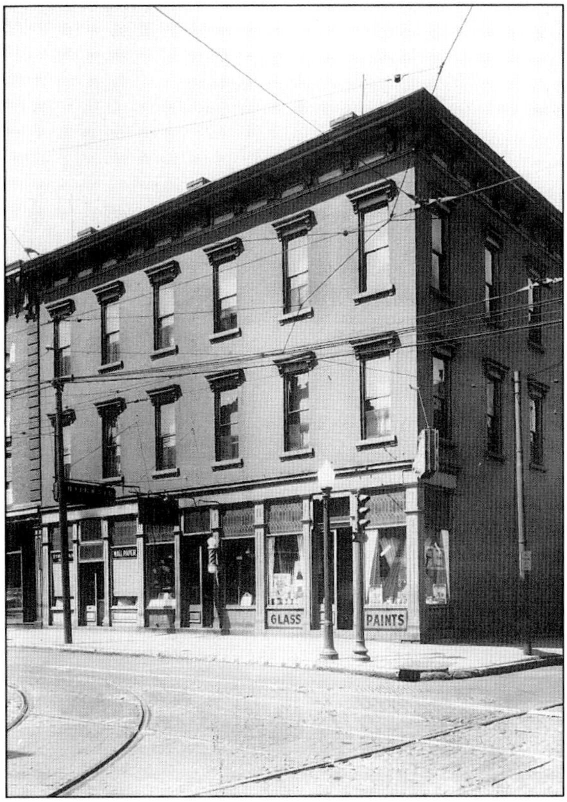

The Allison & Rose Funeral Home was built *c.* 1863 by the Grant family. The building served as a residence for a number of years with both the Hamilton and Ranschell families occupying the building until it was purchased by Allison and Rose in the mid-1920s. The building has functioned as a funeral home since that time. The porte cochere and front porch were added *c.* 1928.

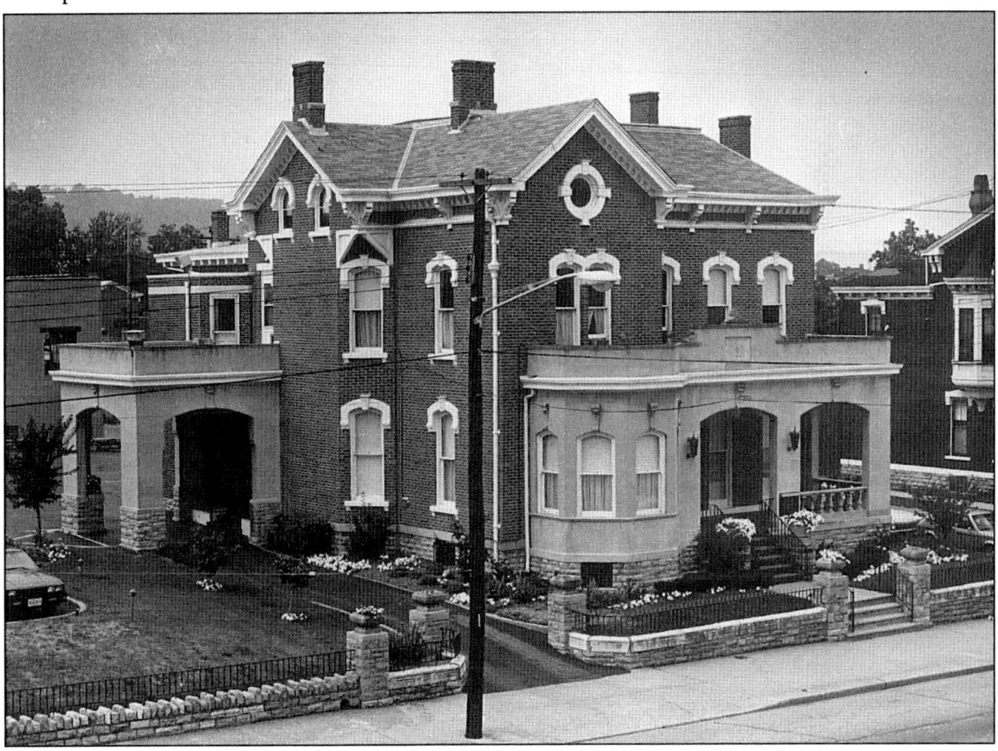

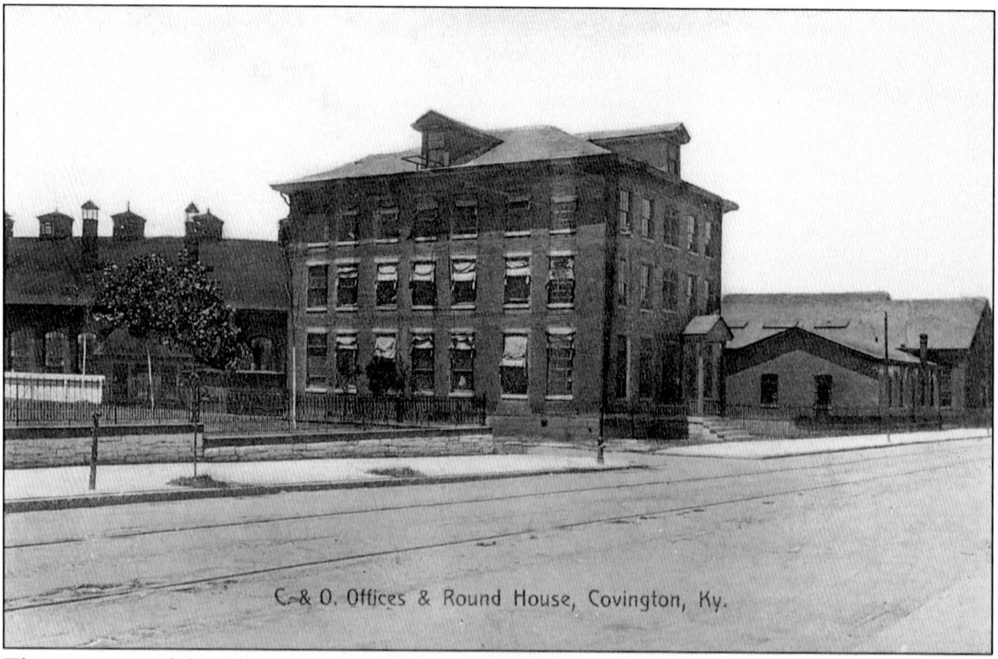

This is a view of the Chesapeake and Ohio Railroad Office Building and Roundhouse, *c.* 1900. The railroad office building was damaged by a tornado in 1914, when the front of the building was destroyed, it was subsequently rebuilt, and the complex functioned as home to the railroad company until *c.* 1940s. The building complex is now owned by the Duro Bag Company. The railroad office building was demolished in 2002 but the roundhouse still stands today.

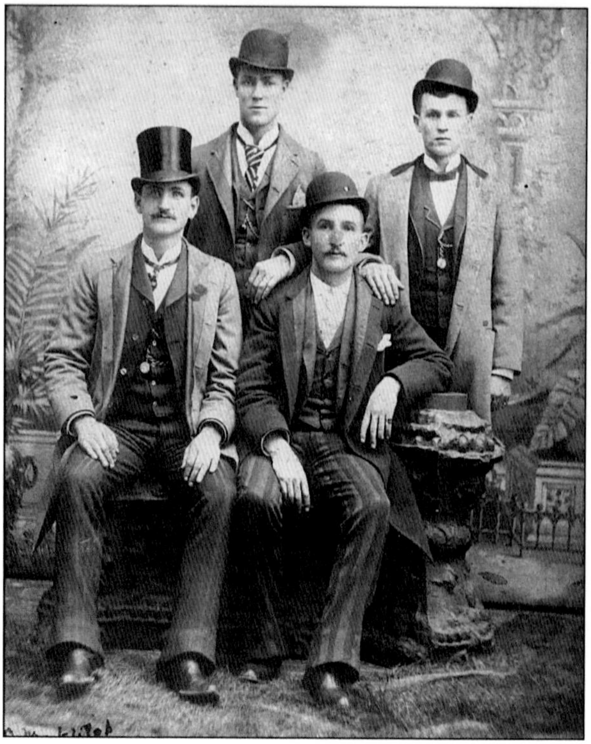

A group of C&O (Chesapeake and Ohio) railroad workers are shown celebrating a payday in 1889. Pictured from left to right are Lou Burns, Cash Hitch, Bill Gaynor, and Al King.

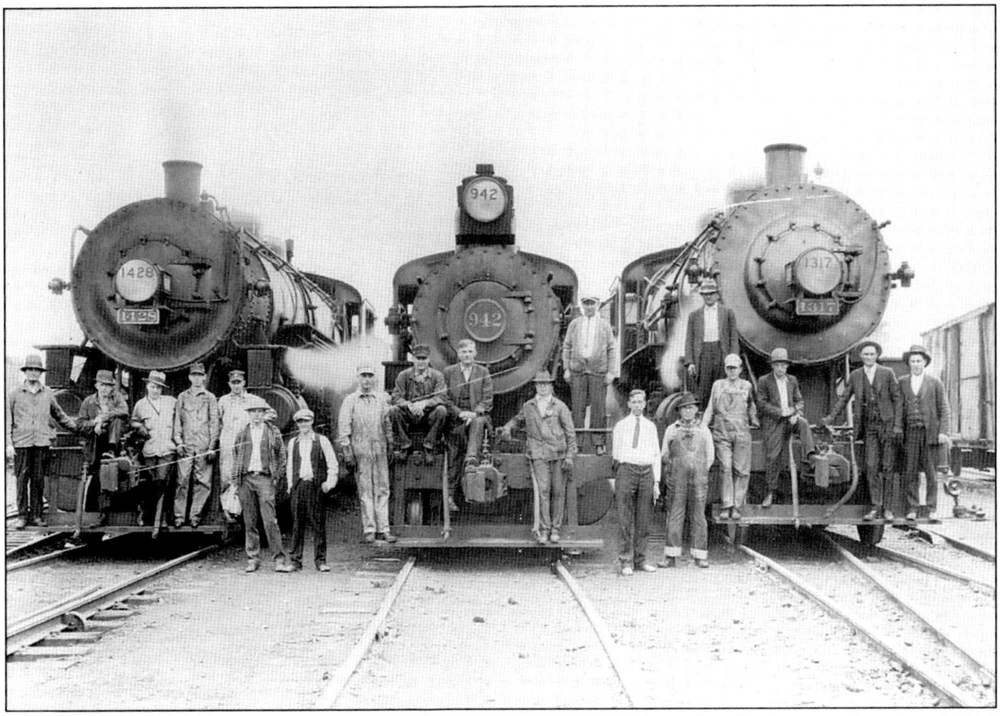

This *c.* 1930 photo shows yardmaster Charles B. Gilham (white shirt) along with other L&N (Louisville & Nashville) railroad workers posing at the old Decoursey Yards, known by the railroad men as "old 26." (Courtesy Lisa Gillham.)

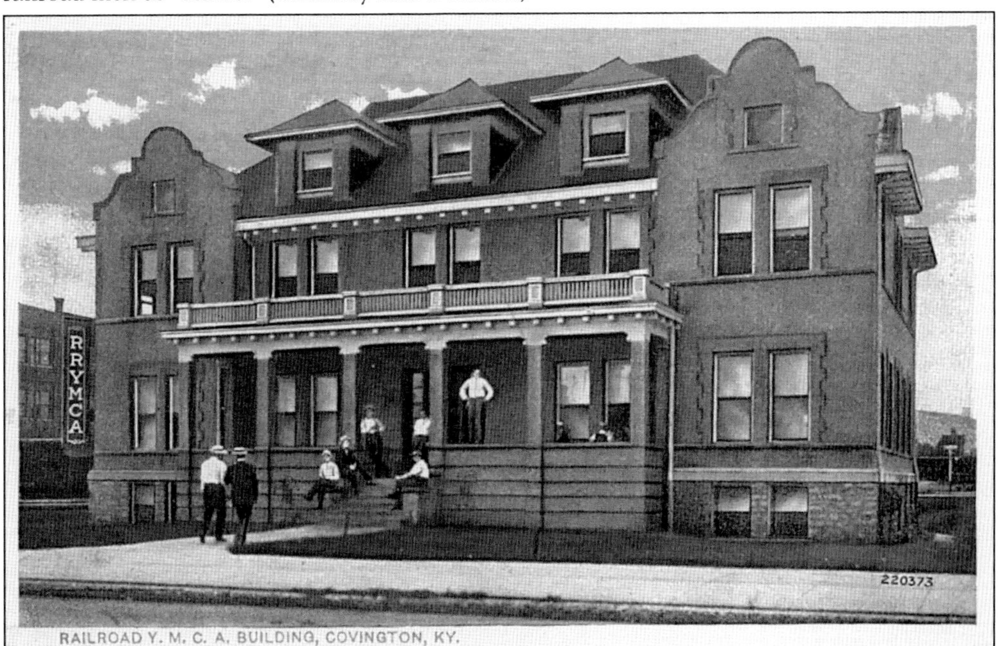

This is a postcard of the Railroad YMCA located at Seventeenth Street and Madison Avenue. The YMCA building was close to the Chesapeake and Ohio railroad complex at Fourteenth Street and Madison Avenue and provided a place for railroad workers to stay.

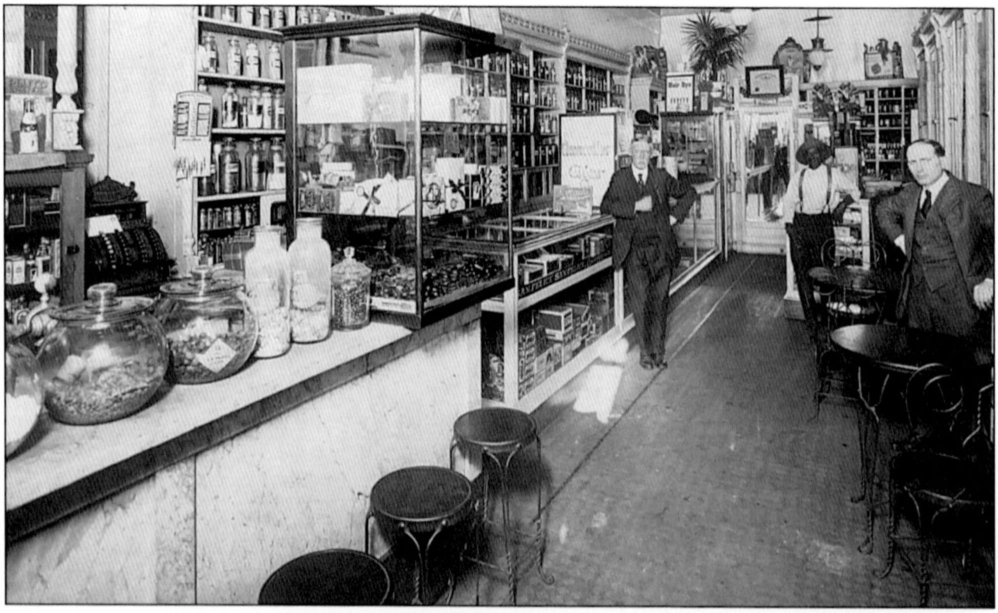

The interior of Hughey's drug store, located at the northeast corner of Eighth and Madison Avenue, is shown here *c.* 1918. Pictured from left to right are Asbury Webb Smith, an unidentified man, and George Hughey, the proprietor of the store. During the mid-20th century, this store and its adjacent storefronts became Tillman's Furniture Store.

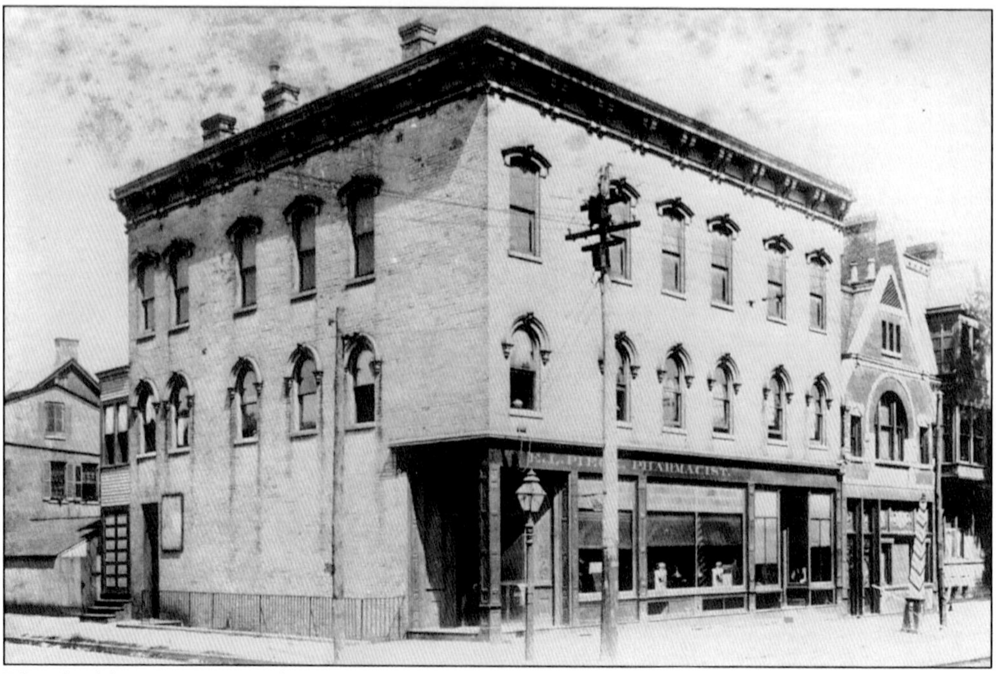

This building, constructed *c.* 1868 at the corner of Sixth and Main Streets, was known as Arnold's Hall. James G. Arnold (1800–1878) was a public school teacher and city council member, as well as a wealthy property developer. This building was built with a commercial space on the first floor and a meeting hall above. In the mid-1880s, E.L. Pieck established his pharmacy there.

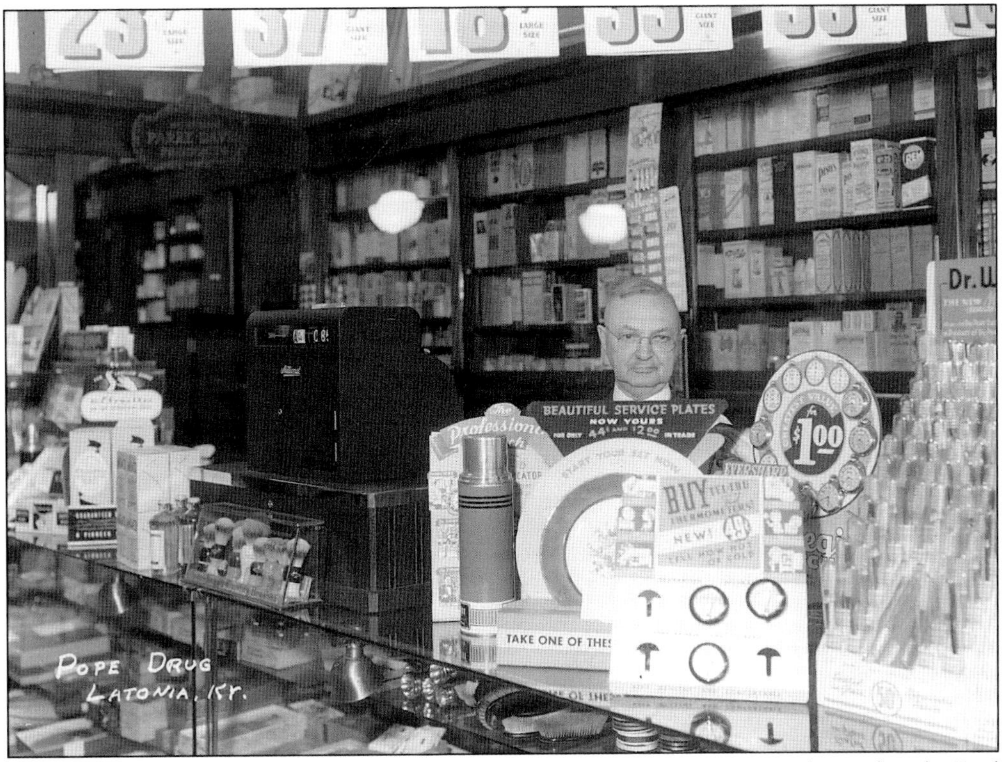

Mr. F.A. Pope stands behind the counter of his corner drug store, Pope Drug, located in the Bird Building at Rittes' corner in Latonia. F.A.Pope died in August of 1941.

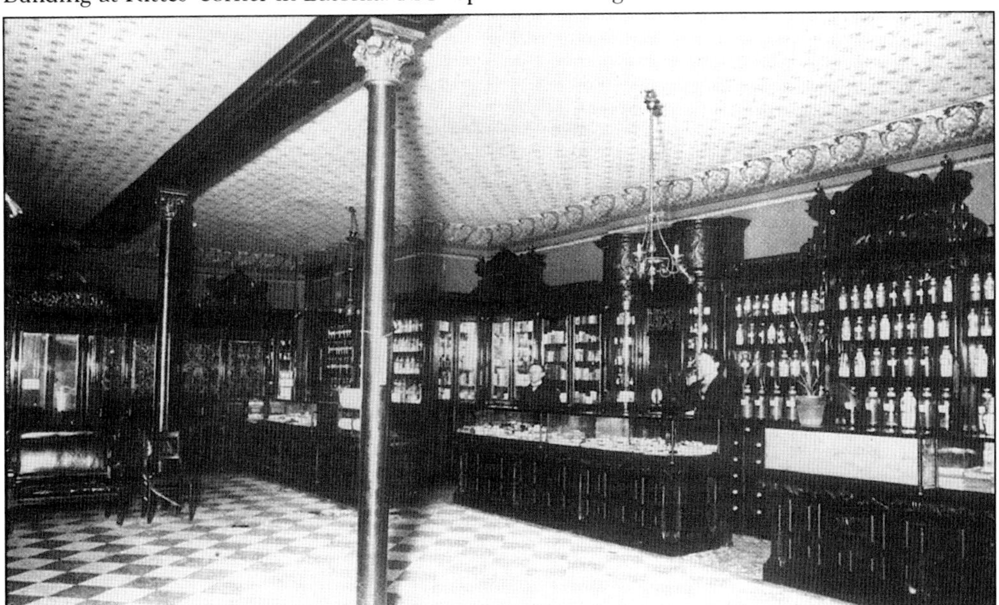

This is the interior of Pieck's Pharmacy, c. 1890. The elaborate interior, typical for its day, featured a polychromed pressed tin ceiling, a marble floor, intricate cabinetry, and elegant lighting fixtures. This interior is one of the few that has survived to this day—it is now the home of Dee Felice Café.

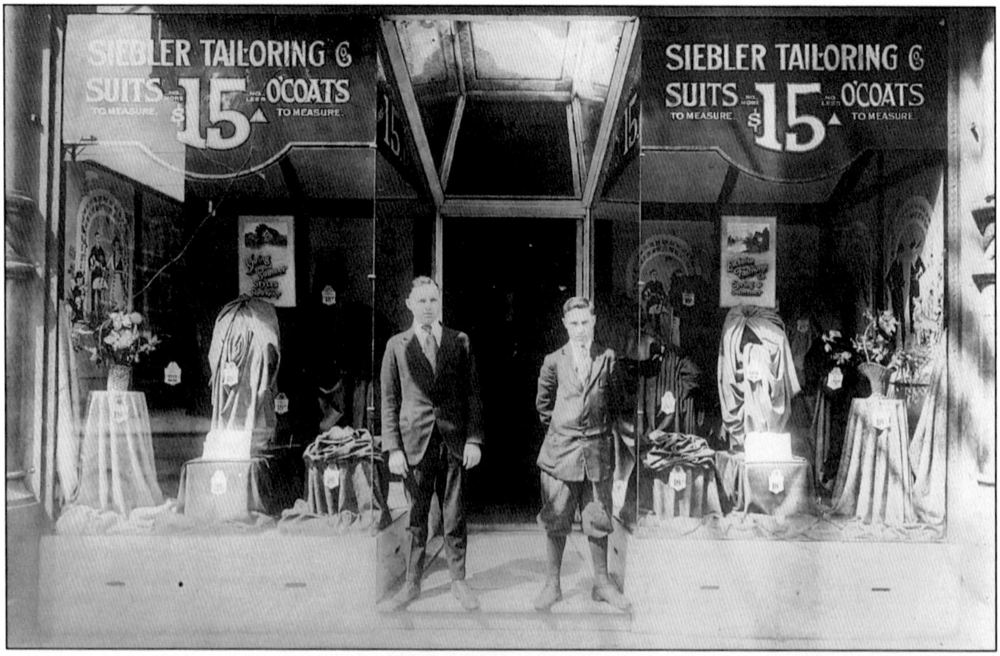

Two serious young men pose outside of the Siebler Tailoring Company, located at 607 Madison Avenue, adjacent to the German National Bank building. Both young men and women were involved in the garment trade as tailors, clothiers, seamstresses, and milliners in the late 19th and early 20th centuries.

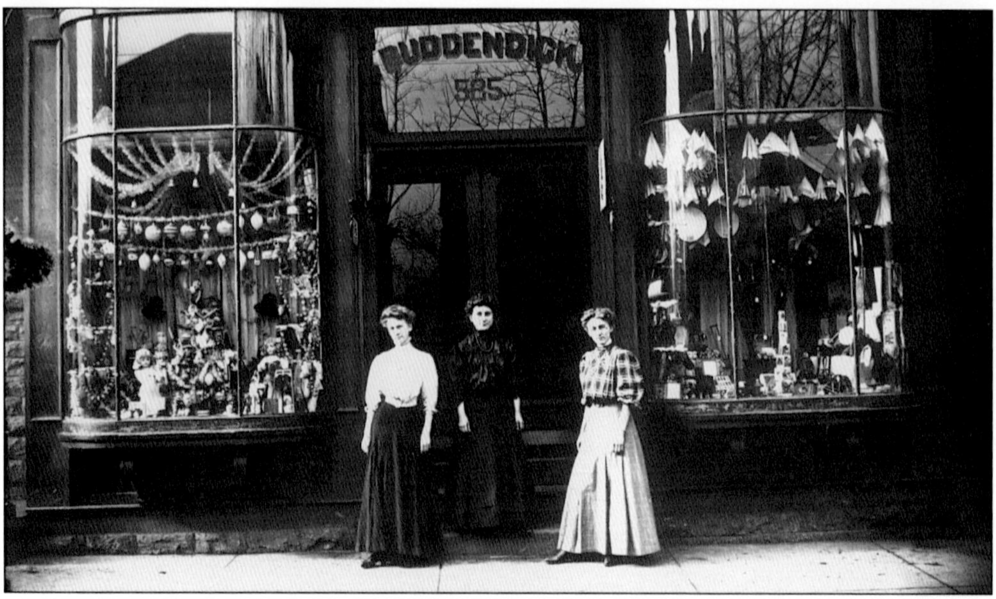

This photo shows Buddendicks, a shop located at 525 (now 521) Main Street during the Christmas season, *c.* 1908. These hardworking and enterprising sisters are first listed in the city directory in 1894 as seamstresses. By 1904, Louisa G. Buddendick opened a dry goods store at the southwest corner of Eighth and Bakewell Streets. By 1906, the name was changed to L.G. Buddendick and Sisters (Clara, Katie, and Mary) Dry Goods, and in 1908 this second store was opened.

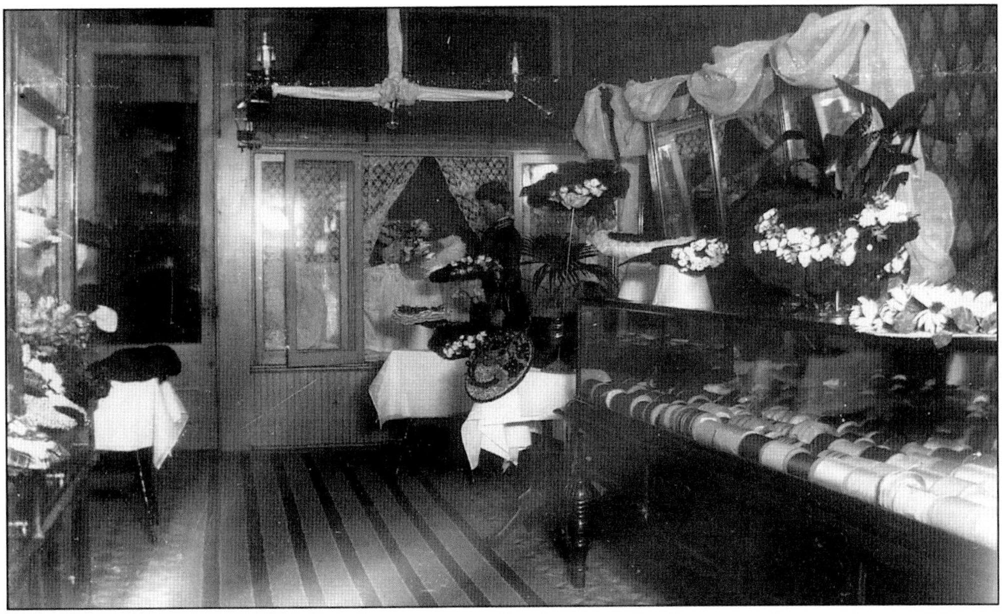

At a time when no woman would ever consider leaving the house without a hat, millinery shops provided the elaborate creations that fashion warranted in the early 20th century. This photo shows the interior of Wessels' Millinery Shop, 806 Madison Avenue. Nora Wessels and her daughter Lillie opened the shop in 1906 and Lillie continued in business there until 1922. (August Koenig, photographer.)

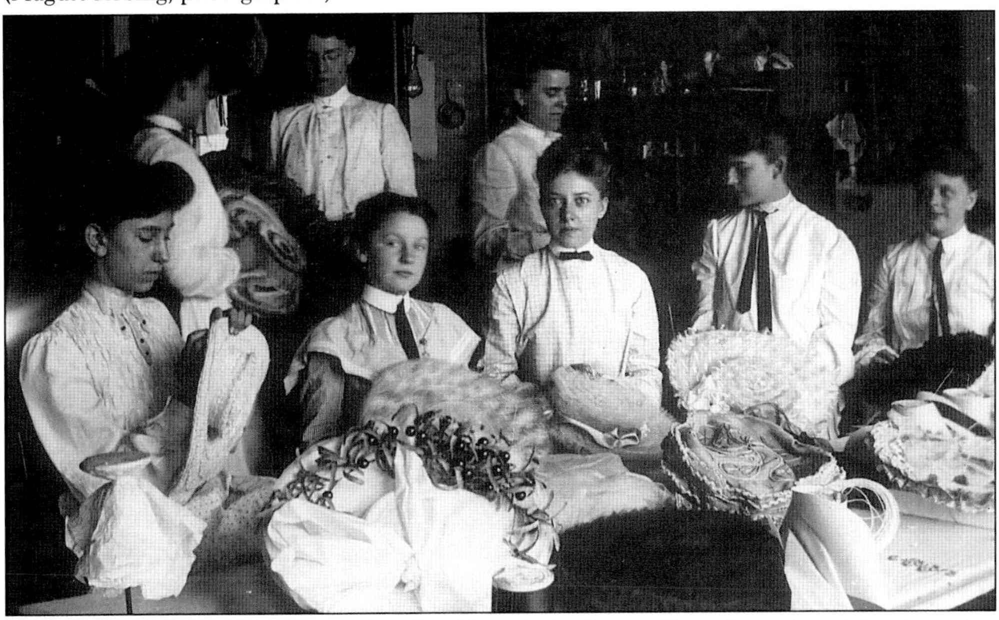

This photo of the many girls employed at Wessels' Millinery Shop shows how labor intensive hat making and trimming were. Millinery and dressmaking shops not only provided respectable employment for young women in the late 19th and early 20th centuries, they were two of the few socially acceptable venues in which an enterprising woman could own and run her own business. Such shops abounded in cities and towns everywhere, only to be put out of business by department stores during the 1920s and 1930s. (August Koenig, photographer.)

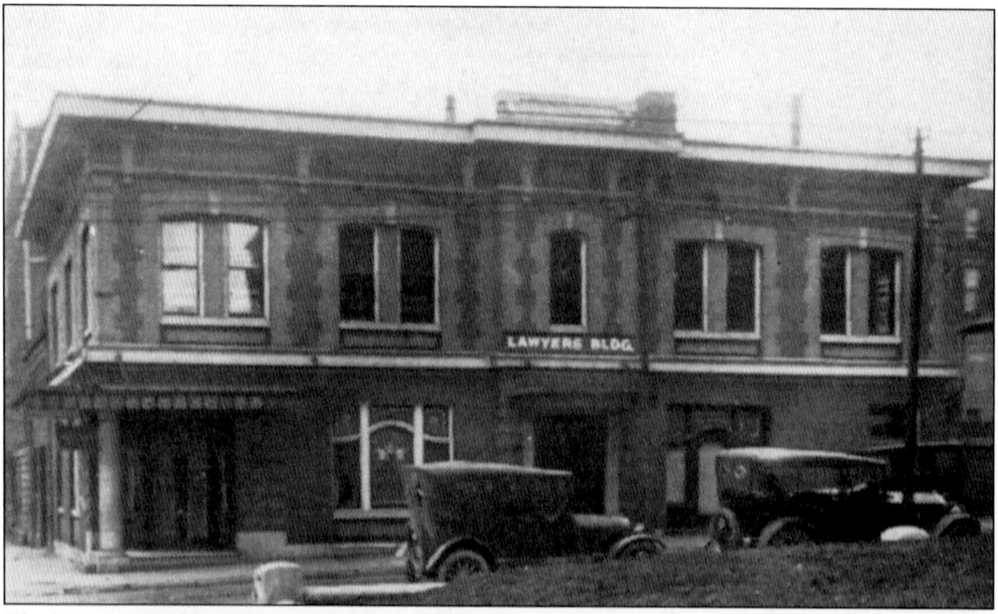

The Lawyers' Building, located on the northeast corner of Third and Scott Streets, was a familiar landmark until it was razed in the early 1990s. Its early history, however, was far different from the professional demeanor it later presented. Attributed to Covington architect Benjamin T. Wisenall, the building was built *c.* 1912 for Thomas R. Cody, a well-known restauranteur. Cody operated a saloon/restaurant in this building until Prohibition forced him to close in 1920. (Courtesy Cincinnati Historical Society Library.)

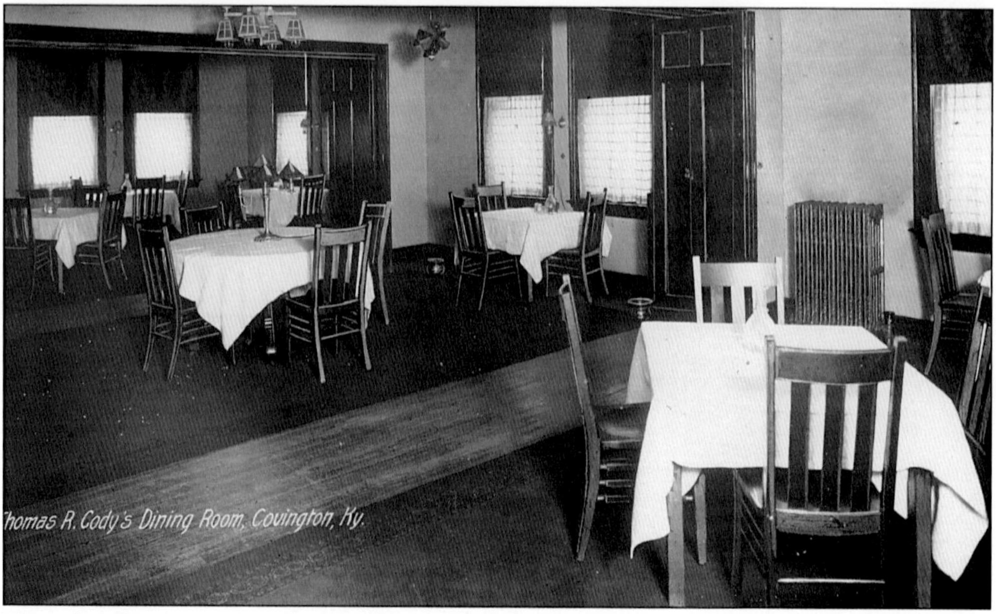

These handsome interior photographs were taken for promotional purposes and were used for postcards advertising Cody's Cafe. This photograph shows the second-floor dining room. With the pink walls, cream ceiling, and maroon carpets, the green glass lights and green window shades provided a striking accent. Note the ceiling fan in the corner and the spittoons on the floor. (Courtesy Cincinnati Historical Society Library.)

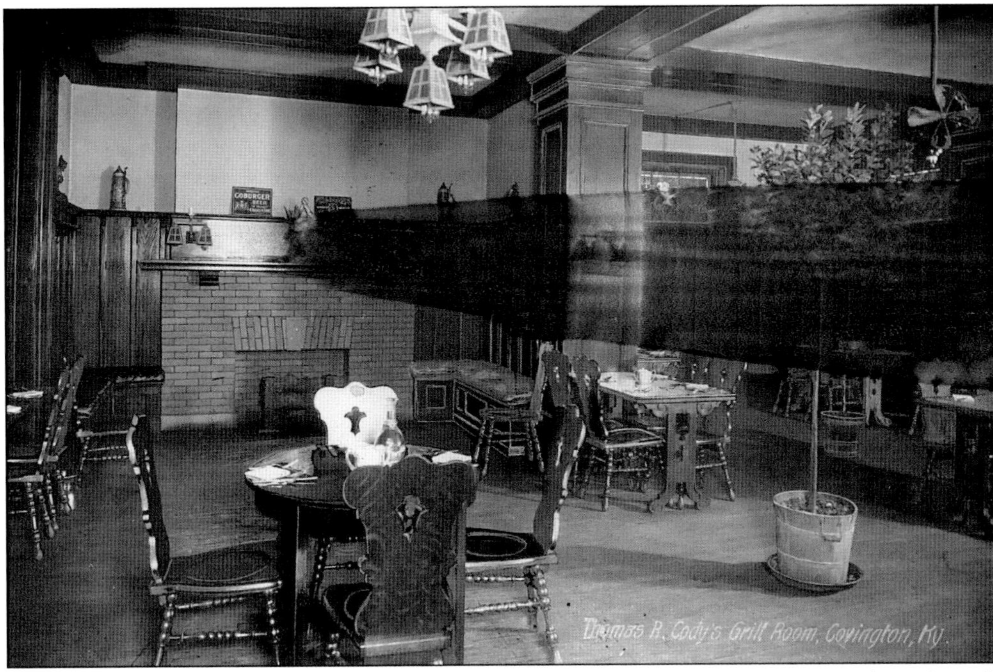

This wood-paneled room was the Grill Room at Cody's. The fireplace alcove, or inglenook, with its bench seating was a common feature of early 20th-century Arts and Crafts design. The light fixtures, dark paneling, and beamed ceilings all identify this handsome room as fine example of a period interior. (Courtesy Cincinnati Historical Society Library.)

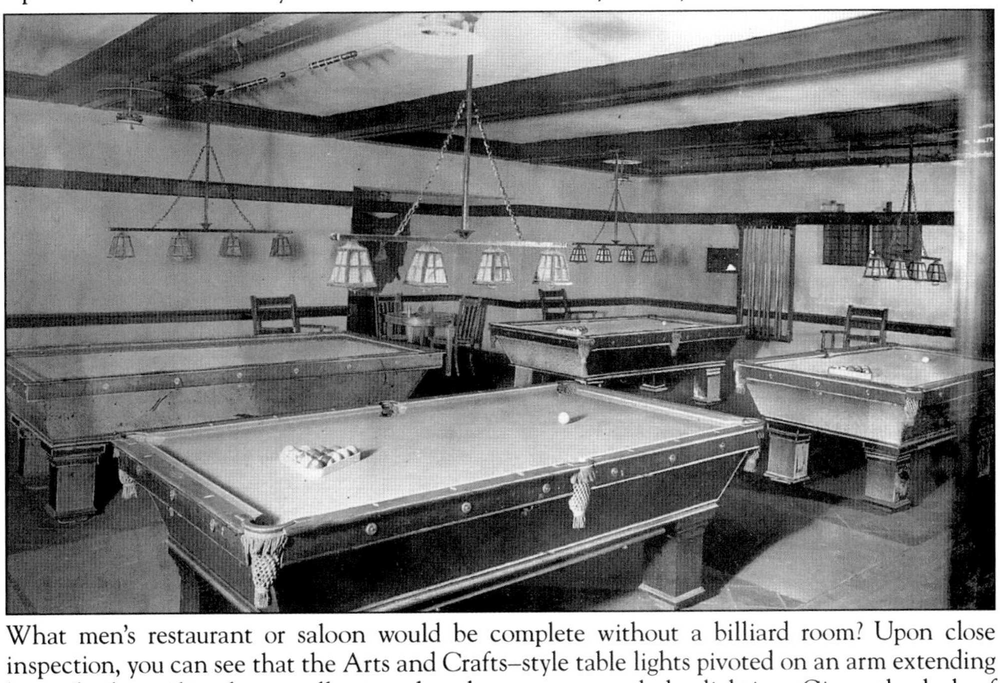

What men's restaurant or saloon would be complete without a billiard room? Upon close inspection, you can see that the Arts and Crafts–style table lights pivoted on an arm extending beneath the ceiling beams allowing the players to control the lighting. Given the lack of windows, this room might have been located in the basement of the building. (Courtesy Cincinnati Historical Society Library.)

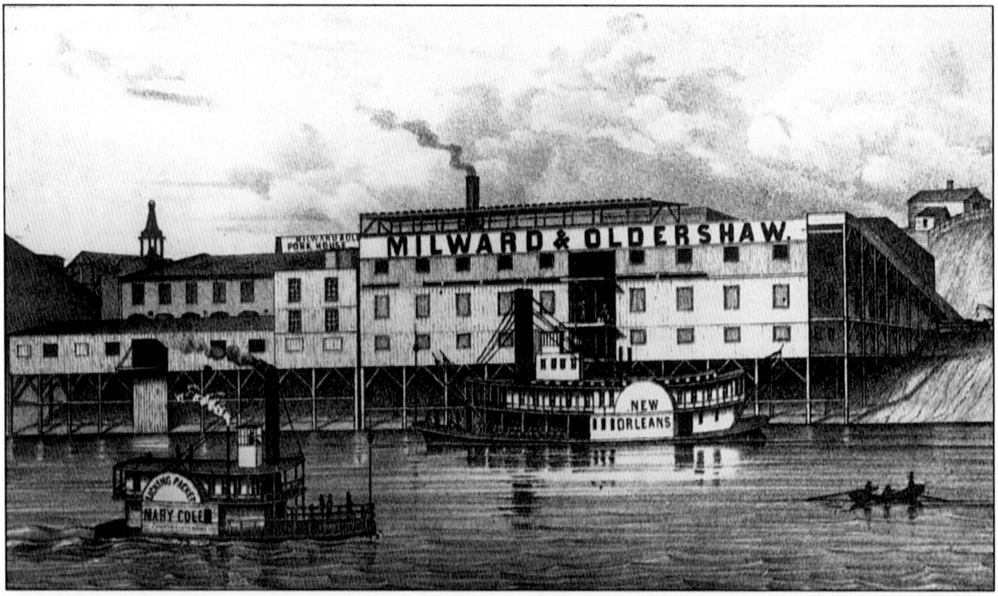

This is the Millward and Oldershaw Company, c. 1850. By the time this image was published, this pork processing plant was slaughtering 3,000 hogs a day and was the largest such plant in the country. Located on the bank of the Licking River between Robbins and Eleventh Streets, the plant burned in 1857 and was never rebuilt.

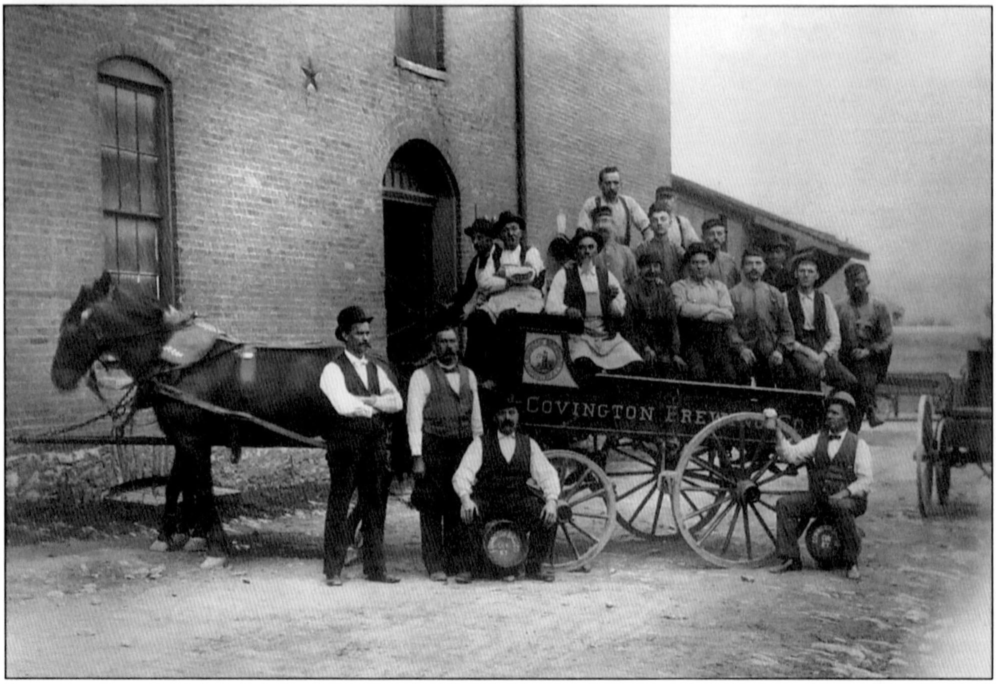

Workers from the Covington Brewing Company pose in the company's horse and wagon during the late 19th century. The Covington Brewery complex was located at the intersection of Scott and Pike Streets. Only the former brewery office building remains of what was once a thriving business. The other buildings were torn down in the 1920s during Prohibition to make way for a hotel which was never built.

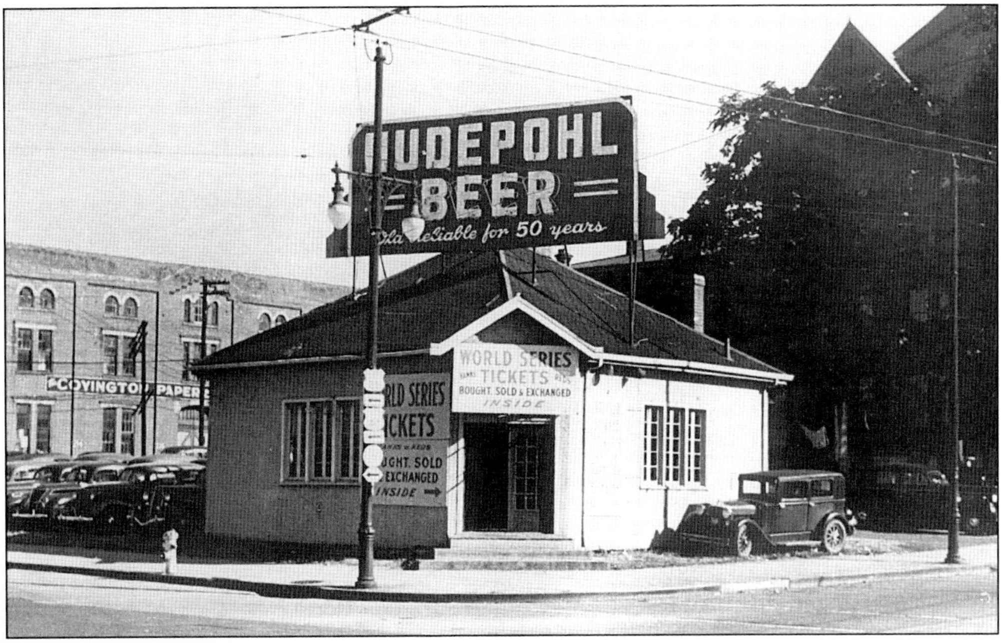

A small corner store located at the foot of the Suspension Bridge at Second and Court Streets advertises both beer and World Series Tickets in 1939. The Cincinnati Reds and New York Yankees played for the championship that year. The Reds lost—four games to none. Joe DiMaggio was one of the Yankees playing in that series.

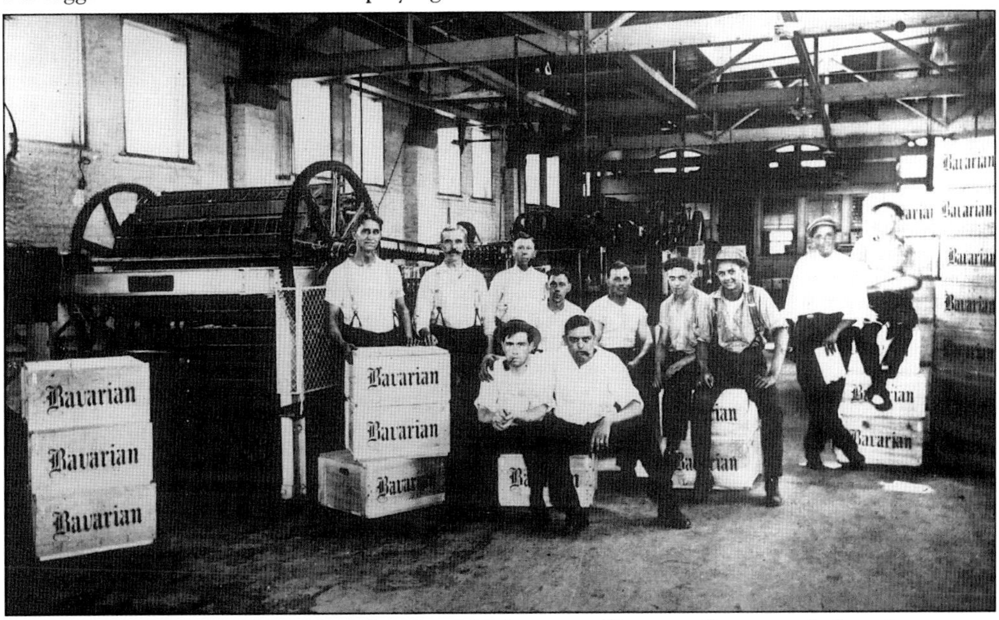

A group of brewery workers take a break at the Bavarian Brewing Company before the passage of the Eighteenth Amendment (Prohibition) in 1919. The brewery, located between Twelfth and Pike Streets, was one of Covington's largest. Bavarian was the brewer and bottler of the famous Bavarian and Reidlin's Select beers. The Bavarian Brewing Company was one of few breweries in Covington which reopened after the repeal of Prohibition. The main building is in use today as Jillian's.

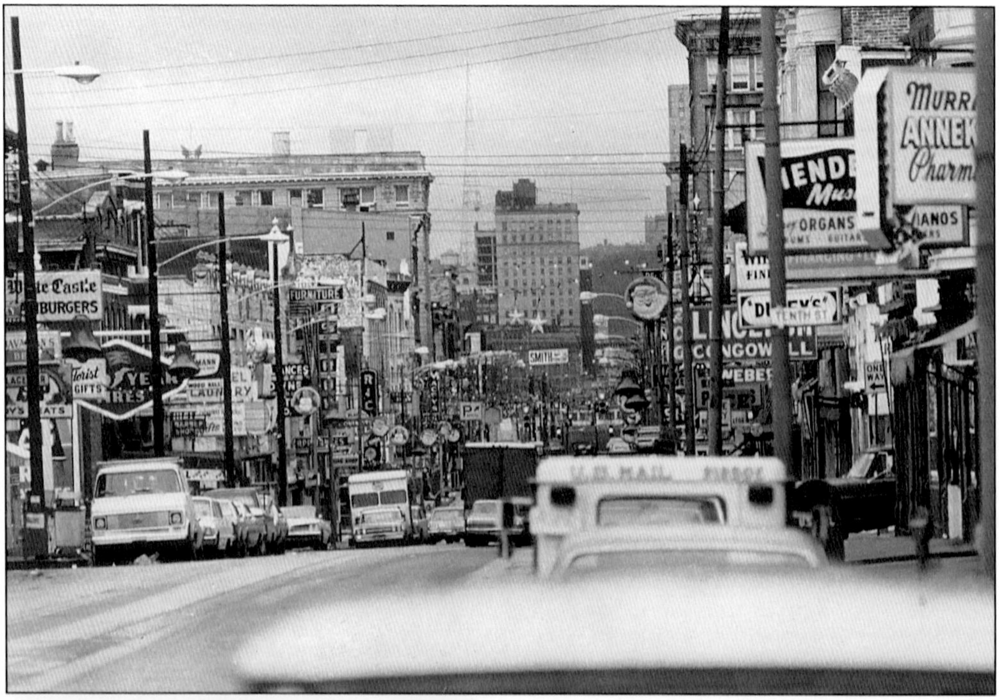

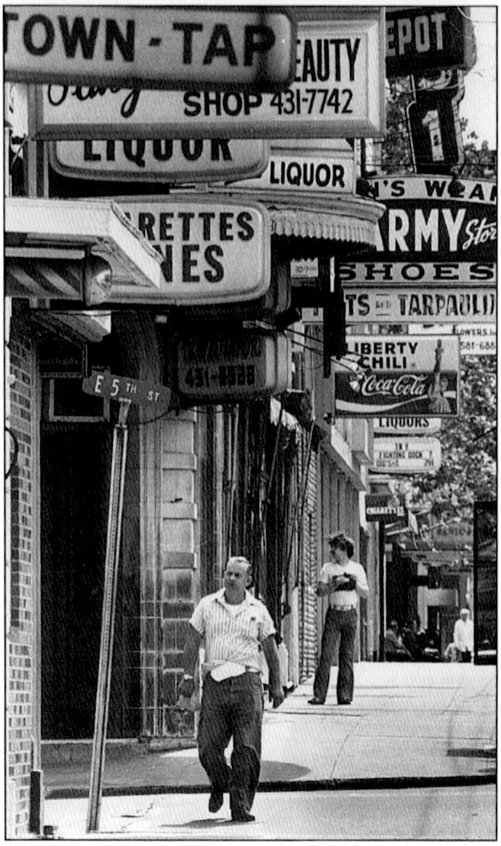

Smiling Santas look down on Madison Avenue, north from Tenth Street in December, 1971. In the distance is Cincinnati's Netherland Plaza Hotel Complex.

This is a more recent view of the corner of Fifth Street and Madison Avenue, facing south. The visual cacophony of signs reflects the vitality of the central business district, which was apparently still thriving in the late 1970s.

Four

NEIGHBORHOODS

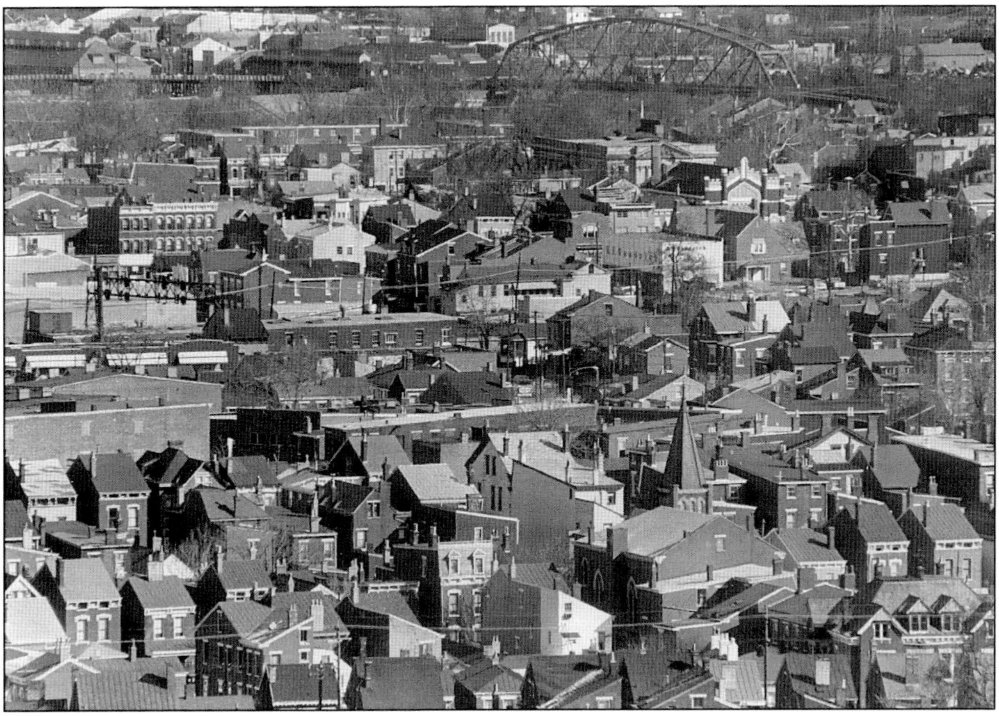

This *c.* 1975 view of Covington is looking eastward toward Newport. The spires of Grace United Church of Christ at Willard and Lockwood Streets are visible in the foreground. In the distance the Madison Avenue Baptist Church and the Carnegie Arts Center can be seen. The Shortway Bridge is at the top of the photo. This patchwork of rooftops displays the continuity of several neighborhoods—MainStrasse, the Central Business District, and the Eastside—as they seem to merge into one. (Terry Duennes, photographer.)

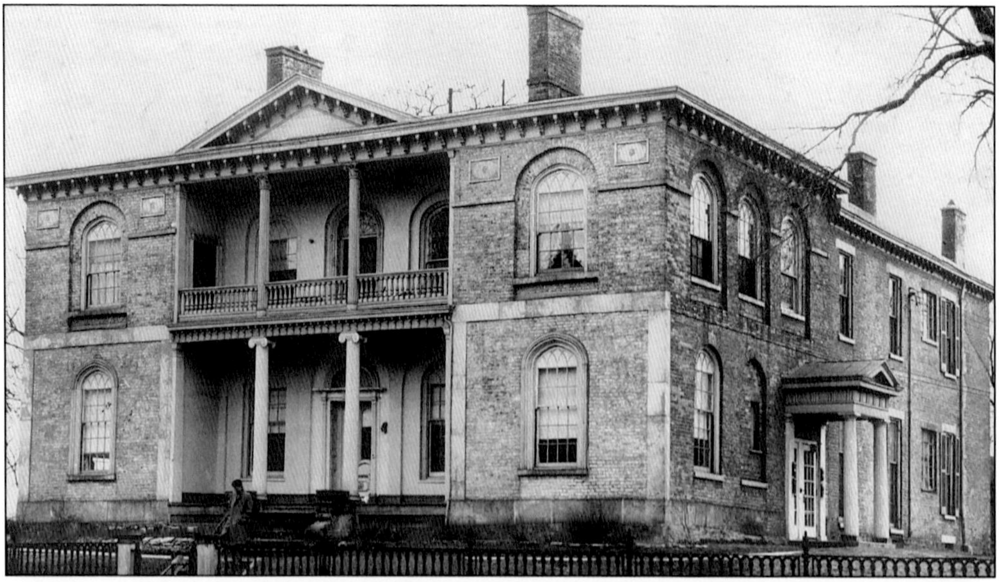

This is a *c.* 1940 photo of the Carneal House, built by real estate developer Thomas Carneal, *c.* 1815. This house, located on East Second Street, was the first brick structure built in Covington. A tunnel connects the basement of the house to the Licking River. Although the tunnel was probably originally built as a service access, rumors persist that the house and tunnel played a role in the Underground Railroad (William Lindsay Williams, photographer.)

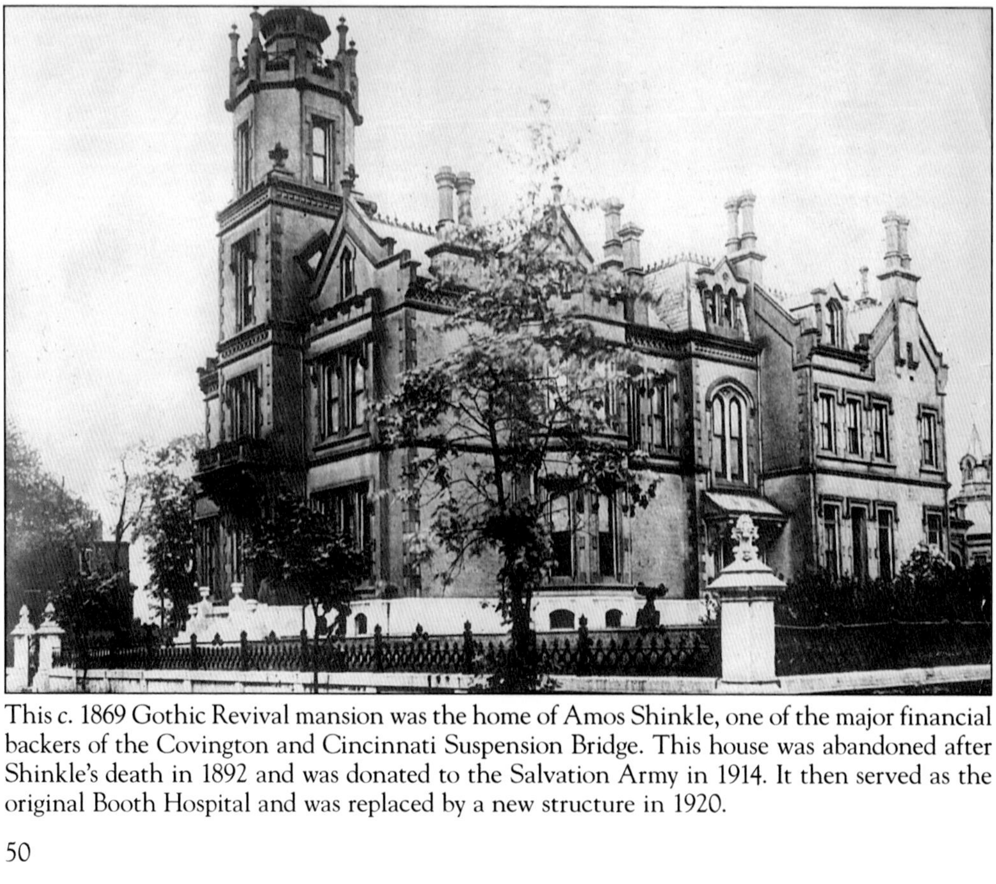

This *c.* 1869 Gothic Revival mansion was the home of Amos Shinkle, one of the major financial backers of the Covington and Cincinnati Suspension Bridge. This house was abandoned after Shinkle's death in 1892 and was donated to the Salvation Army in 1914. It then served as the original Booth Hospital and was replaced by a new structure in 1920.

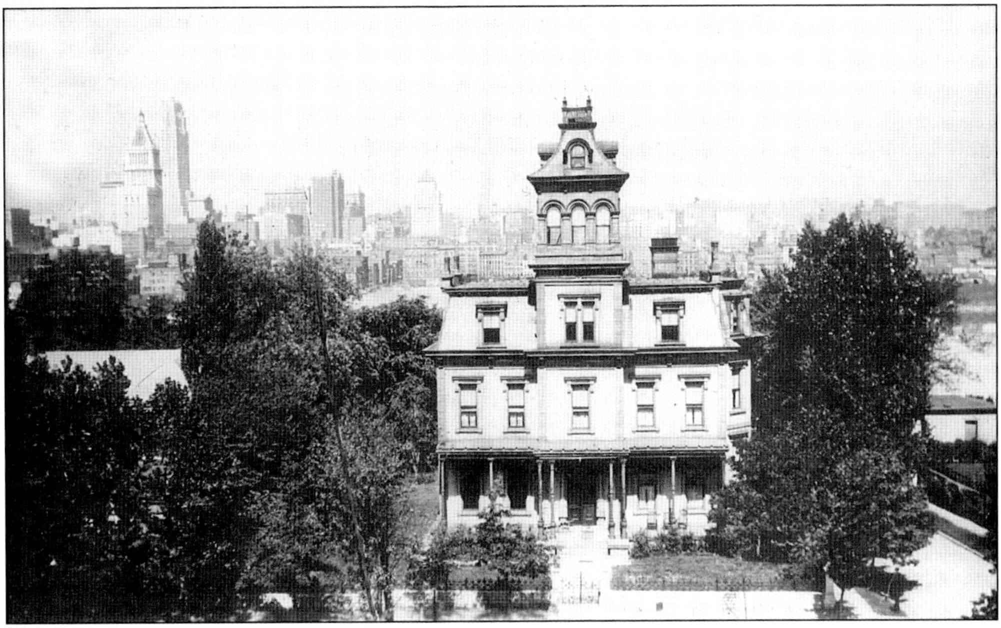

Another fine Second Street home, the Lovell-Graziani House was built for tobacco merchant H.L. Lovell Sr., *c.* 1878. It was later home to noted attorney and reform politician, B.F. Graziani, between 1909 and 1931. The house is a fine example of the Second Empire style with its mansard roof, cast-iron porch, and prominent tower. The tower no longer remains.

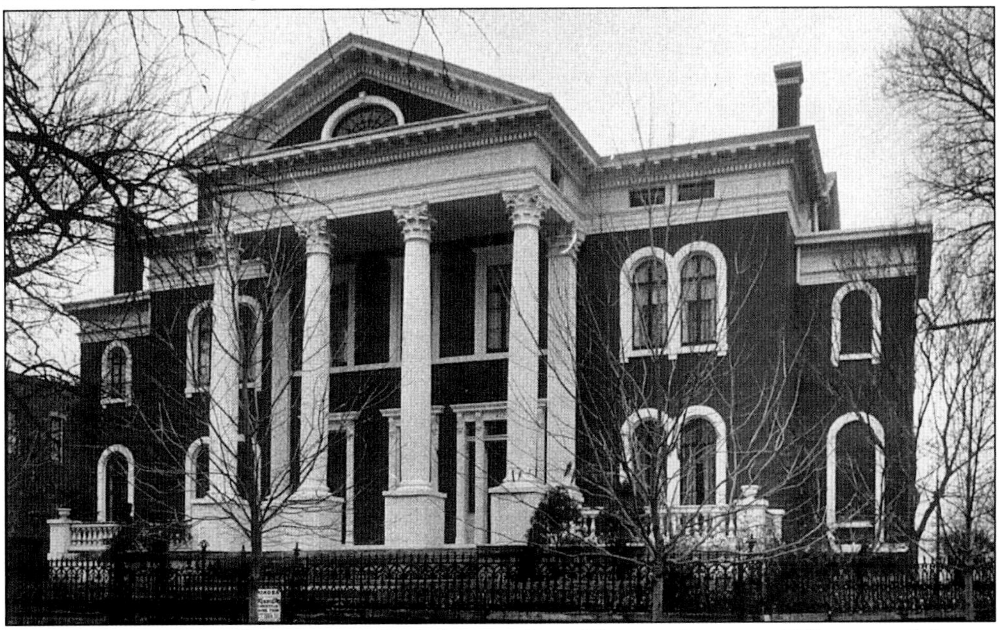

The Porter-Fallis-Lovell House was built by merchant Thomas Porter *c.* 1852, as an elaborate Italianate villa with a belvedere (tower), facing the Ohio River. It was sold to Daniel James Fallis *c.* 1861 and years later May Lovell, his granddaughter, remodeled the house *c.* 1900. The front of the house was then oriented away from the Ohio River towards East Second Street and the large Greek Revival portico was added. The house remained in the Fallis family until 1950, when it was sold at auction.

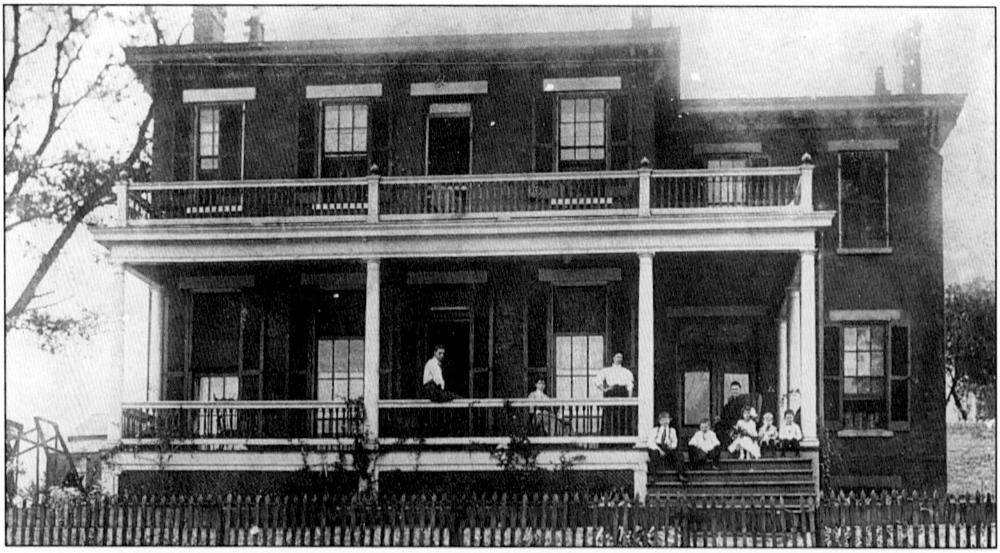

Located at the eastern end of Front Street, now Riverside Drive, this house, built by local attorney Harvey Myers *c.* 1860, has views of both the Licking and the Ohio Rivers. By the time this picture was taken, *c.* 1900, a Colonial Revival porch graced the front of the house. The porch has since been removed.

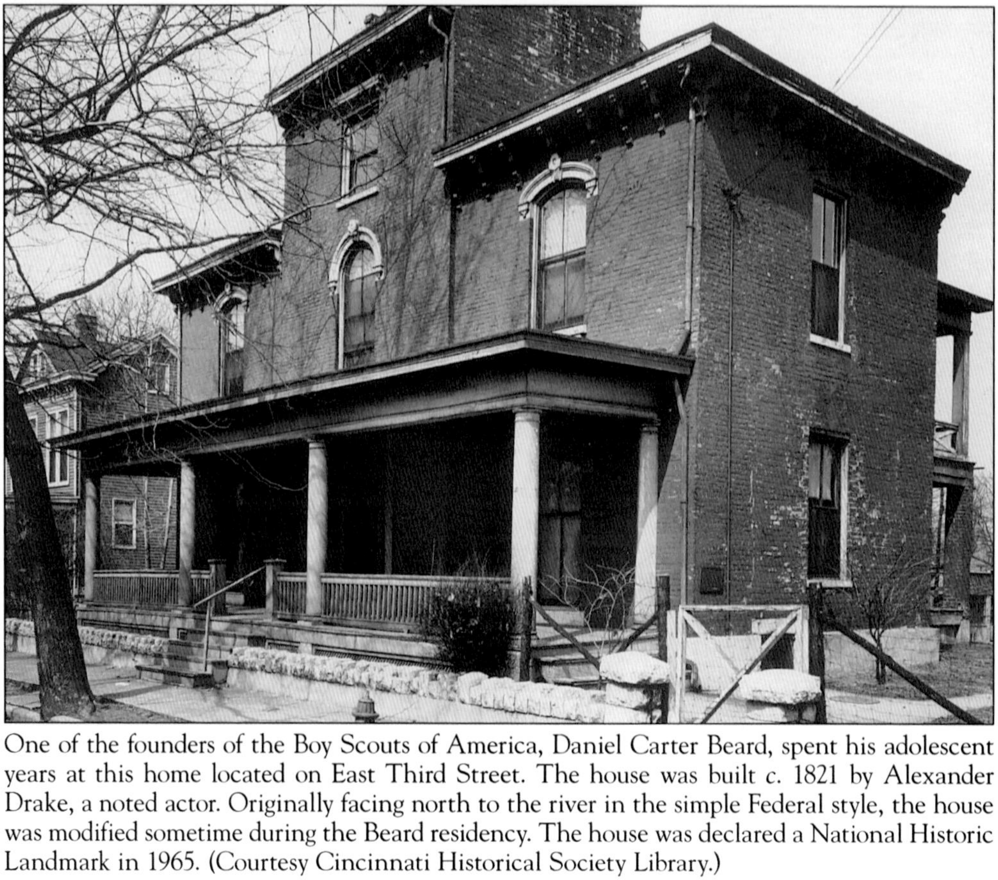

One of the founders of the Boy Scouts of America, Daniel Carter Beard, spent his adolescent years at this home located on East Third Street. The house was built *c.* 1821 by Alexander Drake, a noted actor. Originally facing north to the river in the simple Federal style, the house was modified sometime during the Beard residency. The house was declared a National Historic Landmark in 1965. (Courtesy Cincinnati Historical Society Library.)

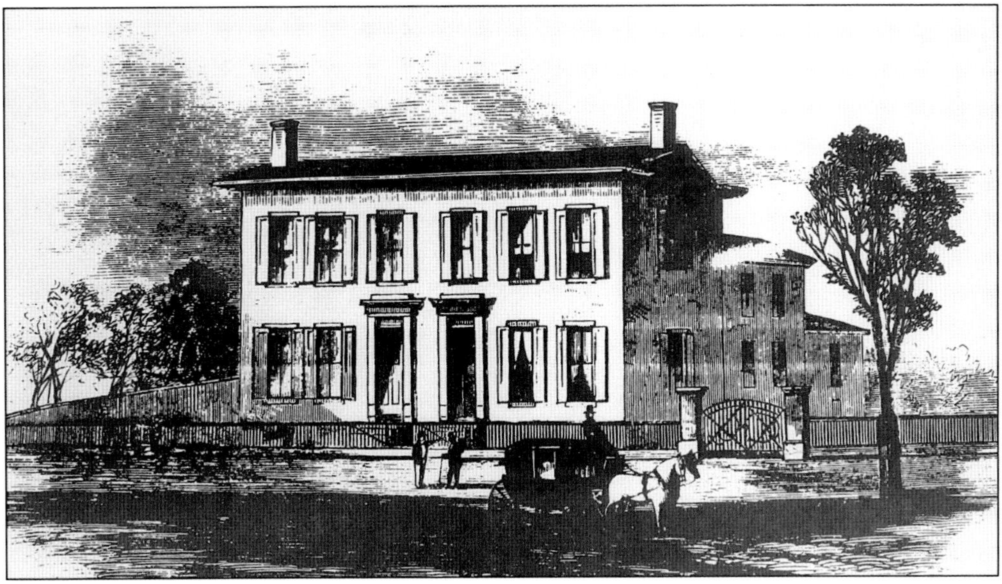

Located at 518–520 Greenup Street, this attached pair of houses was built c. 1850. They were purchased by Jesse Root Grant, father of Ulysses S. Grant, in 1859. He lived there until his death in 1873. A merchant, Jesse Grant was appointed postmaster of Covington by President Andrew Johnson in 1866 and he served in that capacity until 1872. The houses underwent several modifications during the Grant family residency, including the addition of a third floor/ mansard roof.

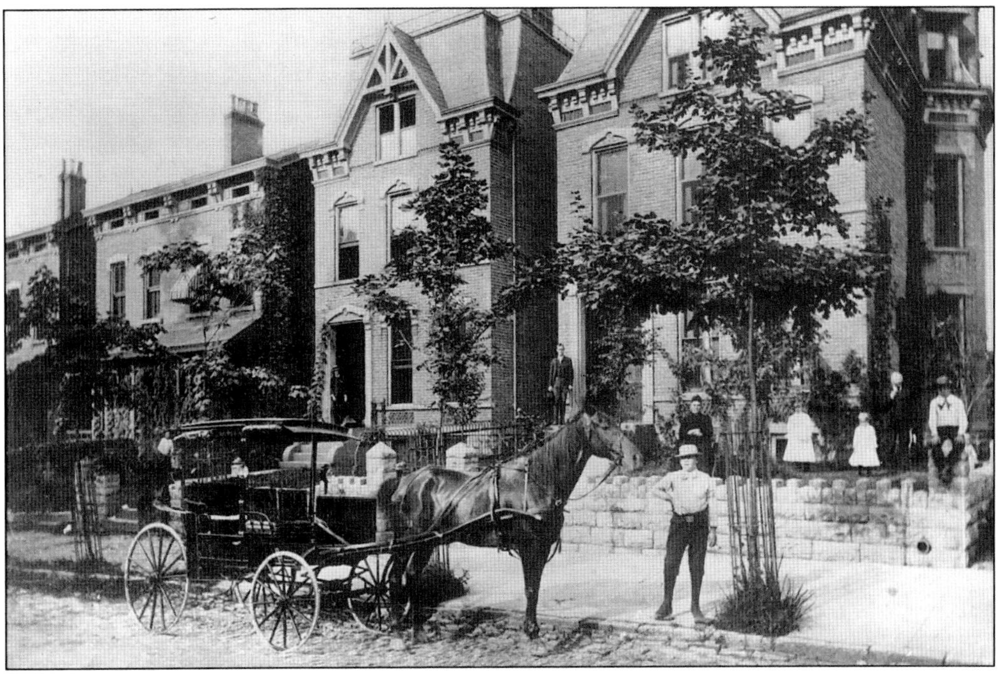

These two houses, located on the northeast corner of Garrard and East Seventh Streets, were built by M.J. Dudley, attorney, c. 1885. The corner house was quickly sold to Mr. and Mrs. August Appel. The Appels owned and operated a millinery shop at 540 Madison Avenue. This photograph is quite possibly a formal family portrait of the Appels.

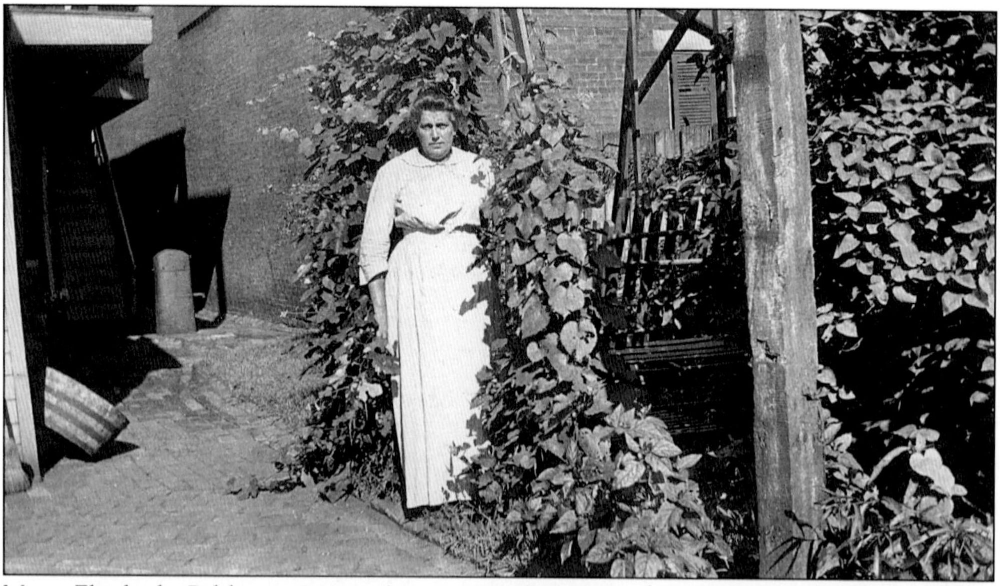

Mary Elizabeth Pohlman Summerkamp was the widow of Frank Summerkamp. Their two sons were Frank, an elevator operator, and L.H., a woodworker at Ohio Scroll and Lumber. Mrs. Summerkamp (*c.* 1914) is surrounded by items from her life as a housekeeper on Craig Street. Note the broom, the washtub, and the water pump adjacent to the house, now demolished.

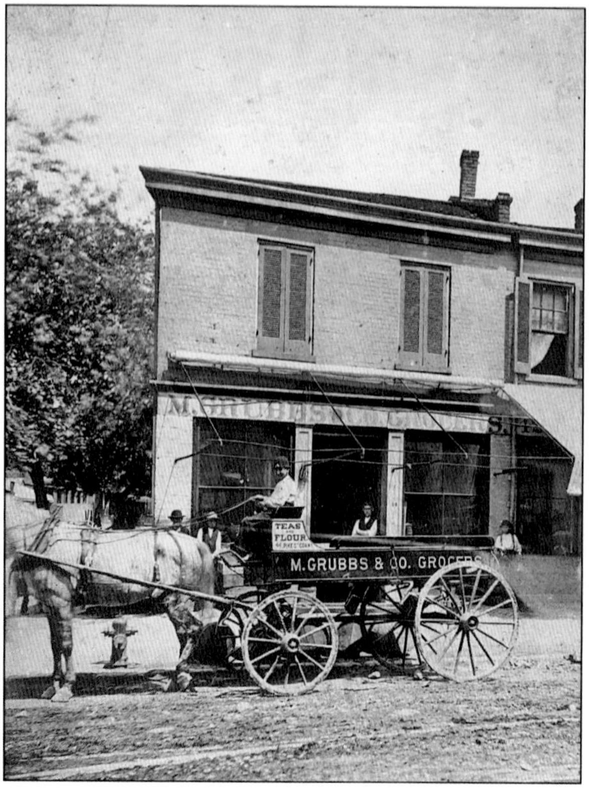

Marion G. Grubbs operated this wholesale and retail grocery on the northeast corner of Pike and Washington Streets *c.* 1875–*c.* 1894. This pre-Civil War building, then typical of that block of Pike Street, was demolished to make way for Parisian's Department Store, approximately 10 years after this photo was taken.

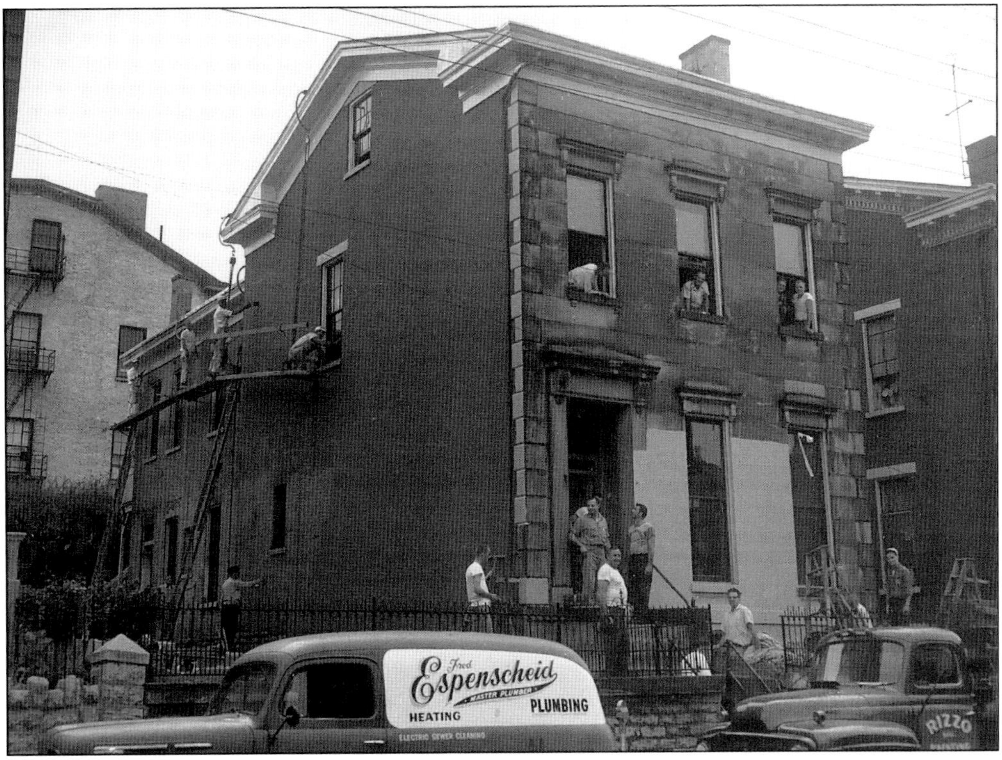

By the time this photo was taken shortly after World War II, this *c.* 1870 townhouse on West Fifth Street was due for some long-deferred repairs. The housing shortage of the post-war years spurred much activity as many historic homes were renovated into multi-family dwellings. Both Espenscheid Plumbing of Fort Thomas and Rizzo Painting of Fort Wright are still in business. How many workmen can you find? (Raymond E. Hadorn, photographer.)

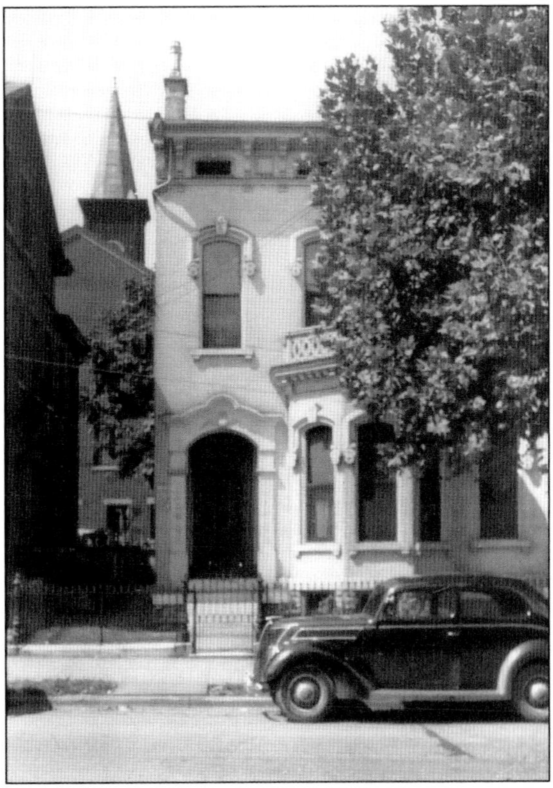

This *c.* 1874 house was built on Russell Street for Harriet Albro and her teenage children after the death of her husband, Henry Albro, a Cincinnati dealer in fine woods and veneers. Italianate in style, the interior detailing includes elaborate plasterwork, doors, and windows in fine woods and a curved staircase. Harriet Albro lived there until her death in 1904.

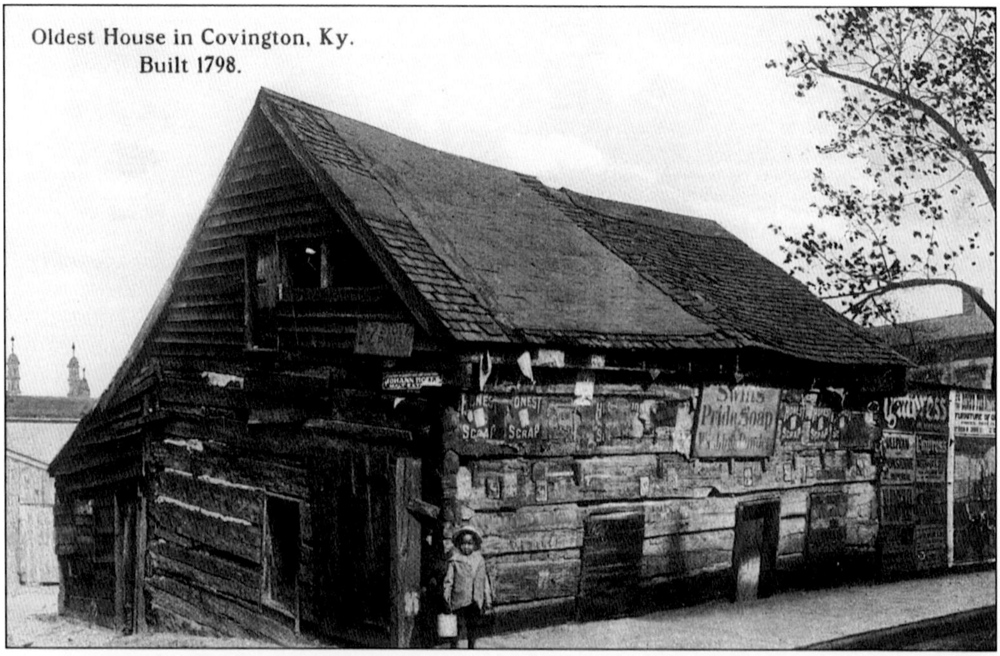

This log house, located on West Ninth Street, between Russell and Banklick Streets, was the center of quite a controversy when, in 1916, the city decided to demolish it because of safety concerns. Reported (erroneously) to have once been occupied by Simon Kenton and visited by Daniel Boone, the house was moved to this site from a location adjacent to the courthouse, where it had been used as a schoolhouse early in the 19th century. Note the little boy carrying a lard or beer bucket and the spires of Mother of God Church in the background.

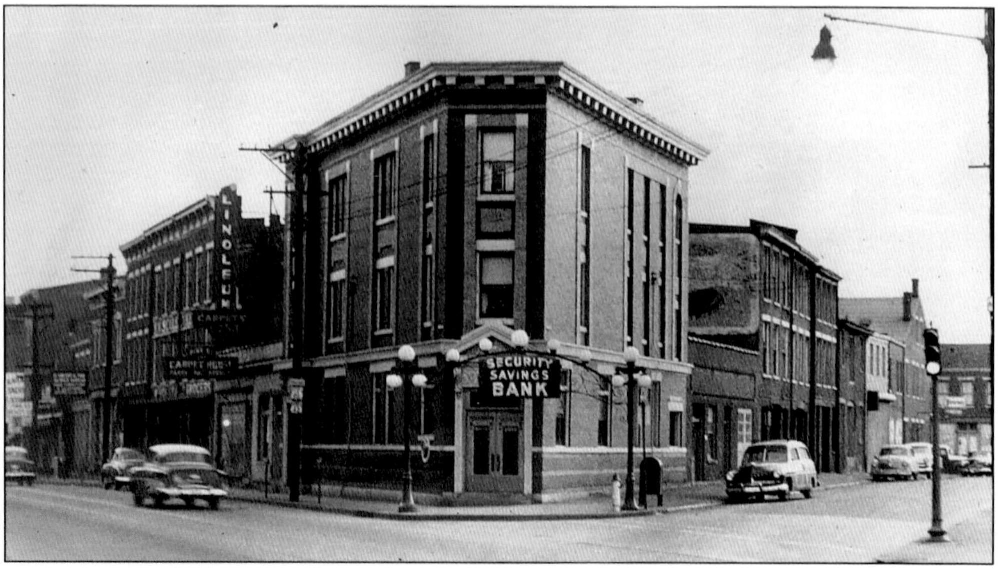

Located at the corner of Pike and West Ninth Streets, this bank was originally built as the Western German Savings Bank, *c.* 1910. Anti-German sentiment during World War I caused the bank to be renamed the Security Savings Bank, which it remained until the late 1980s, when it was taken over by Fifth Third Bank. Today the building is owned by the Covington Board of Education. Note the elaborate arch supporting the sign.

Edward Schneider built and opened this sample room on the northwest corner of West Twelfth and Bullock Streets in 1912, a scant seven years before Prohibition. He continued in business there, however, first as a soft drink establishment and later as a grocery store. Note the sign for a public telephone pay station on the side of the building and the woman and child waiting for a streetcar. The building was demolished in the 1990s.

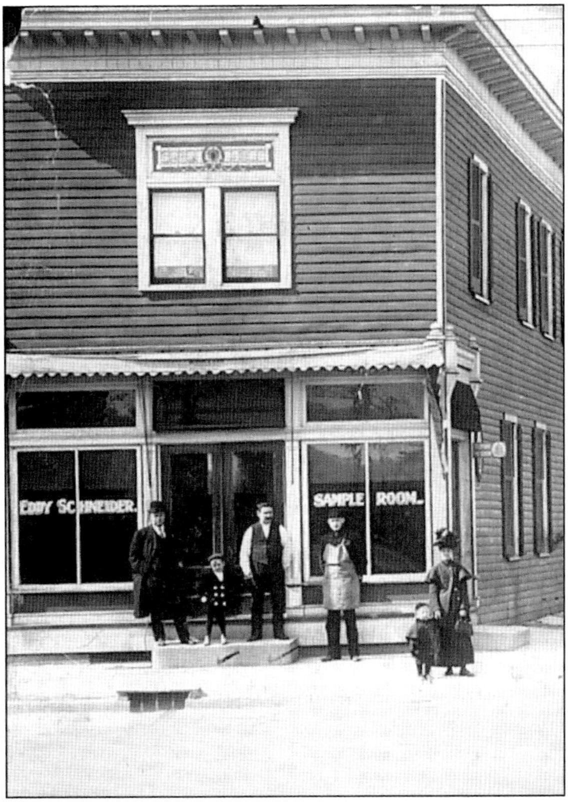

A group of men enjoy a pint at the Lewisburg Tavern, located at the corner of Worth and Lewis Streets, c. 1894. This very possibly could have been a portrait of a meeting of the Scheuetzengesellschaft or the Lewisburg Scheutzen (Shooting) Society, because most of the men are wearing ties and hats and at least one has a gun in his hand.

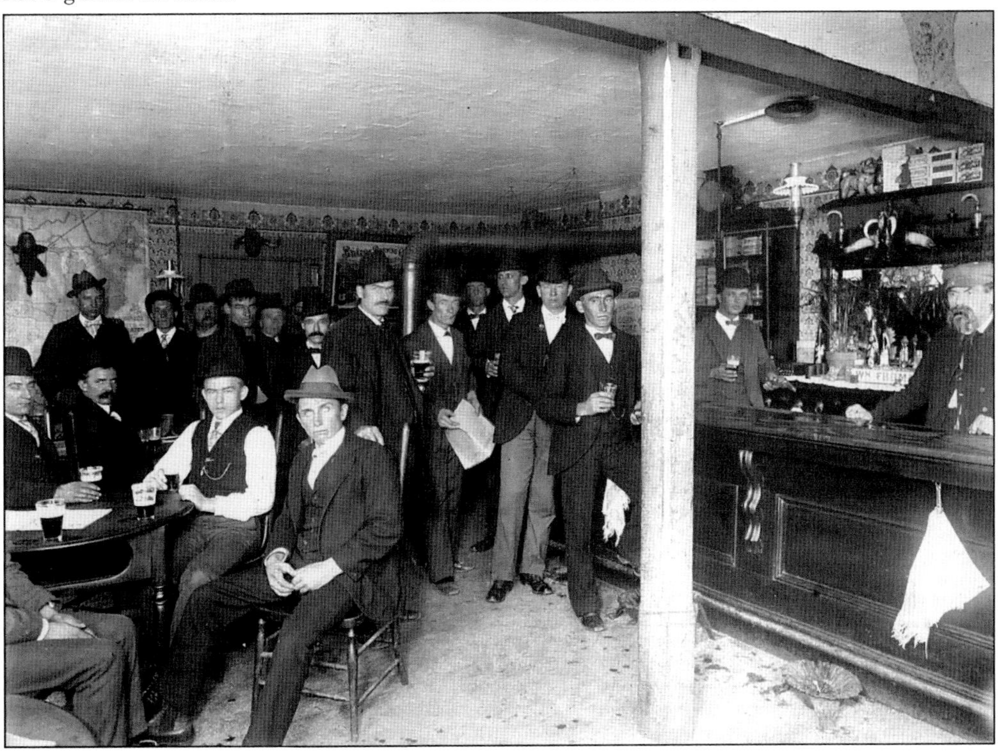

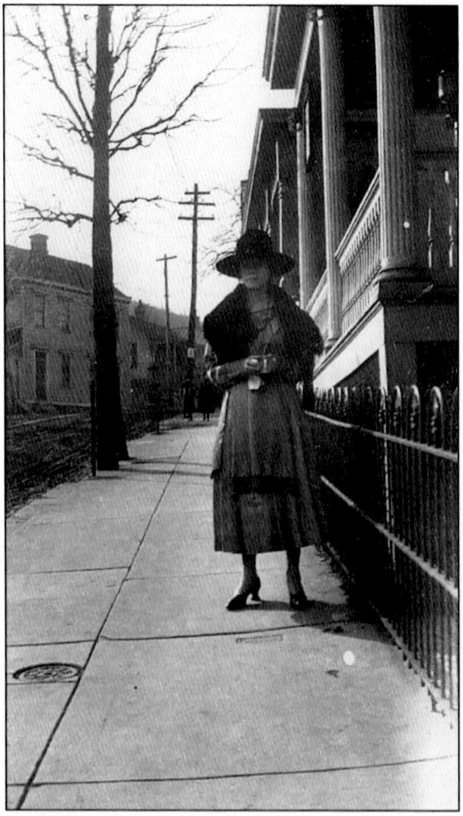

Laura C. Nienaber is pictured in front of her home at 6 (now 808) Montague Street. At the time this photograph was taken, c. 1914, Laura resided there with William T. Nienaber, insurance agent; William J. Nienaber, painter; and Frances Nienaber. Both the Nienaber house and the house seen in the background still stand. Even though the sidewalks had been paved, Montague Street was still a dirt road.

This 1915 photo shows the laying of the tracks for the Ludlow streetcar line. The tavern, located on the corner of Highway and Hayman (now Altamont) Avenues, was owned by Christ Barkhau. What was originally known as St. John's First German Evangelical Protestant Church can be seen in the background. (Courtesy Joseph Gastright.)

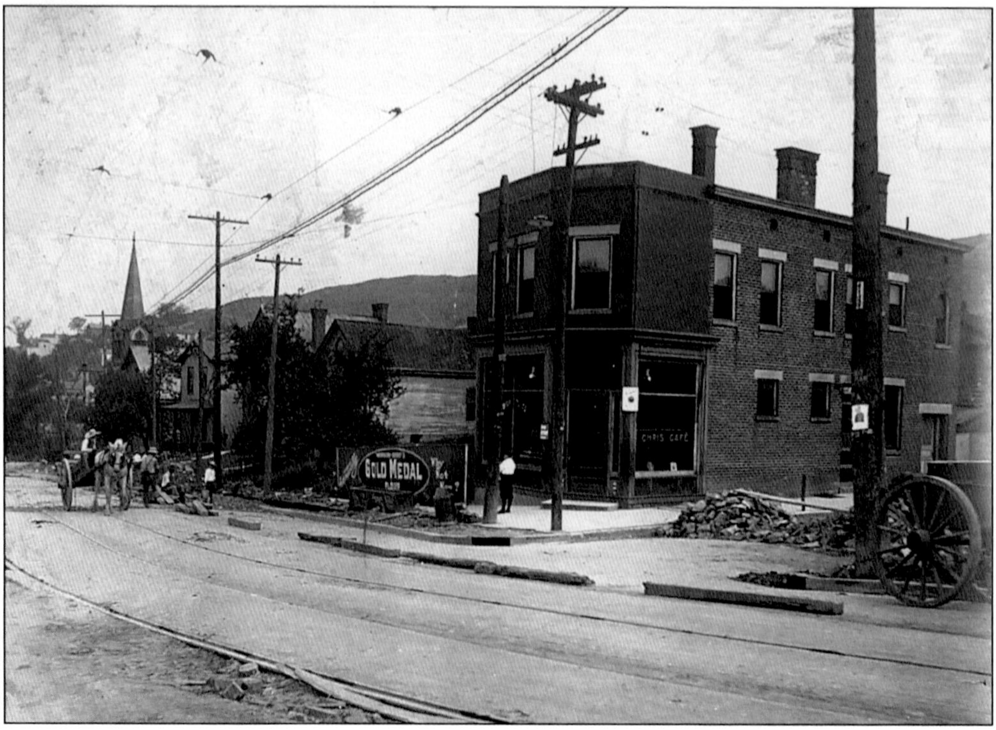

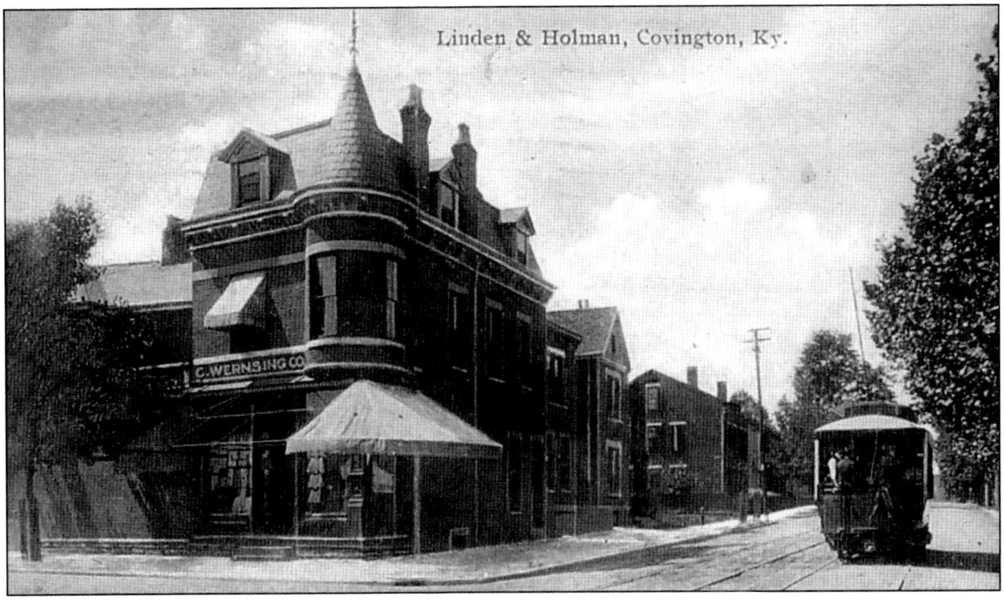

This postcard depicts the C. Wernsing Company, a dry goods store located on the northwest corner of Linden and Holman Streets. C. Wernsing was probably Clara Wernsing, a widow. The store was operated by her children while the family lived upstairs. In the late 20th century it was a tavern, and, according to rumor, contained the old bar removed from the Latonia racetrack clubhouse.

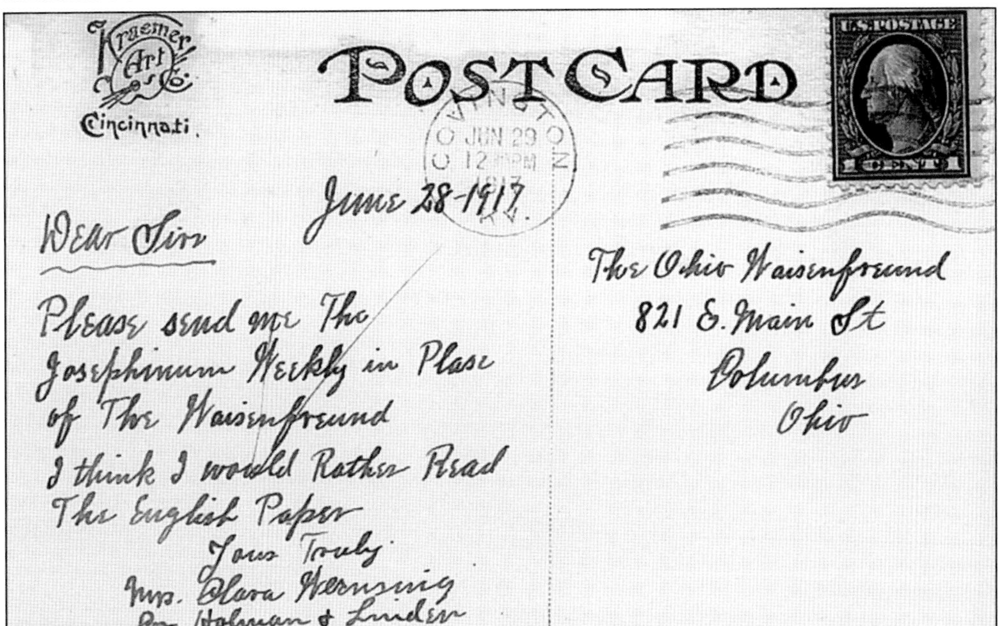

June 28-1917

Dear Sir

Please send me The Josephinum Weekly in Plase of The Waisenfreund
I think I would Rather Read The English Paper
Yours Truly
Mrs. Clara Wernsing
Cor Holman & Linden
Cov Ky.

The Ohio Waisenfreund
821 E. Main St
Columbus
Ohio

Mrs. Clara Wernsing wrote this postcard in 1917 to the Ohio-based *The Waisenfreund*, a German-language publication, requesting that her subscription be changed to the *Josephinum Weekly*, an English-language publication concerned with German American activities. She was the proprietor of the corner store seen above, and was fortunate to have commercial postcards of her store and home available to her!

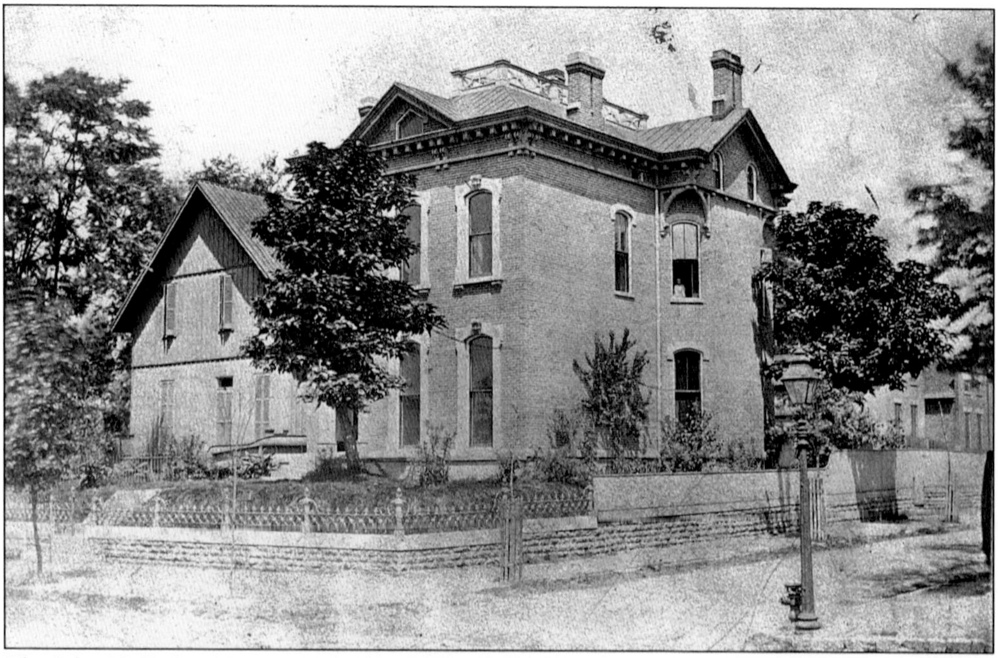

The John N. Furber House was built *c.* 1870 on the northeast corner of Scott and Lynn Streets. Furber was a Covington attorney. In 1880, his widow was listed in the city directory as residing there and by 1890, their son, Charles S. Furber, also an attorney, was living there. During the 1930s the Temple Israel Synagogue was built on the site.

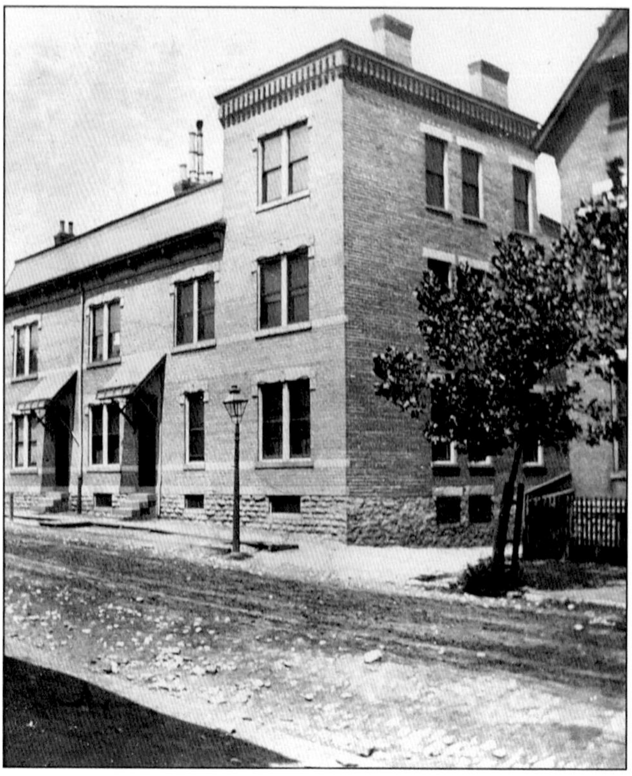

These handsome buildings, on Robbins Street west of Madison Avenue, were known as the Furber Block and built by Charles S. Furber *c.* 1893, who resided there until 1905. One was his home and the others were apartments. They were later renamed the Maurice Apartments and were demolished *c.* 1960 as part of the bridge right-of-way.

The Covington High School Alumni Association

(INCORPORATED)

HISTORICAL DEPARTMENT,
CHAS. S. FURBER, HISTORIAN.

COVINGTON, KY., JUNE 4, 1902.

DEAR FELLOW-GRADUATE:—This Association is looking forward to the preparation of a History of the Covington High School, its teachers and alumni. To that end it is collecting material from every available source, such as personal and family histories, personal and class reminiscences and anecdotes, individual and class pictures, and other things of interest.

There have been over five hundred and forty graduates. They are scattered to all parts of the globe, they have entered all the walks of life, and they are represented in all professions, trades and business enterprises. About sixty of these are known to be dead, some we have been unable to locate. (A list of the latter accompanies this letter; can you not tell us who and where some of them are?)

If this work be deferred much longer what is difficult now will become an impossibility.

Will you not aid us by filling and returning at once the enclosed blank, thus giving us authentic information concerning yourself and your family? The material you send us will not go out as your autobiography. In many cases modesty would forbid. It will, however, in the hands of the historical department, serve as a reliable basis from which to verify and correct the matter accumulated. Later on we will need your assistance in making up the missing links, and in testing for and correcting errors, in this way making the work as accurate and complete as practicable.

If I were to write you a letter containing just such information about your old schoolmates, whom you knew so well and have probably not seen for years, as we are asking you to send us about yourself, you could not but be both interested and pleased. Then rest assured they will be interested in hearing from you.

Kindly fill out the enclosed blank and add on the back anything which you think may be of interest, and especially suggestions as to where we may obtain matter of interest, and return it within the next two or three days, as we wish to use a portion of it, properly compiled, at the coming banquet. Don't put it off. We will be glad to hear from you again later on.

Counting on your co-operation, and thanking you in advance, we remain

Fraternally yours,

CHAS. S. FURBER, Historian.

Postoffice addresses are wanted of the following: Miss Anna Garner, '84; Miss Maud Germain, '95; Miss Emma Thompson, '96; Miss Alice C. Gunning; Miss Mabel Shaw, '87.

This 1902 letter was written by school historian and attorney Charles S. Furber beseeching Covington High School alumni for information to compile a comprehensive history of the school and its students. Experience has shown us just how difficult a task he had before him! (Courtesy Judith Boyers Gee.)

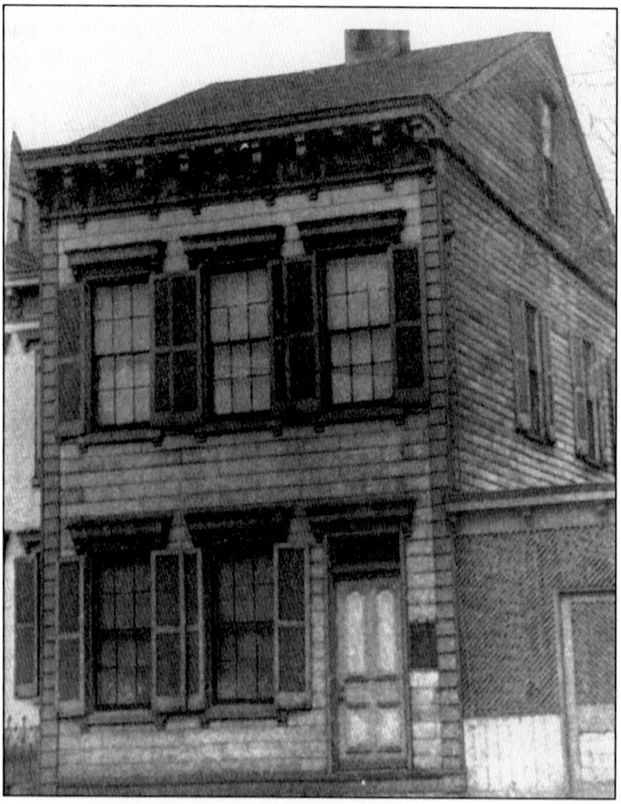

This modest frame dwelling was home to Covington artist Frank Duveneck (1848–1919) for most of his life. Built by his stepfather, Joseph Duveneck, c. 1861, the family home and property was also the family business, a beer garden. It was expanded several times as the family grew, and when Duveneck returned permanently to the area in 1900, a painting studio was added to the rear of the house. The house remained virtually unchanged by the time of this c.1940 photograph. Both the house and the studio are currently being restored as part of the Frank Duveneck Arts and Cultural Center.

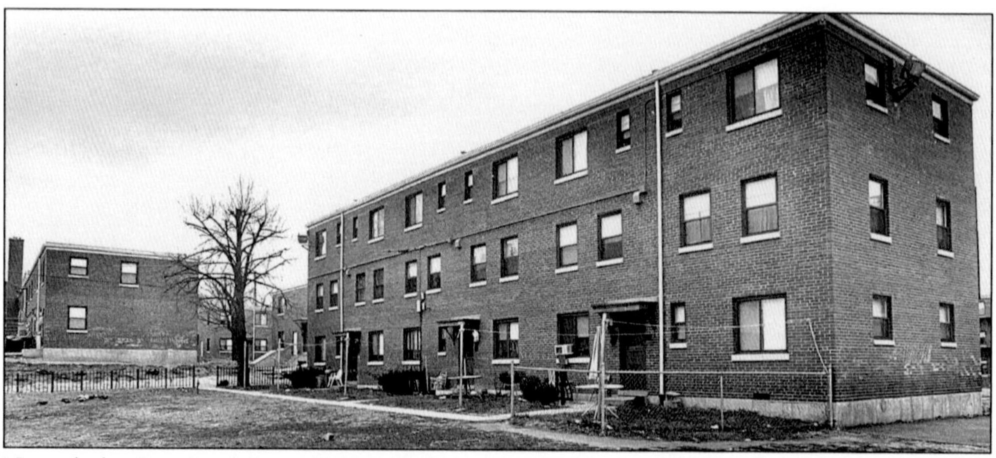

Named after Rev. Jacob Price (1839–1923), a successful African-American lumber dealer, pastor, and civic leader, these Greenup Street homes were originally intended as federally sponsored public housing for the city's African Americans. They have, in fact, been integrated since their opening in 1939.

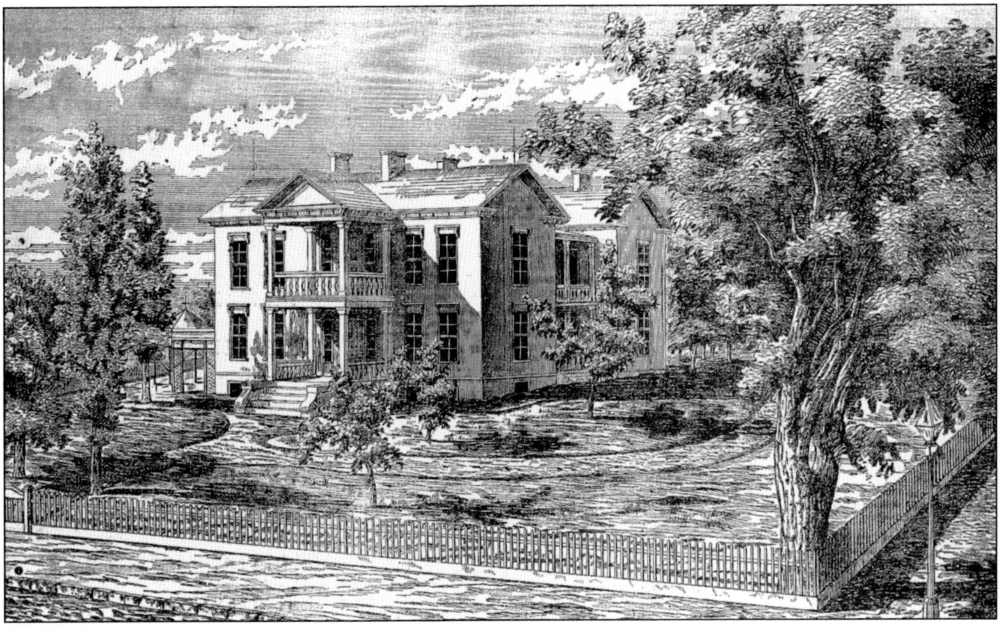

The Patton-Carlisle House is located at 1533 Garrard Street. Robert Patton was an attorney and a real estate developer. In 1853 he established a subdivision on the east side of Covington, constructing his own home as its centerpiece. By 1856, John G. Carlisle, attorney, senator and later United States Treasurer, was living there. The original porch shown here was replaced late in the 19th century with its current Victorian porch.

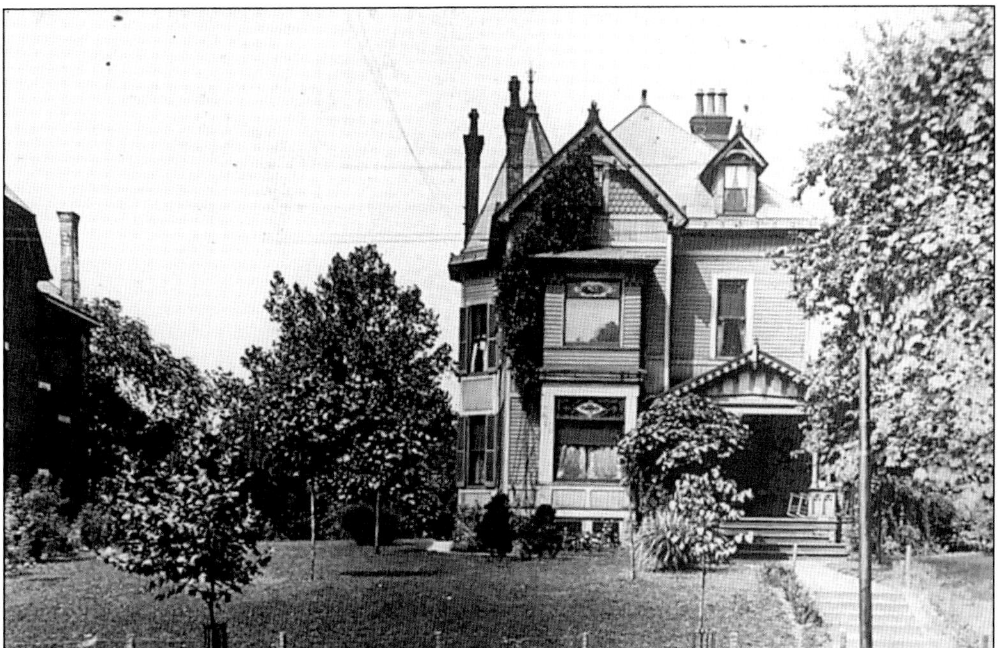

This elaborate Queen Anne house at 1553 Madison Avenue was built by Arthur E. Motch, a prominent Covington jeweler, *c.* 1884. It remained the family home until the late 1920s. The house was replaced in 1954 by the Masonic Temple.

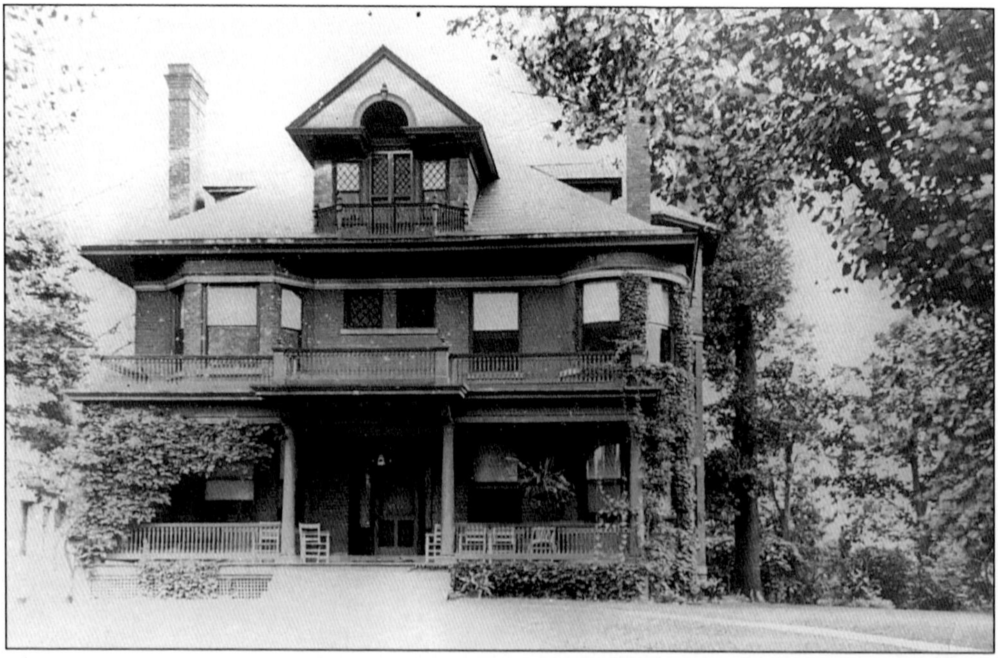

This *c.* 1895 Colonial Revival house, built for Jennie Holmes, granddaughter of Robert Wallace, replaced the original Wallace Family farmhouse, Longwood. The original farmlands were subdivided and developed after 1894, making way for one of Covington's most fashionable neighborhoods. (Courtesy Joseph Gastright).

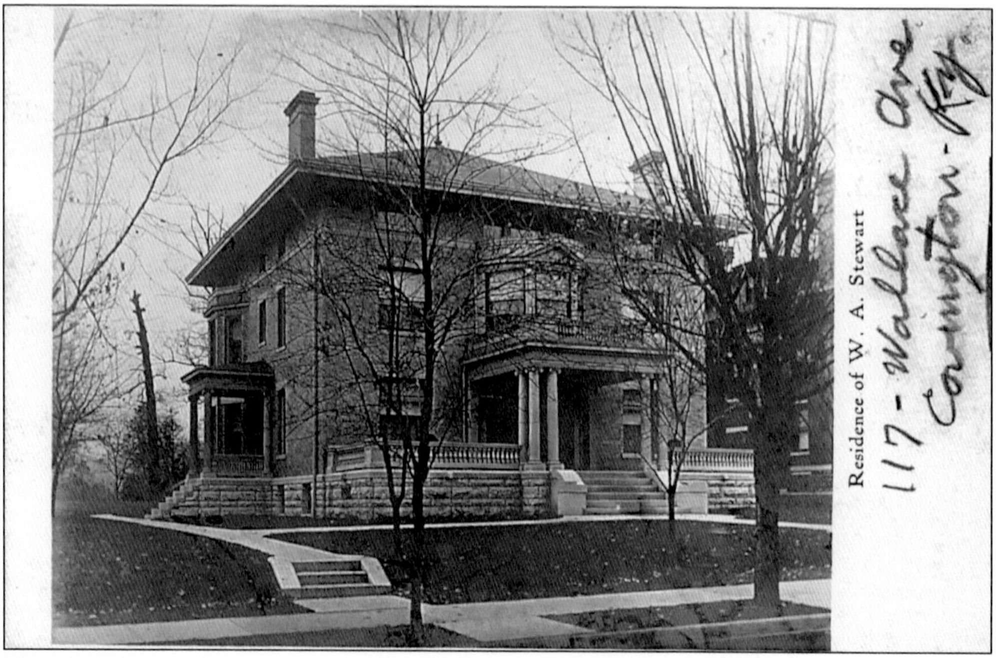

The 1909 Stewart Mansion on Wallace Avenue was designed by Cincinnati architect Harry Hake for William A. Stewart, a partner in the Stewart Iron Works. This must have been a popular design for Hake; at least two other examples of this house still exist in Greater Cincinnati. (Courtesy Joseph Gastright.)

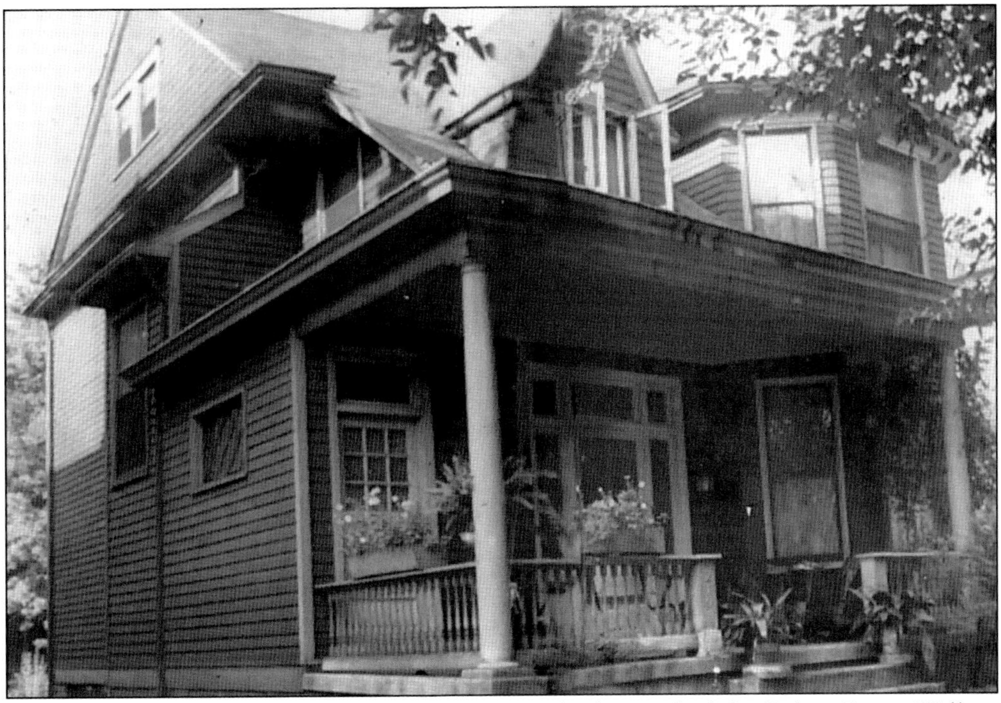

The John R. Coppin Jr. House was one of four similar houses built by Robert Bruce Wallace as rental property on Wallace Avenue c. 1898. He was the son of the founder of the John R. Coppin Department Store in downtown Covington and became vice-president of the store upon his father's death in 1913. Coppin lived in this house from 1920 until his death in 1954.

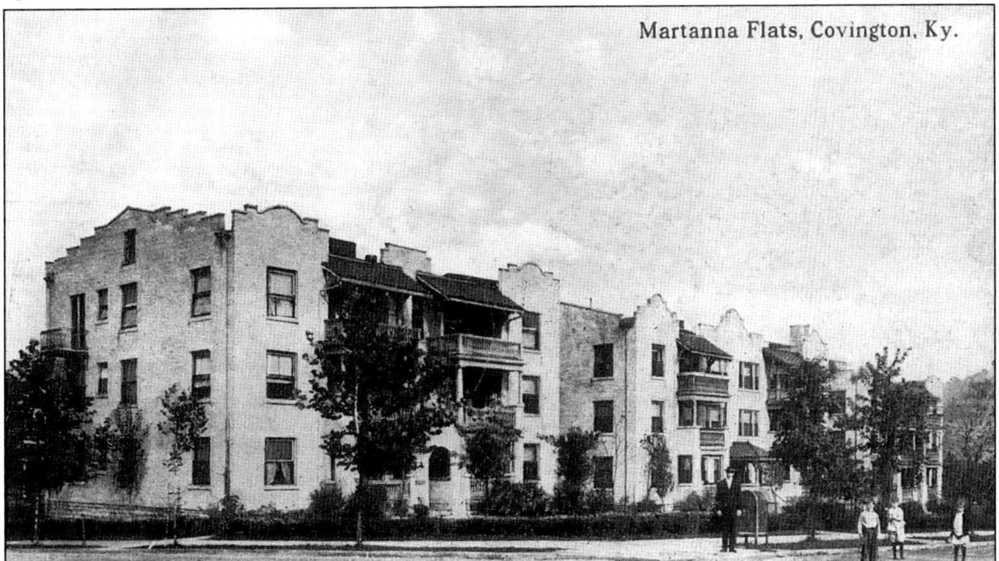

The Martanna Flats are located near the eastern end of Wallace Avenue. These Spanish Revival apartment buildings were built by and named after Martin and Anna Durrett c. 1908. Martin Durrett was a prominent local attorney. Like the Virginia Flats at the western end of Wallace Avenue, the Martanna was located at the terminus of a streetcar line, thus providing convenient rental housing for those wishing to live in the desirable Wallace Subdivision.

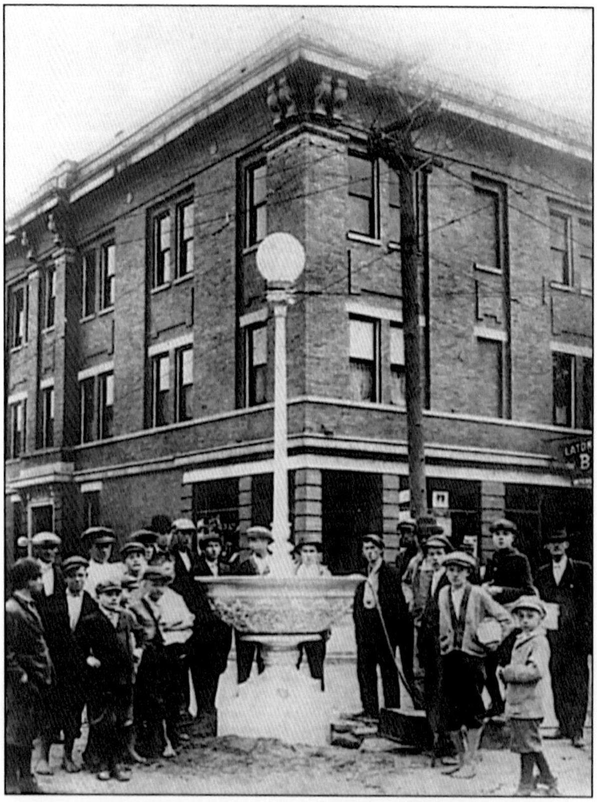

This elegant fountain was erected by Dr. Robert E. Carlton at Ritte's Corner in 1915 in honor of the Latonia men serving in World War I. According to local lore, it was destroyed by the popular, but far from sober, Doc Fenton Adams, who had not yet made the transition from the horse-drawn carriage to his Reo automobile. In the background is the *c.* 1902 Bird building, erected by Dr. R.B. Bird, a physician and surgeon. He was also dealer in drugs, chemicals, and perfumery.

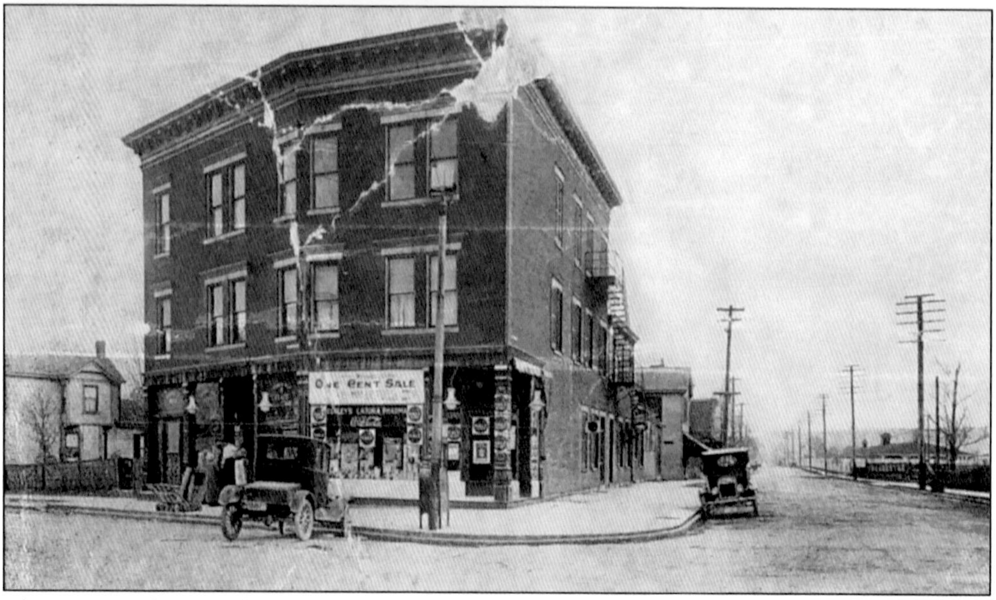

This *c.* 1908 photograph shows Boeckley's Drug Store in its original location at the southwest corner of Decoursey and Main Street (now Winston Avenue). Boeckley built his own building across the street in the 1930s and this building was later demolished. It is now the site of the Korean Conflict Memorial Fountain. Note the Latonia Racetrack out-buildings in the background.

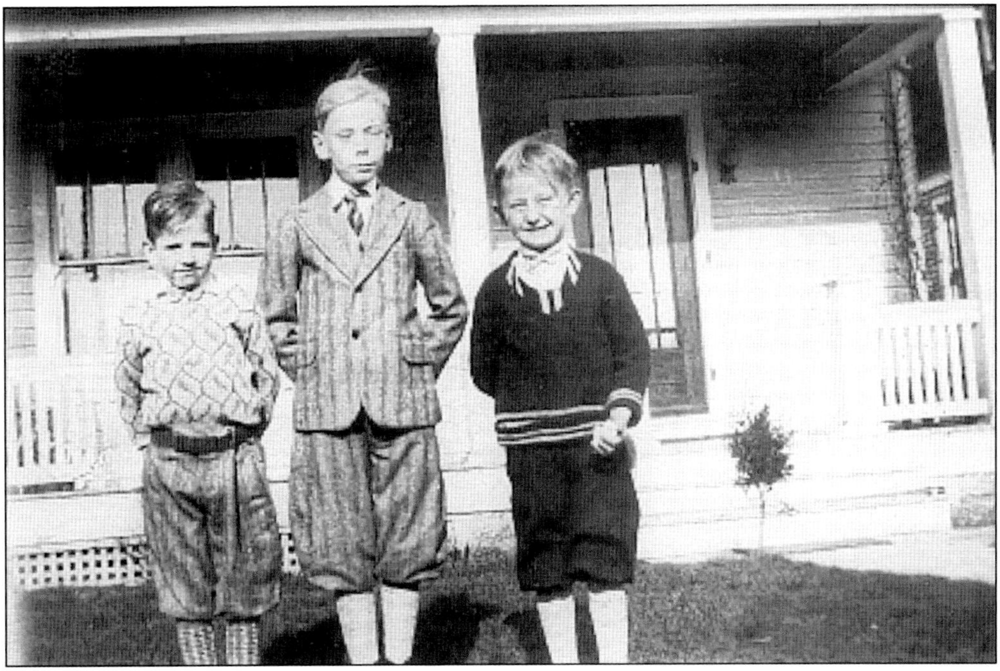

These three dapper young men, (from left to right) Jack Silver, Charles L. Gillham, and Charles Rieger, seem quite pleased with themselves! They are standing in front of the Gillham home at 2731 Iowa Avenue sometime in the mid-1920s. (Courtesy Lisa Gillham.)

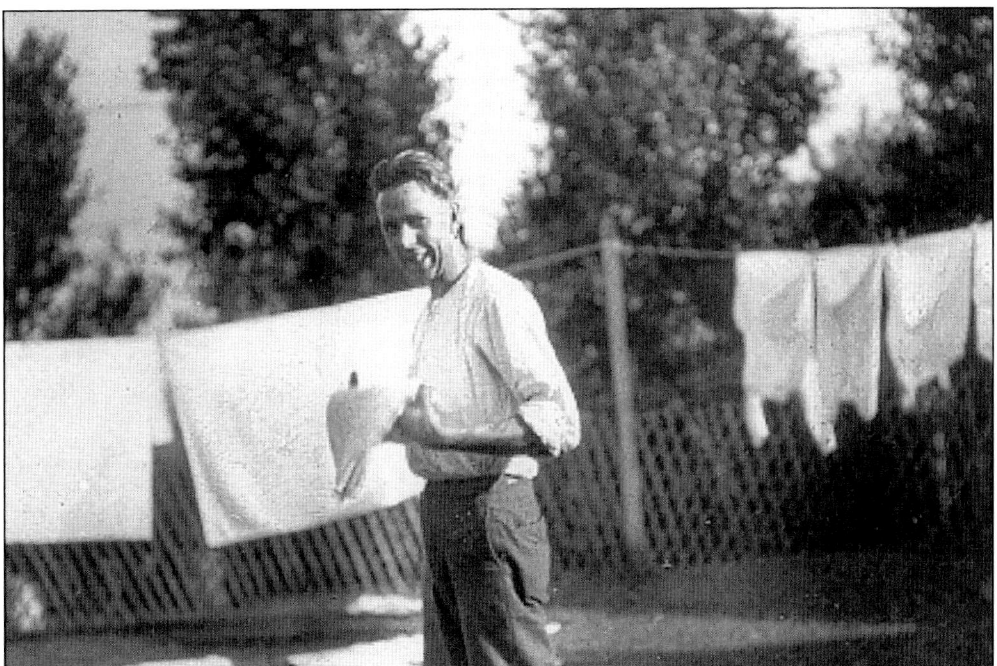

Not dressed as formally as his son, Charles B. Gillham is nonetheless happily at work hanging the family laundry at the rear of their Iowa Avenue home. Gillham was a yard master at the Decoursey railroad yards at the time of this *c.* 1926 photo. (Courtesy Lisa Gillham.)

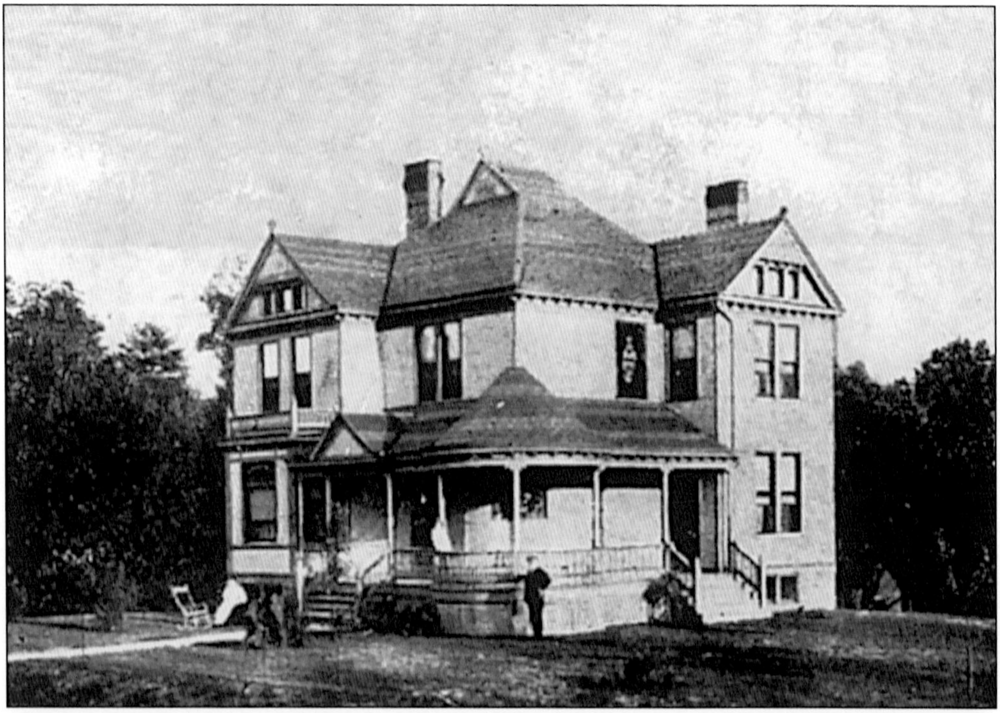

The James T. Earle home was built *c.* 1897 and this photo was taken shortly thereafter. Pictured are James T. Earle, the last mayor of the City of Latonia before it was annexed into Covington in 1909, his wife, and his infant daughter. Earle was also a railroad agent and president of the Latonia First National Bank. (Courtesy Karl Lietzenmayer.)

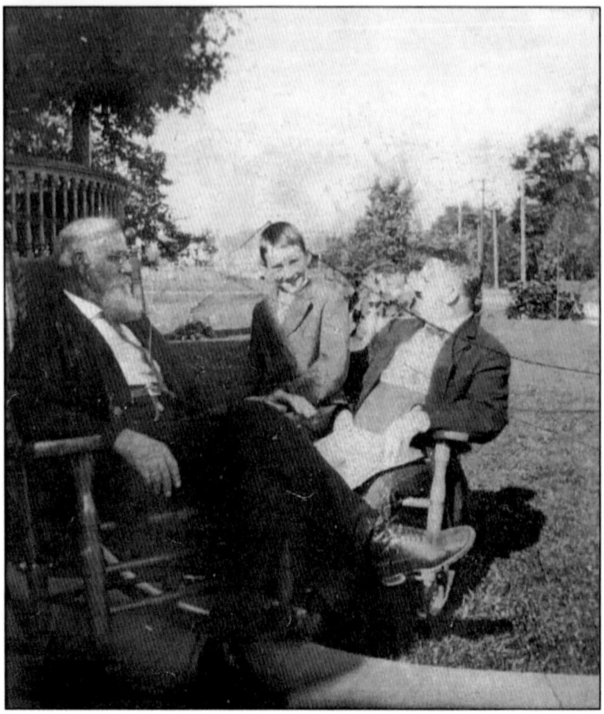

Three generations of the Earle family are captured in this photograph taken in front of the Earle house at 501 East Southern Avenue, *c.* 1905. Seated on the left is Jonathan Earle, standing is James Dewey Earle (born in 1897, he was named after Admiral Dewey), and James T. Earle is seated on the right. (Courtesy Karl Lietzenmayer.)

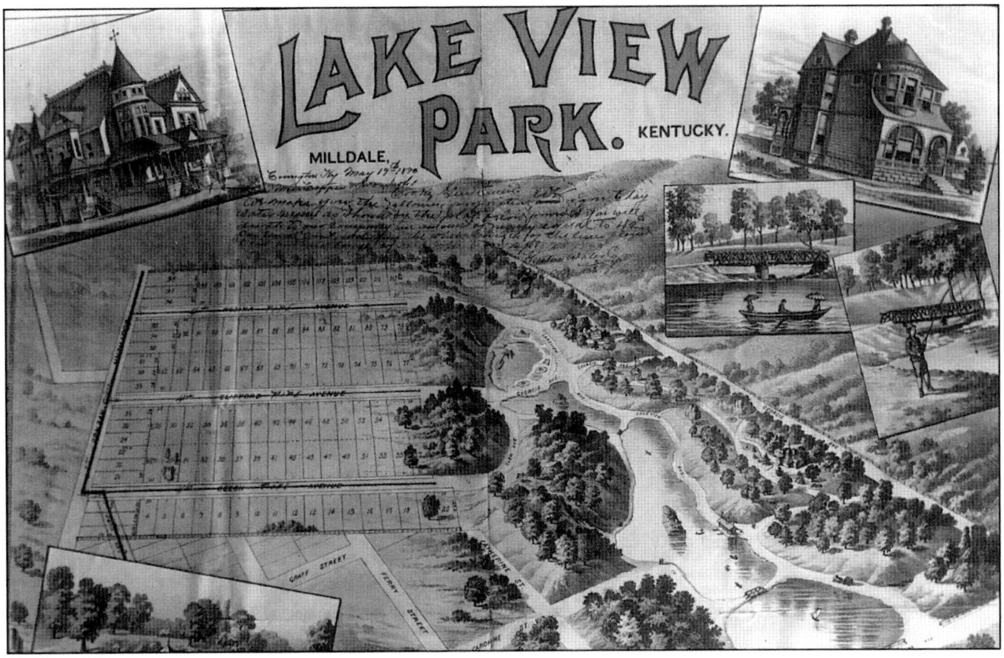

The promise of electric streetcars and water mains drew people to the subdivision of Lake View Park, Milldale, now part of the Latonia neighborhood of Covington. John R. Coppin, owner of the John R. Coppin Department Store, was the developer of the project and built his own home here.

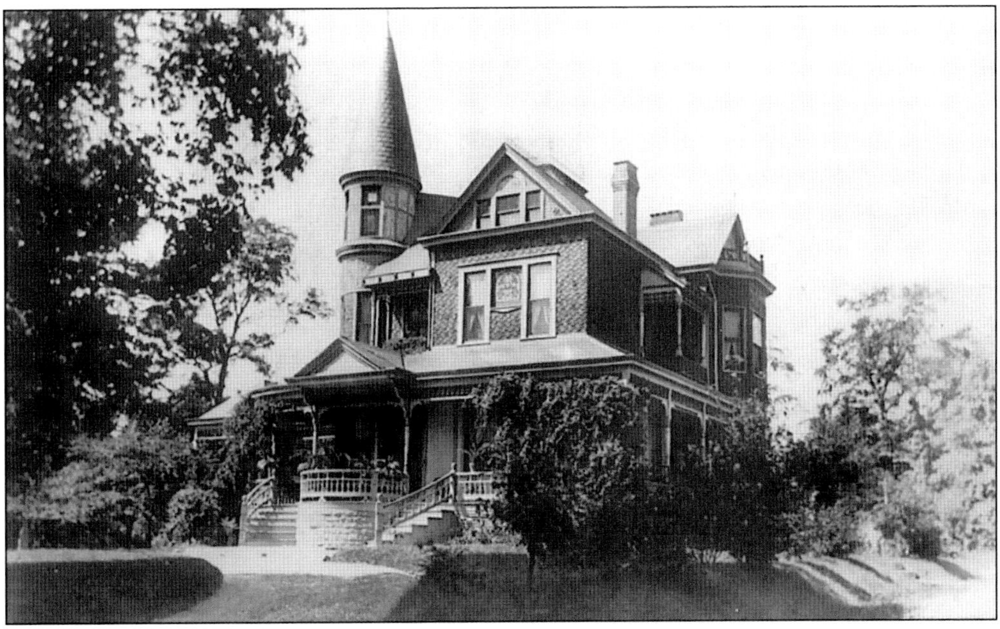

This Queen Anne–style house was designed for John R. Coppin by Covington architect Daniel Seger c. 1892. It was located in what was then a suburb of Covington, Milldale, as the centerpiece of Coppin's Lakeview Park Subdivision. Coppin was the founder of the John R. Coppin Department Store, Northern Kentucky's largest store. The house was razed in 1957 to make room for Covington's Ninth District School.

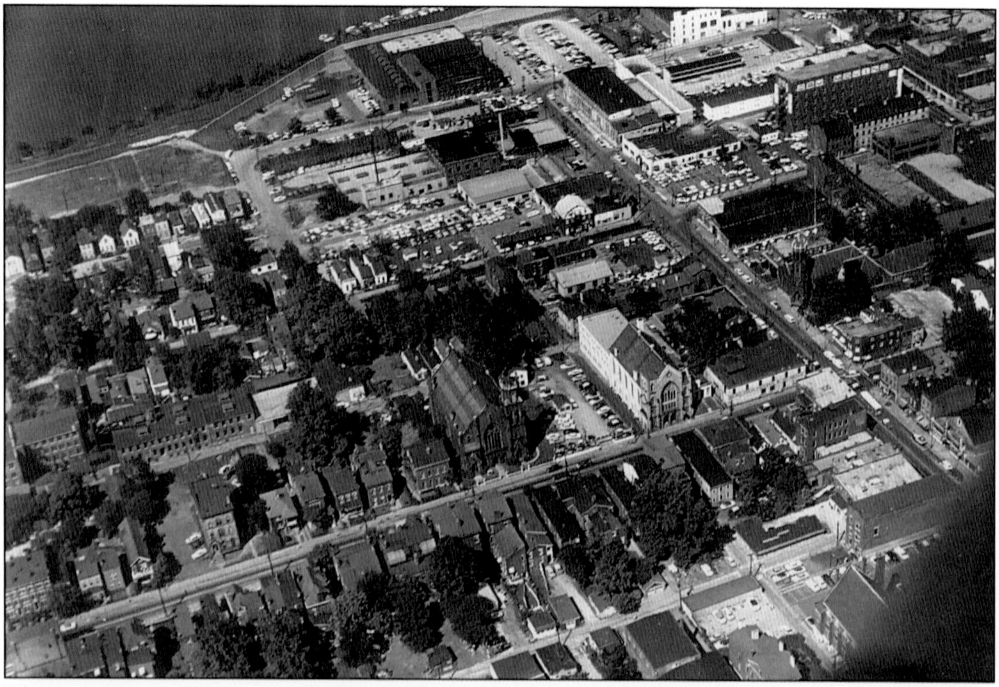

This *c.* 1950 aerial view of downtown Covington shows the density of this residential neighborhood before the building of the IRS Center and I-71/75. The two churches in the center of the photograph are located on West Fourth Street, just west of Madison Avenue. Only the First Baptist Church on the right still stands.

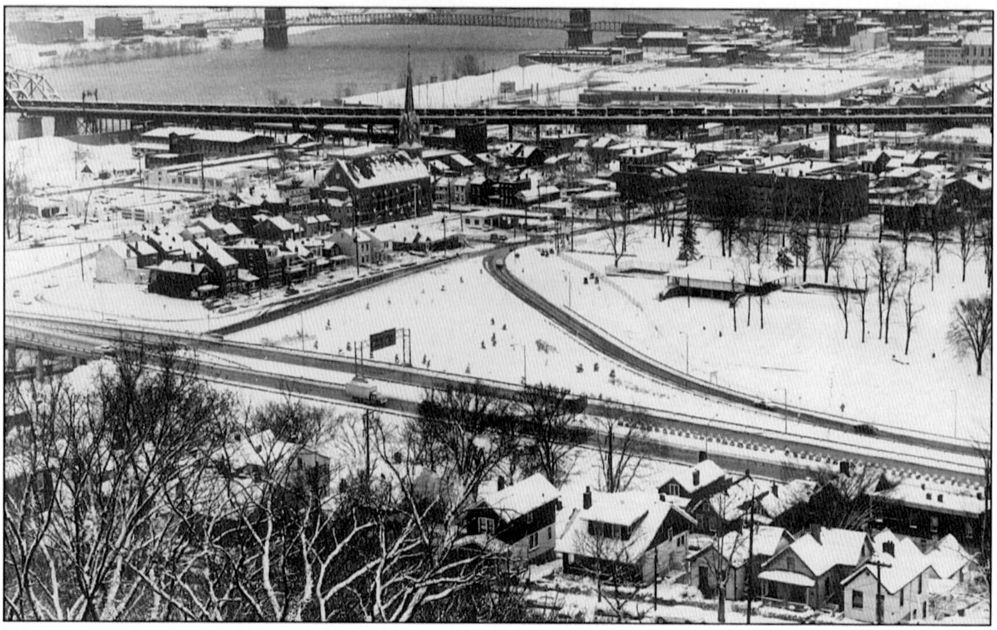

This *c.* 1965 aerial view, taken after the construction of the interstate, clearly shows the beginning of the neighborhood's eventual change in character from a residential area to a commercial area. St. Patrick Catholic Church (now demolished) is visible to the left and the IRS Center is in the background.

Five

HAPPENINGS

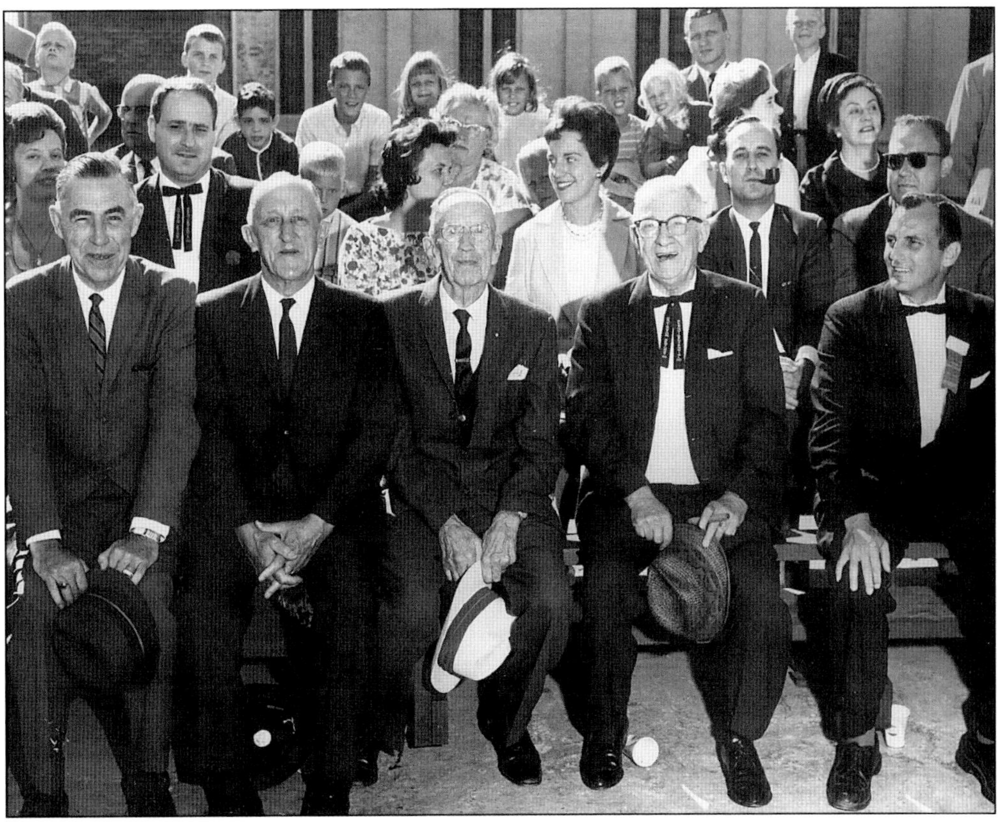

Four former mayors watch the Covington Sesquicentennial Parade from the reviewing stands on Sunday, August 29, 1965. Pictured from left to right are John J. Moloney (1952–1955 and 1960–1963), William Beuttel (1940–1945), Henry Knollman (1936–1939), and Harry Schneider (1956–1959).

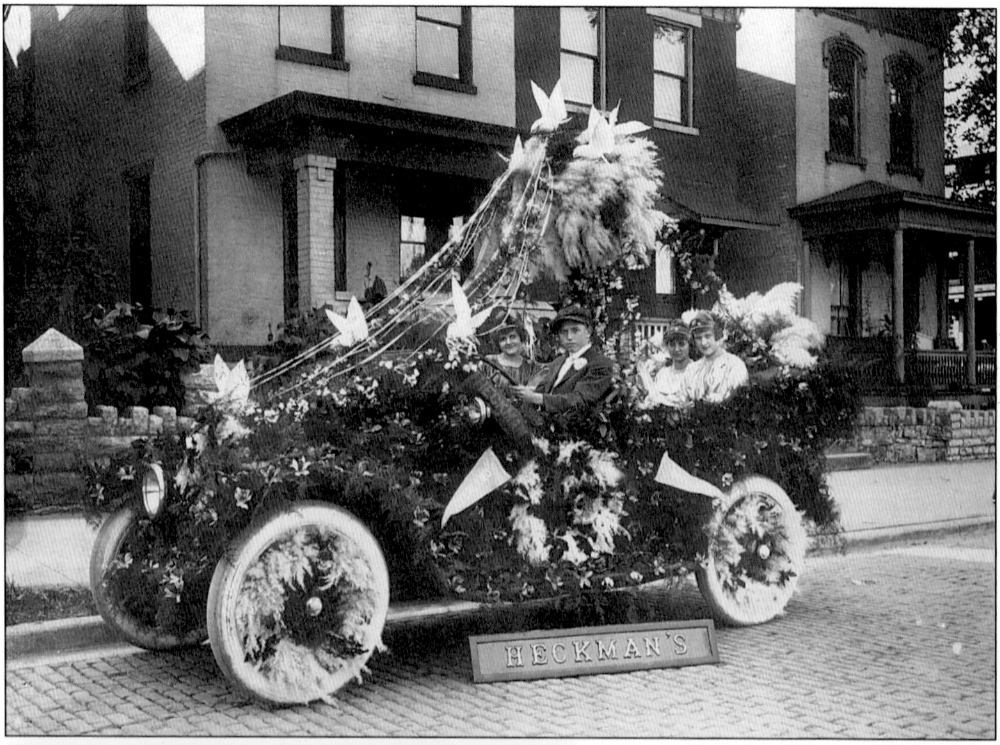

This elaborately decorated float was the Heckman Floral Company parade entry for the 1914 Centennial Parade in Covington. Heckman's motto was "Artistic Floral Work a Specialty." The Centennial was held a year early due to a misreading of historic records.

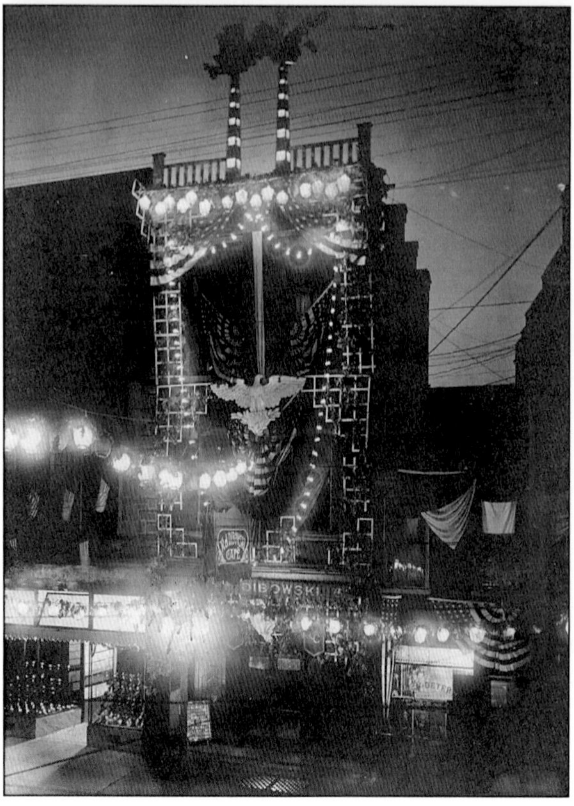

R.J. Dibowski's Café at 6 Pike Street was all decked out for the Covington Centennial celebration in 1914. Note the elaborate lighting and decorations applied to the building, along with the American flags and eagle. On the sidewalk, the illumination from the underground marble bathrooms is visible through the grillwork.

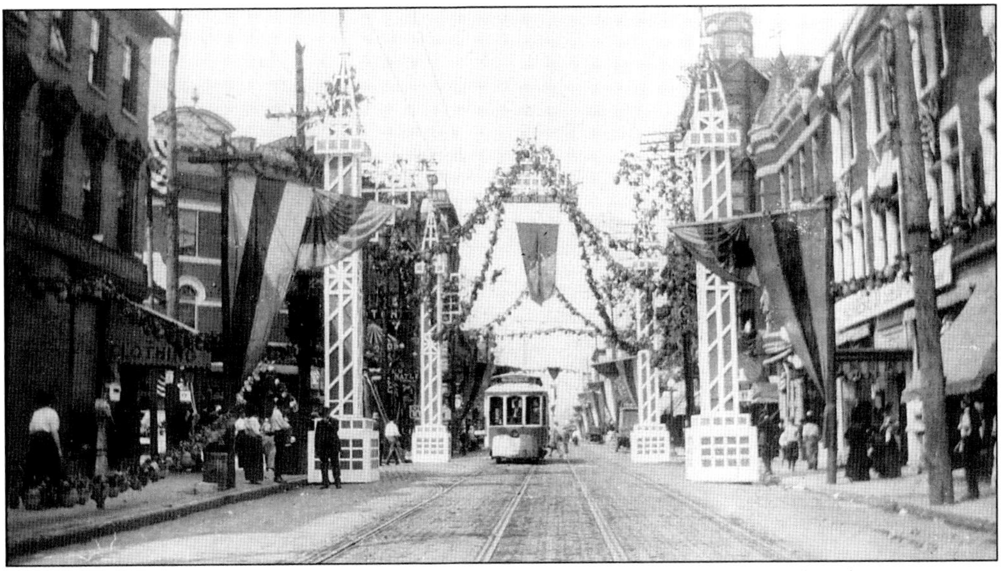

A trolley rumbles south on Madison Avenue through the decorations for the Covington Centennial celebration in 1914. Note the double sets of trolley car tracks down the middle of the street. Flags hang from the light poles down both sides of the street. (Frank Sommerkamp, photographer.)

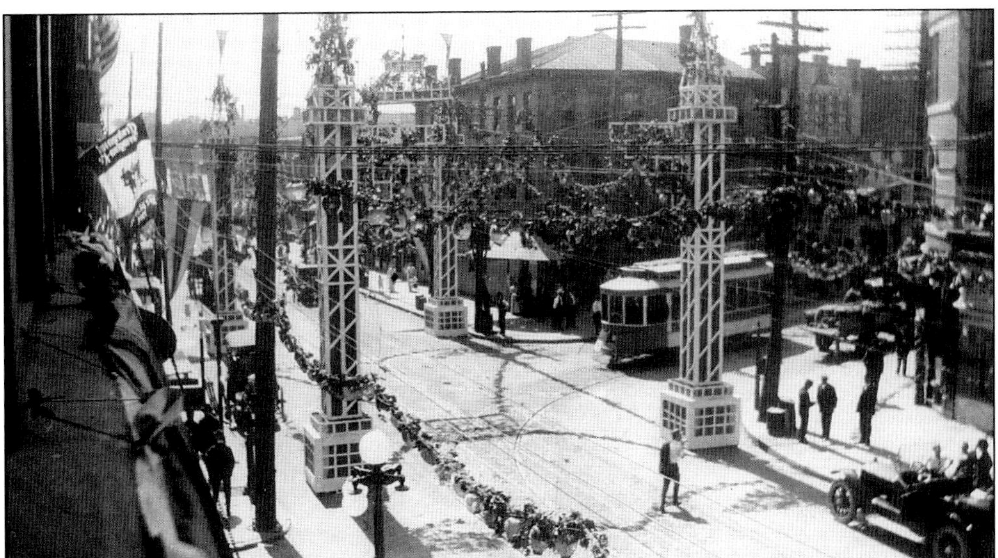

This is another view of Covington's Centennial celebration in 1914 as seen from the corner of Pike and Madison. A trolley car is turning north onto Madison. Note the towers with floral decorations and the lights between them. (Frank Sommerkamp, photographer.)

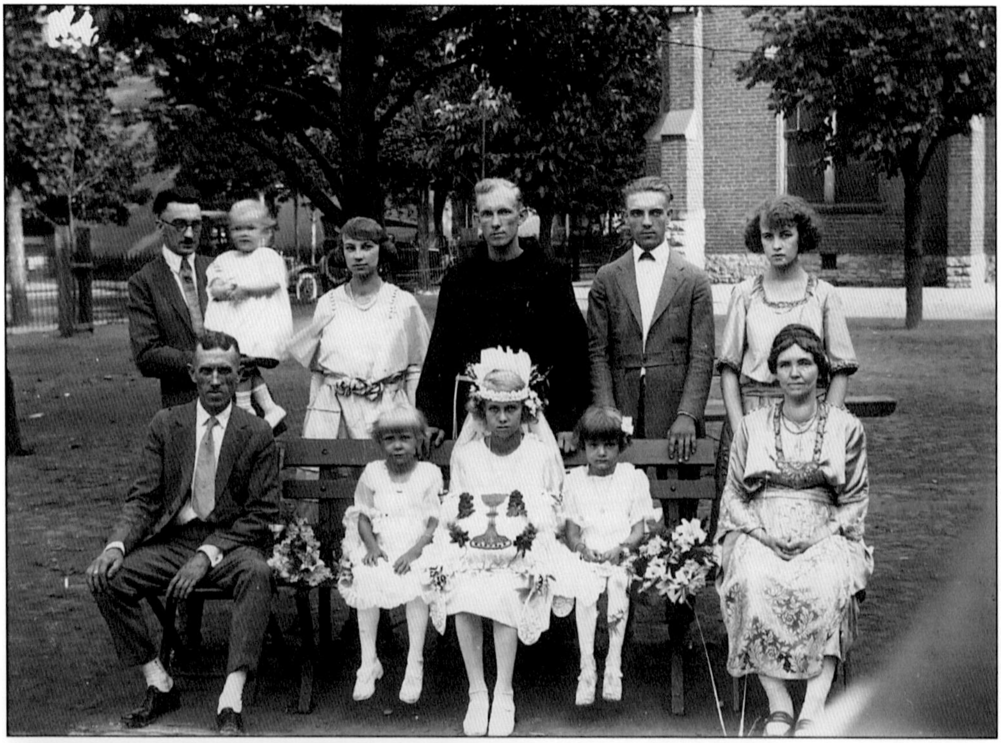

This is a Hengehold family First Communion at Holy Cross Catholic Church in the Latonia neighborhood, *c.* 1920. Latonia still retains its separate identity almost a century after being annexed to Covington. (August Koenig, photographer.)

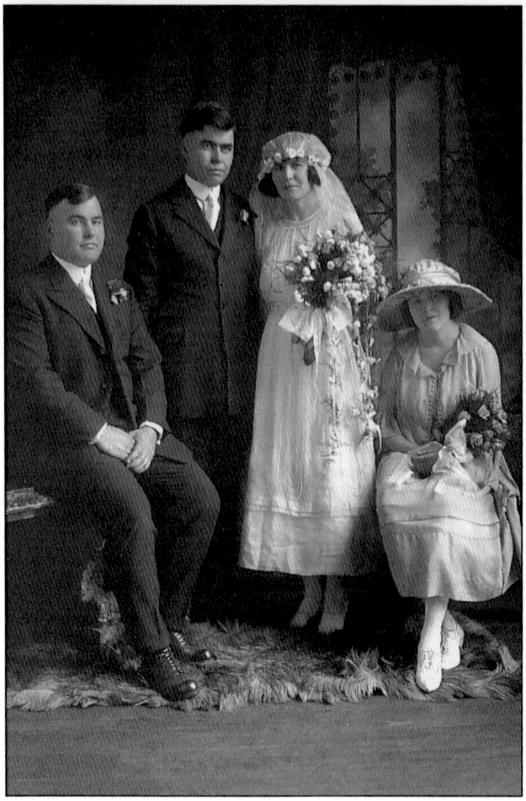

This *c.* 1920 wedding portrait is of a couple married at Saint Patrick Catholic Church. Located on West Third Street and Elm Streets, Saint Patrick was the center of the Irish community. After suffering years of flood damage, the church and the neighborhood were torn down for urban renewal. The area is now a collection of fast food restaurants. (August Koenig, photographer.)

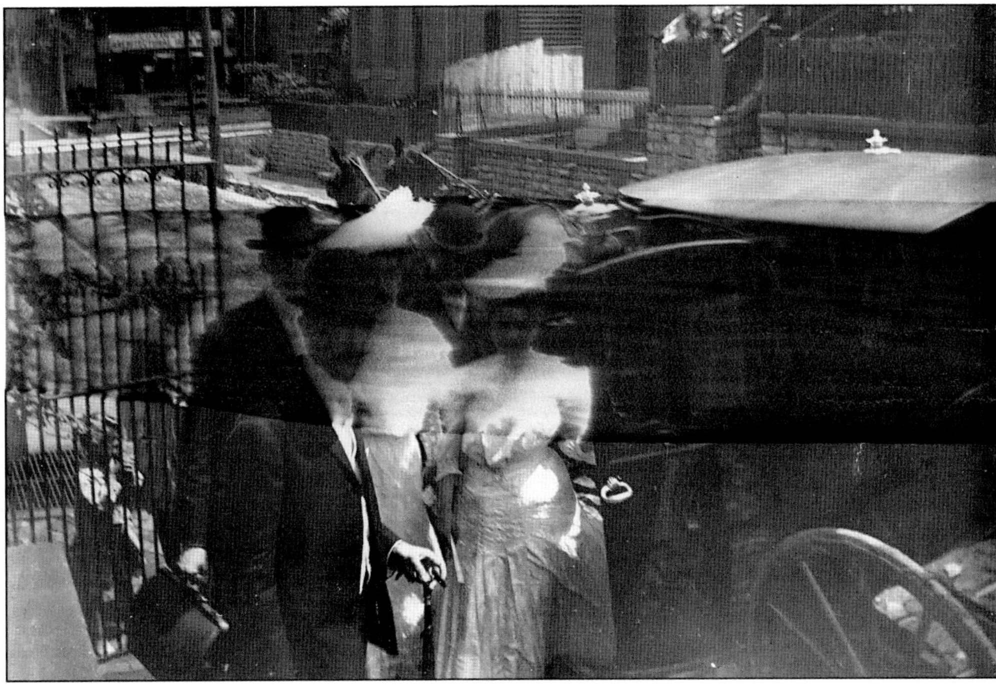

Katie Wessels Ratterman and husband George Ratterman arrive at the family home on West Ninth Street after their wedding. Note the Covington Architectural Iron Works building. The rough condition of the street must have made for an uncomfortable ride over those ruts and stones. (August Koenig, photographer.)

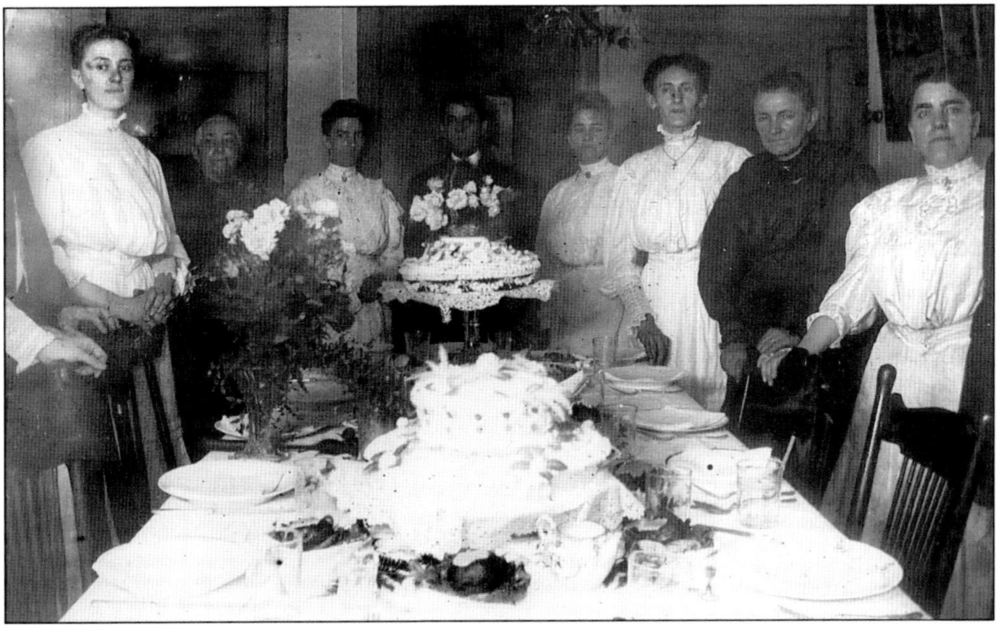

This is Katie Wessels Ratterman's wedding reception with the Wessels family *c.* 1910. Katie is on the far right. The elegance this middle class family of milliners was able to display is an example of the strivings of family life in the early 20th century. Nora Wessels, owner of the Wessels Millinery Shop, is fourth from the right. (August Koenig, photographer.)

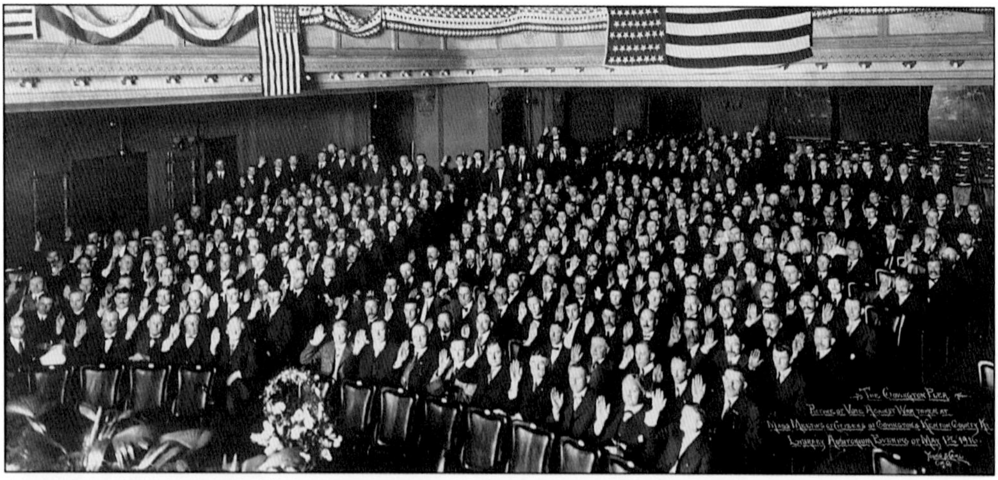

A mass meeting was held in Covington in 1916 in support of peace and against the United States entering World War I. The auditorium, then part of the Covington Library, is now part of the Carnegie Arts Center. When the war came, it forced the local German community to drop its language and to blend into the larger English-speaking community.

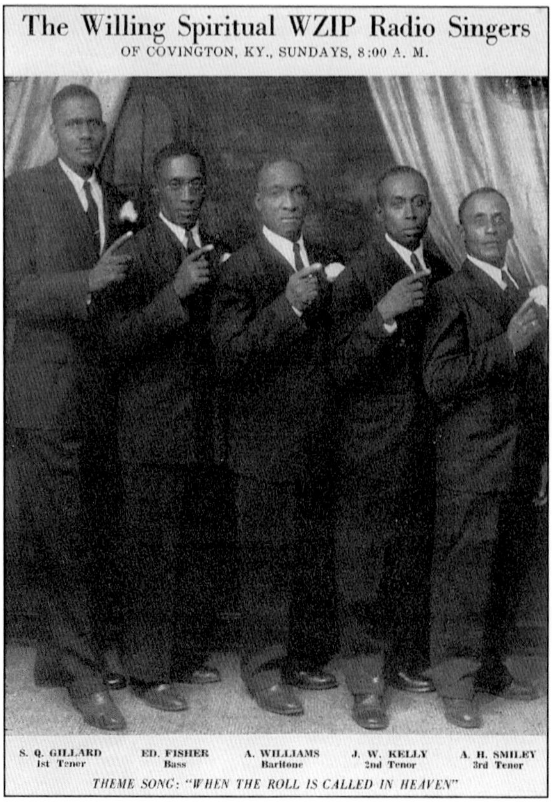

This is a 1940s photograph of a gospel group who sang regularly on WZIP, the second station in Covington after WCKY. It was developed by Carmen and Arthur Eilerman.

As part of a larger campaign against segregation, demonstrators demanded the integration of movie theaters in Covington in December, 1960. The Liberty Theatre was originally owned by L.B. Wilson and Richard P. Ernst.

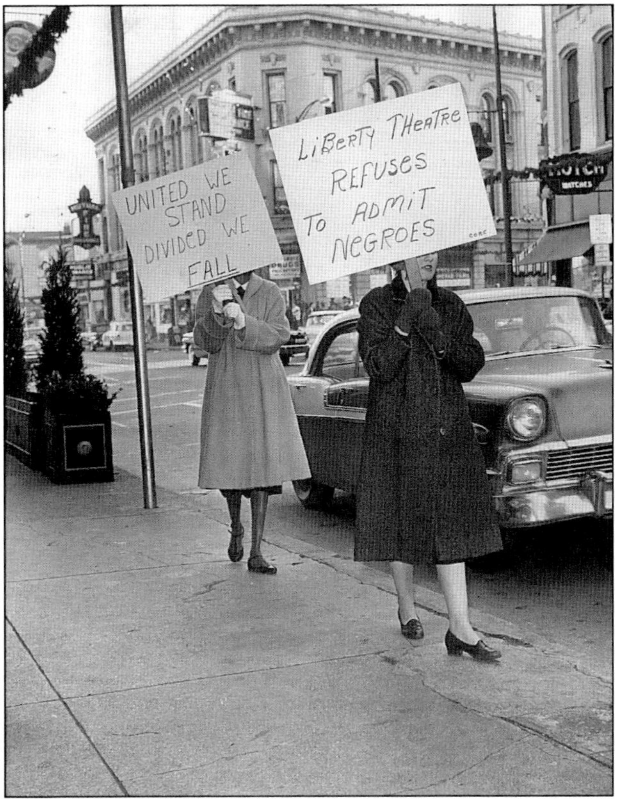

In 1970, a protest was held at Holmes High School over the lack of African-American history and culture courses. This was at the height of the black power movement across the United States.

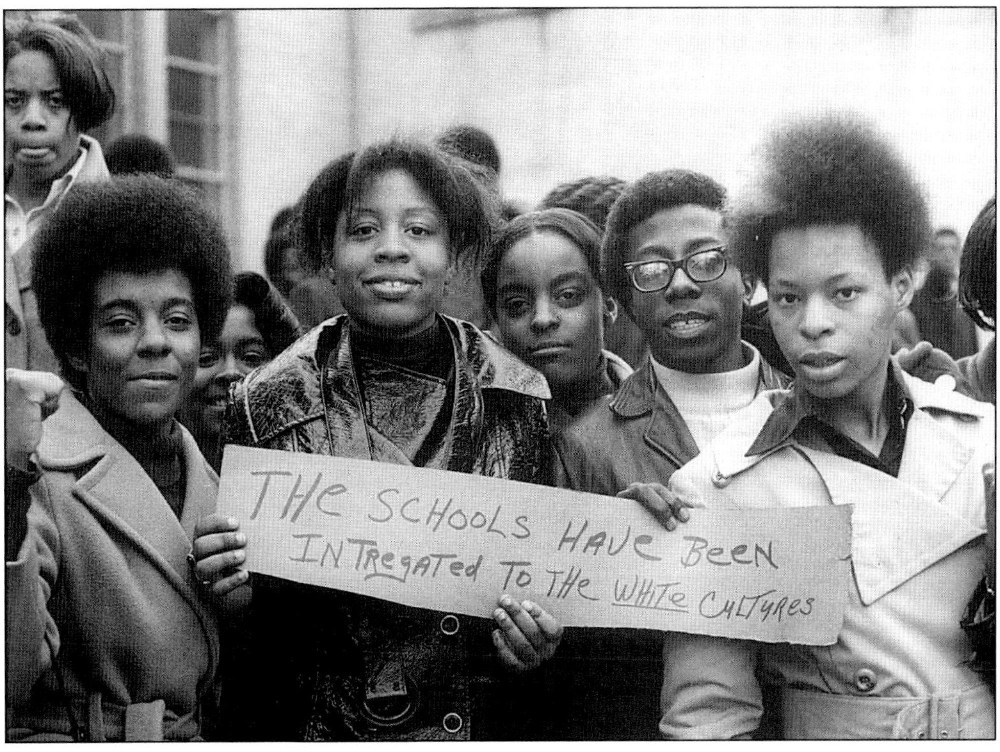

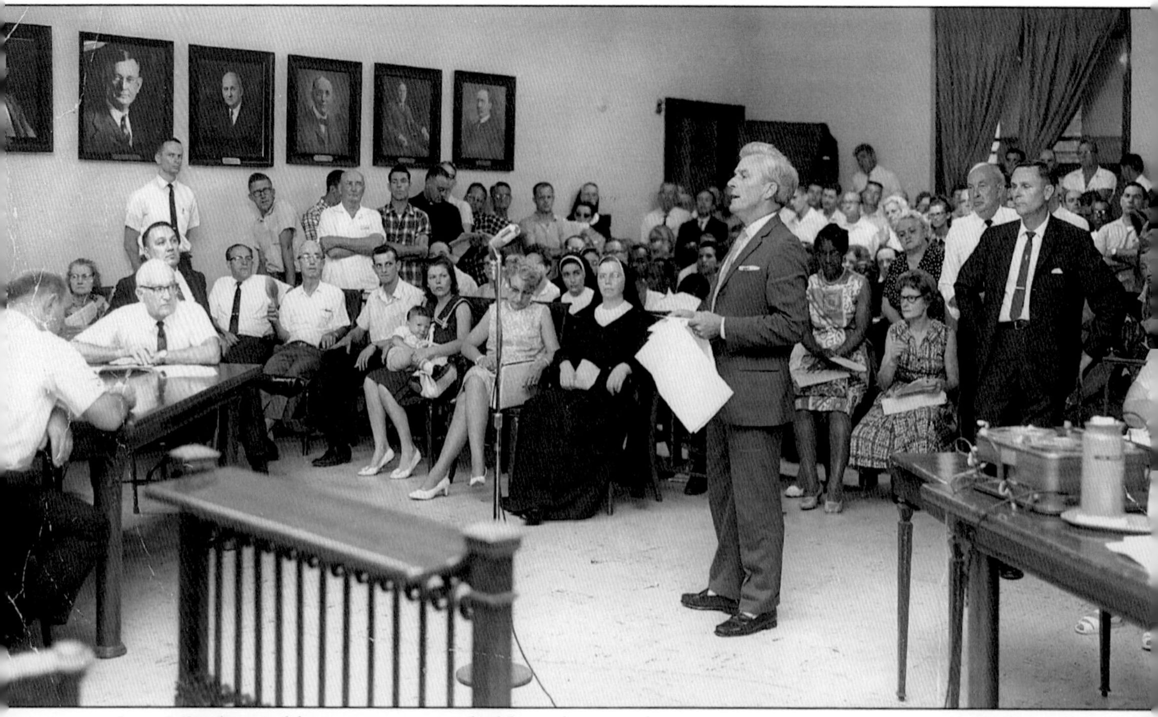

In 1967, this public meeting was held to discuss the Open Housing Ordinance pertaining to race, which was being considered by the City of Covington. Like many communities, Covington has had problems with race relations, but has in the last few decades made earnest efforts to eliminate discrimination. Free blacks were living in Covington before the Civil War, and the African-American community has long played an important role in the history of Covington. (Richard Pridemore, photographer.)

Six

DISASTERS!

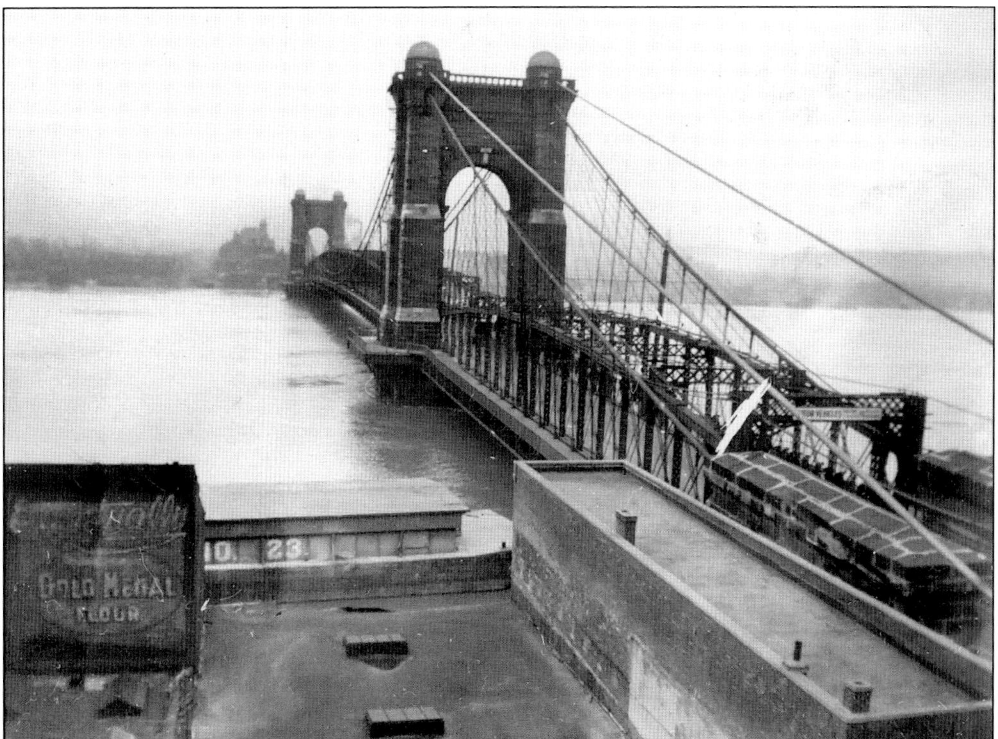

The 1937 flood was the worst flood in recorded history on the Ohio River. The water is lapping at the bottom of the Suspension Bridge.

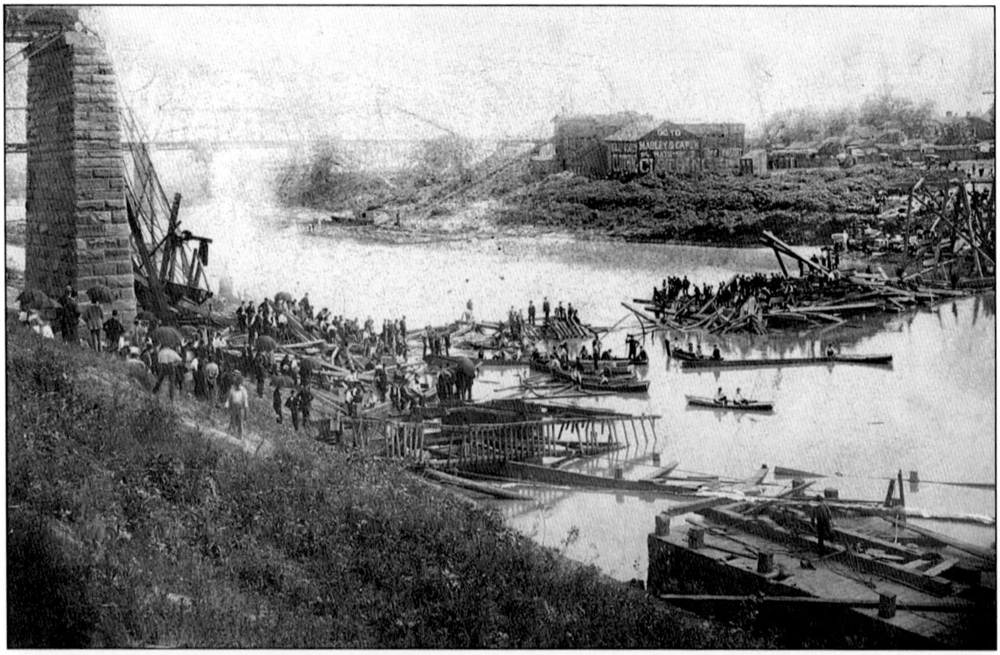

The Shortway, or Eleventh Street Bridge, was being built by the Green Line Trolley Company in 1892 to connect Covington and Newport when it collapsed. The bridge was rebuilt and operated as a toll bridge for many years. It was replaced in 2002.

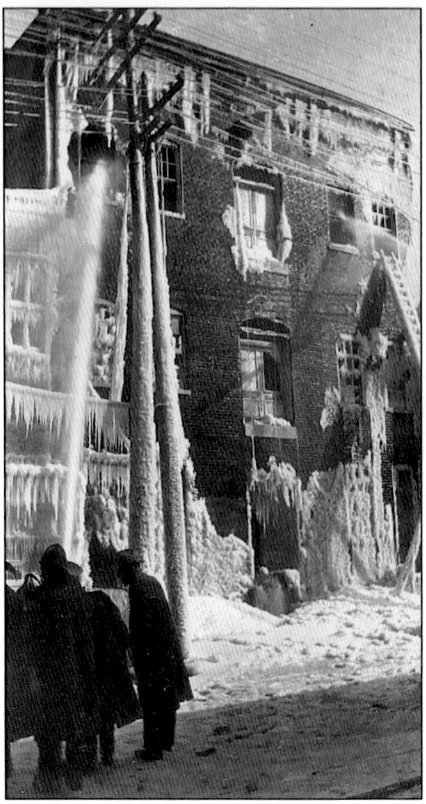

This winter fire took place in 1914 fire at the Hippodrome Theater (also known as the Broadway) at Seventh and Washington Streets. This area is still part of the historic downtown shopping and theater district.

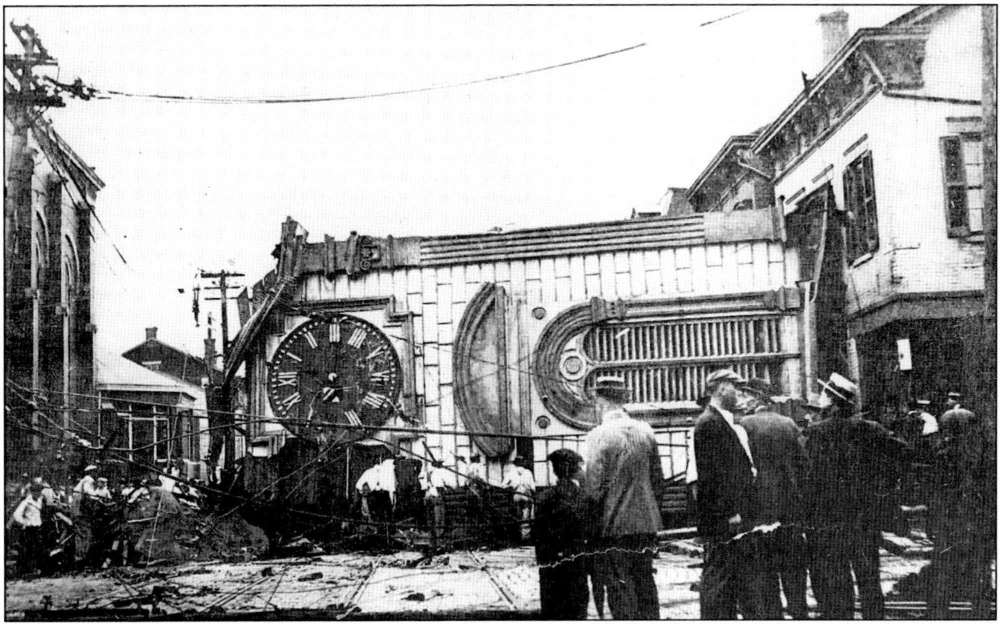

This destruction of the tower of Saint Joseph Catholic Church at Twelfth and Greenup was caused by a tornado in 1915. Many windstorms have caused damage to Covington through the years. In 1986 a wind burst struck that caused a great deal of damage to the downtown area.

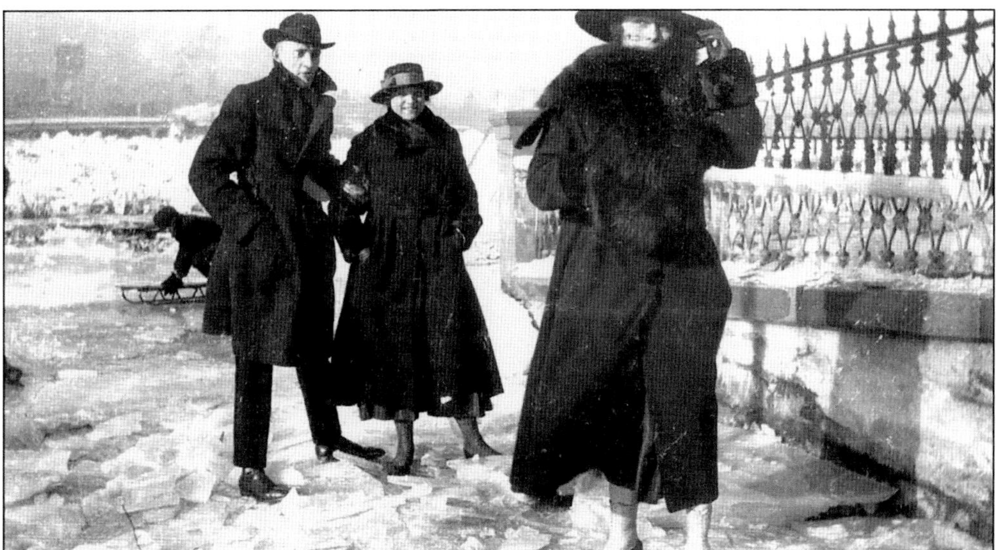

This 1918 view of Front Street, now Riverside Drive, showed the ice caused by flooding of the Ohio River. Through the years, the river has frozen over several times allowing people to walk across to Ohio. The women's boots are a distinctive fashion statement.

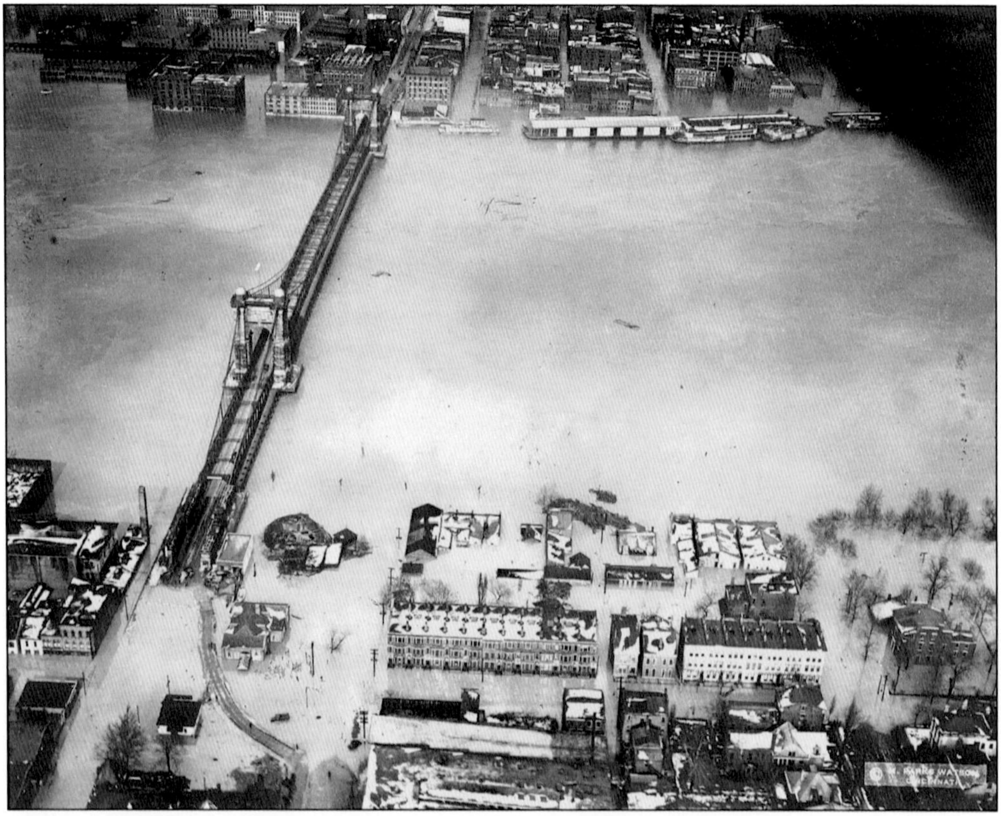

This is an aerial view of the Riverside Neighborhood during the 1937 flood. Most of the buildings on the right side are still standing and a condominium tower has replaced those just to the right of the bridge. (Courtesy Cincinnati Historical Society.)

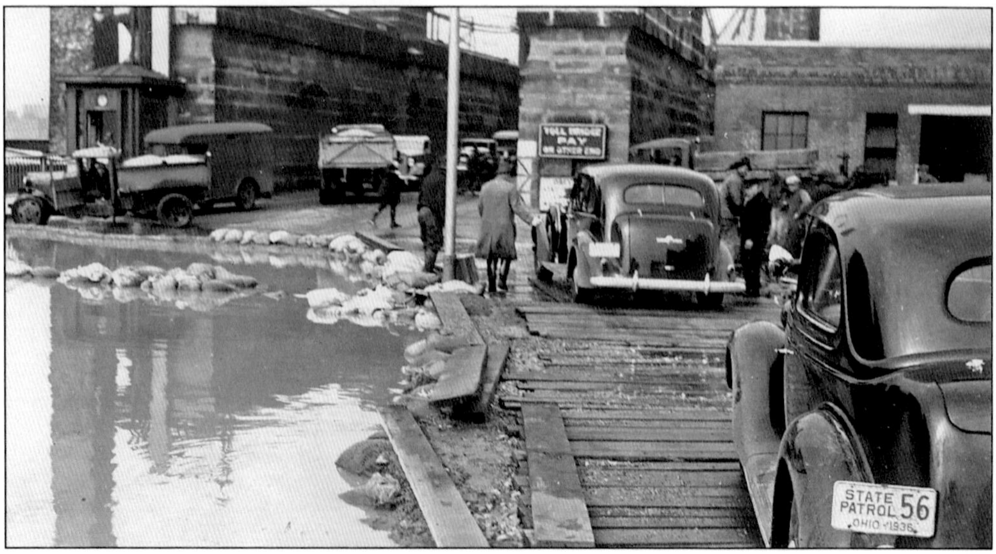

The 1937 flood was the most devastating flood in the region's history, cresting at 80 feet, almost 30 feet above flood stage. Shown here is a ramp leading to the Suspension Bridge. At the height of the flood this was the only remaining connection across the Ohio River.

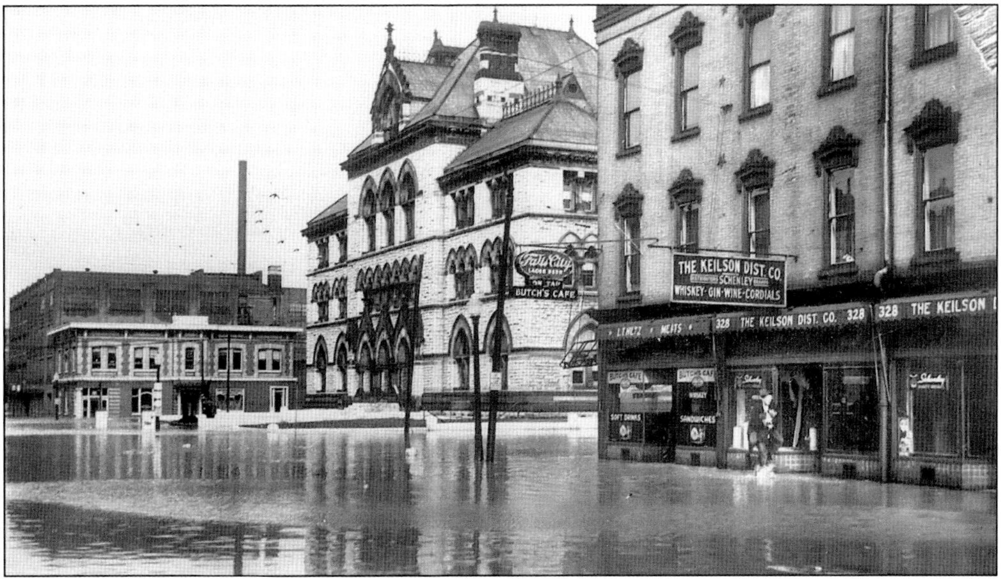

This view is looking north along Scott Street between Third and Park Streets during the 1937 flood. The Lawyers' Building can be seen in the background. The building in the center is the Federal Building and to the right is the Bradford Block named for Bradford Shinkle, a son of Amos Shinkle, who was the president of the Suspension Bridge Company. The Federal Building was demolished in the early 1970s to make way for the Kenton County Building.

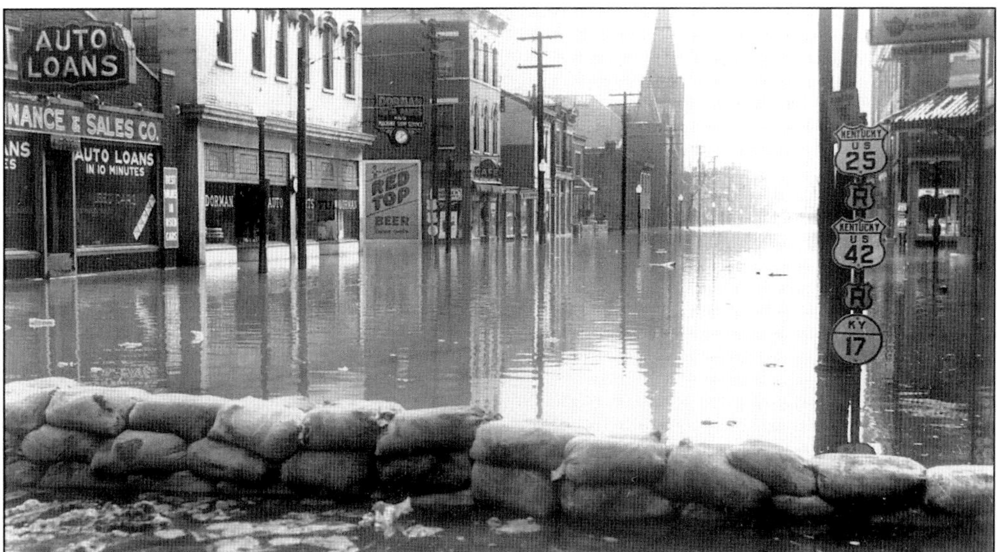

This view is looking south along the 400 block of Scott Street during the 1937 flood. The buildings just across Fifth Street, in the center of the picture, were replaced by the Kenton County Public Library in the early 1970s. The church in the background is Scott Street Methodist Church South (now demolished), which broke away from First Methodist Church over slavery and rejoined in the 1930s.

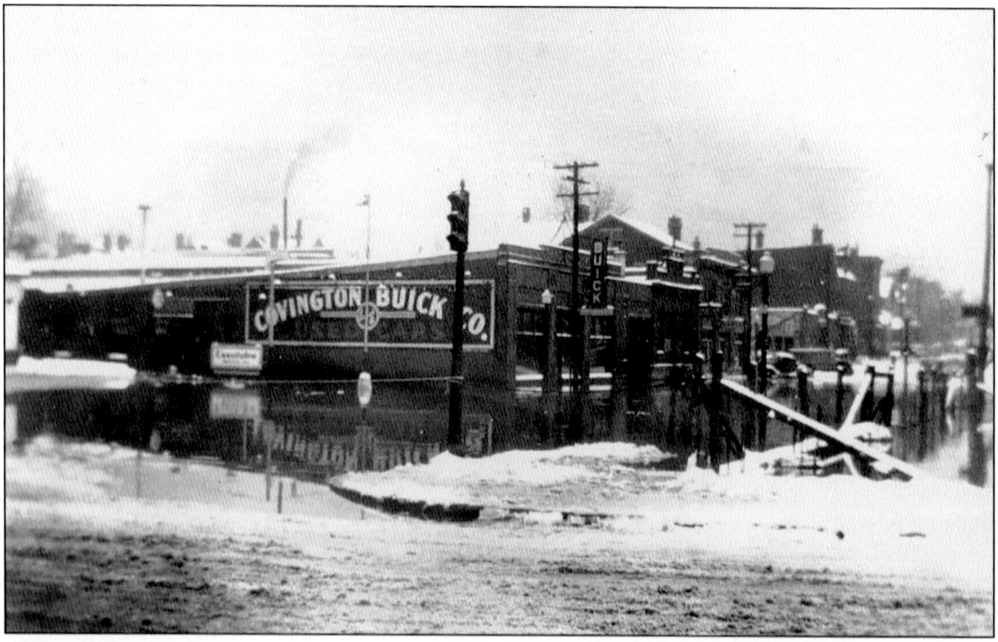

The 1937 flood waters reached still further south on Scott Street to Sixth Street. The Covington Buick Building is still in use today as an office building. The rear of the building was originally a stable and is today again being used for the carriage livery trade.

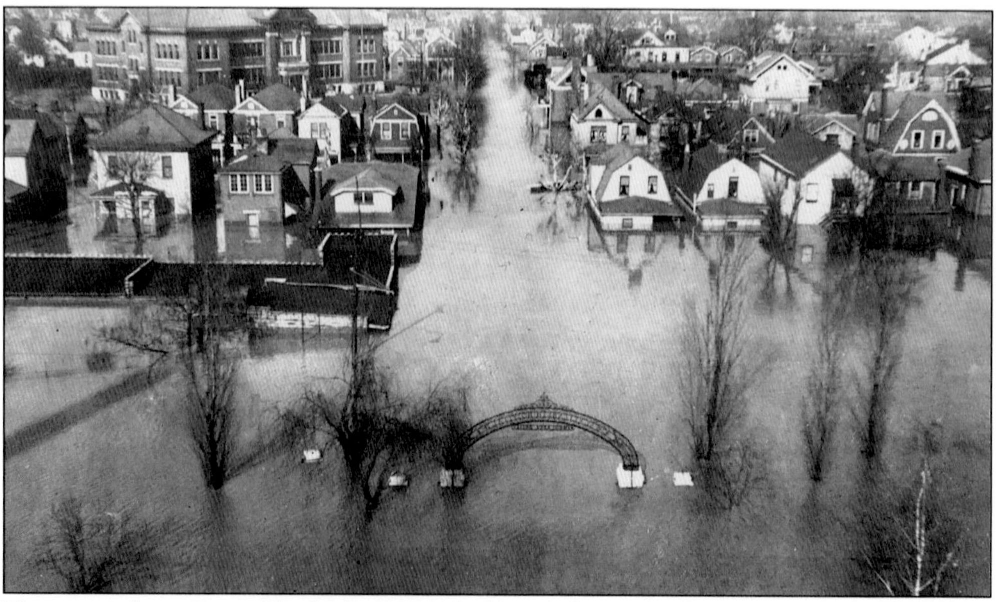

This view from Saint Elizabeth Hospital during the 1937 flood shows the Austinburg neighborhood under water from the flooding of the nearby Licking River. Sixth District Elementary School is visible in the background.

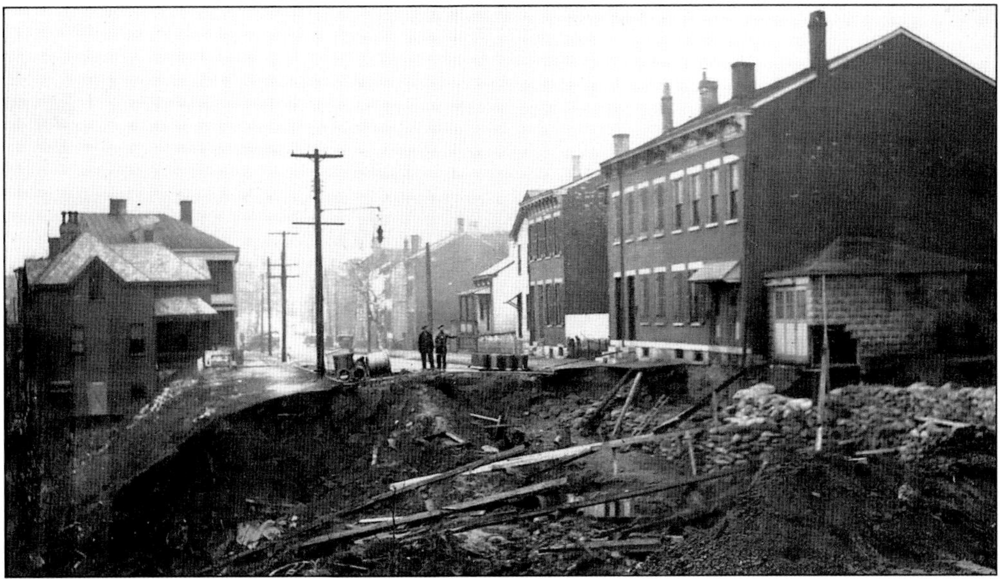

Not just the areas adjacent to the Ohio or Licking Rivers suffered during the 1937 flood. Here a view of Philadelphia Street north of Ninth Street shows the street caved in from underground water from the nearby Willow Run. (Courtesy Joseph Gastright.)

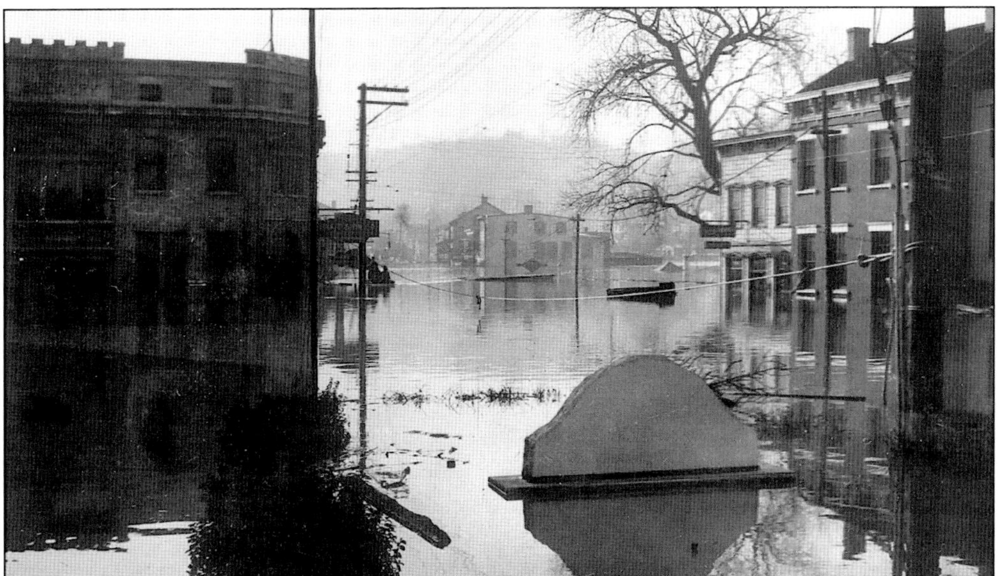

This 1937 view looking west along Pike Street shows how connected the Lewisburg neighborhood was to the rest of the city before the construction of I-71/75. Part of the Bavarian Brewery complex can be seen on the left. Most of the buildings on the right have since been demolished. (Courtesy Joseph Gastright.)

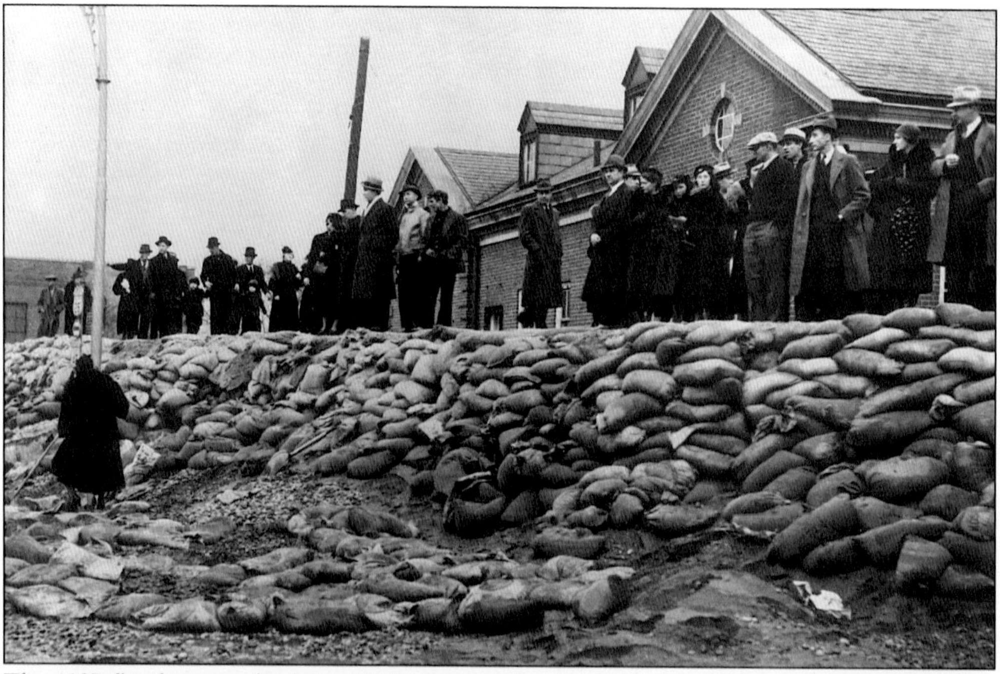

The 1937 flood waters slowly receded, after weeks of unprecedented disaster. The building in the rear housed the Suspension Bridge Company offices and is still in use today. (Courtesy Cincinnati Historical Society.)

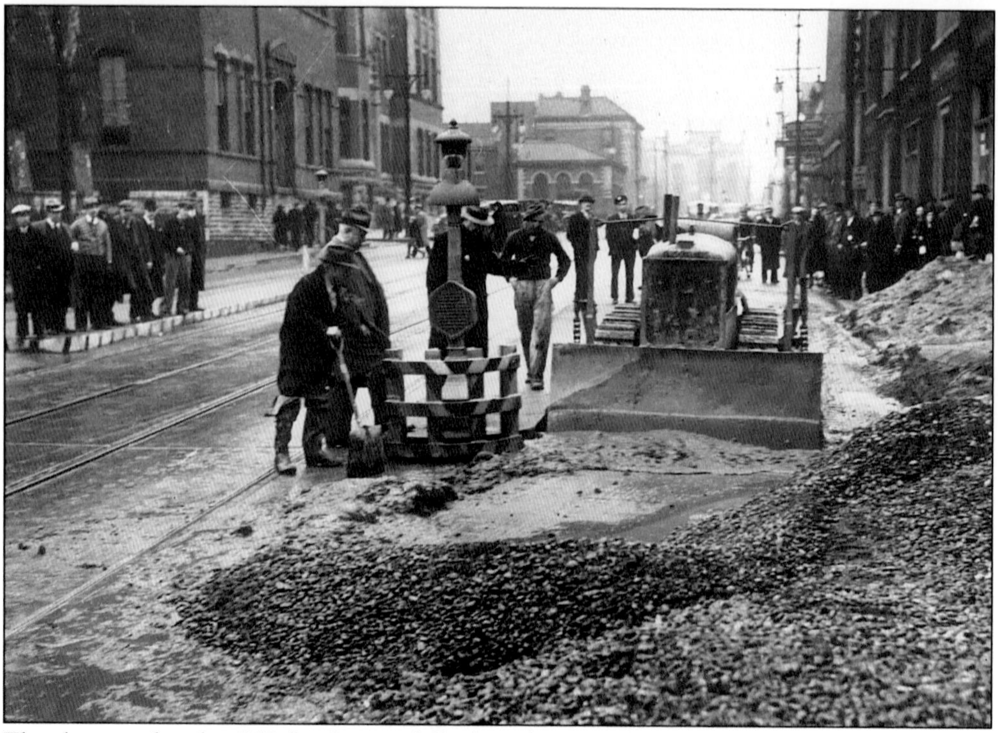

The cleanup after the 1937 flood was a difficult and messy job. This view is looking north along Court Street. The city hall and the jail are to the left. (Courtesy Cincinnati Historical Society.)

Seven

Parks and Recreation

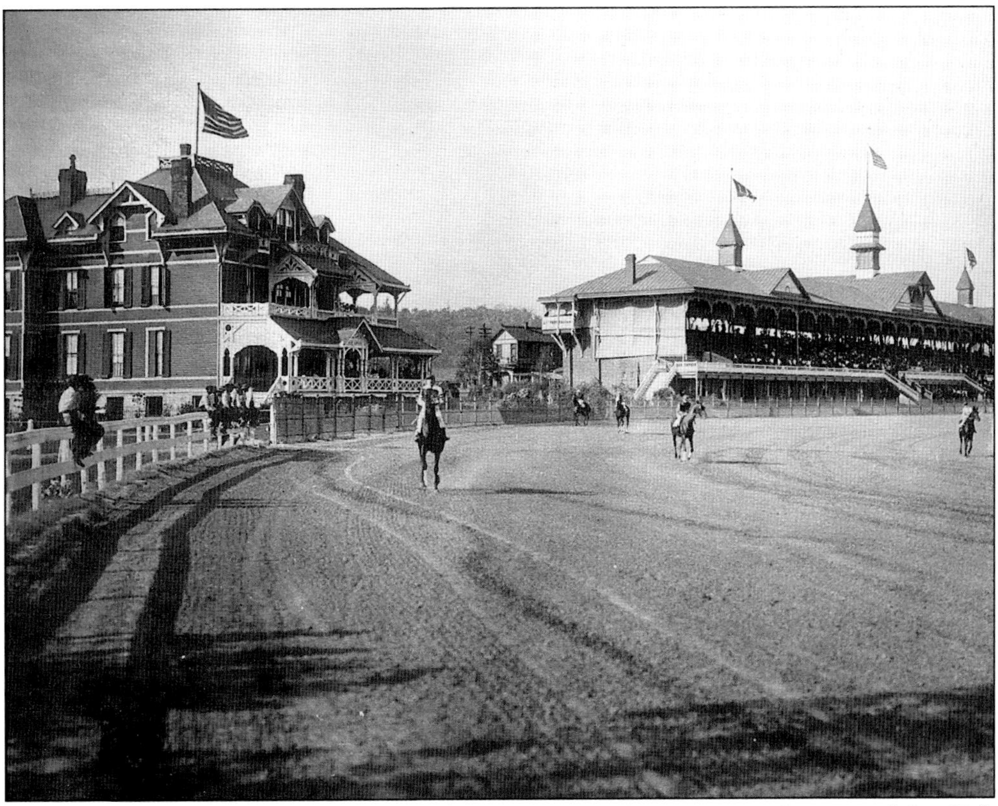

One of the main tourist and recreational attractions in Covington at the turn of the 20th century was the Latonia Race Track. The track was established in 1883 and operated each season until its closing in 1939. The highlight of each season was the running of the Latonia Derby. The derby attracted tens of thousands of spectators and offered large purses. (Barney Graue, photographer.)

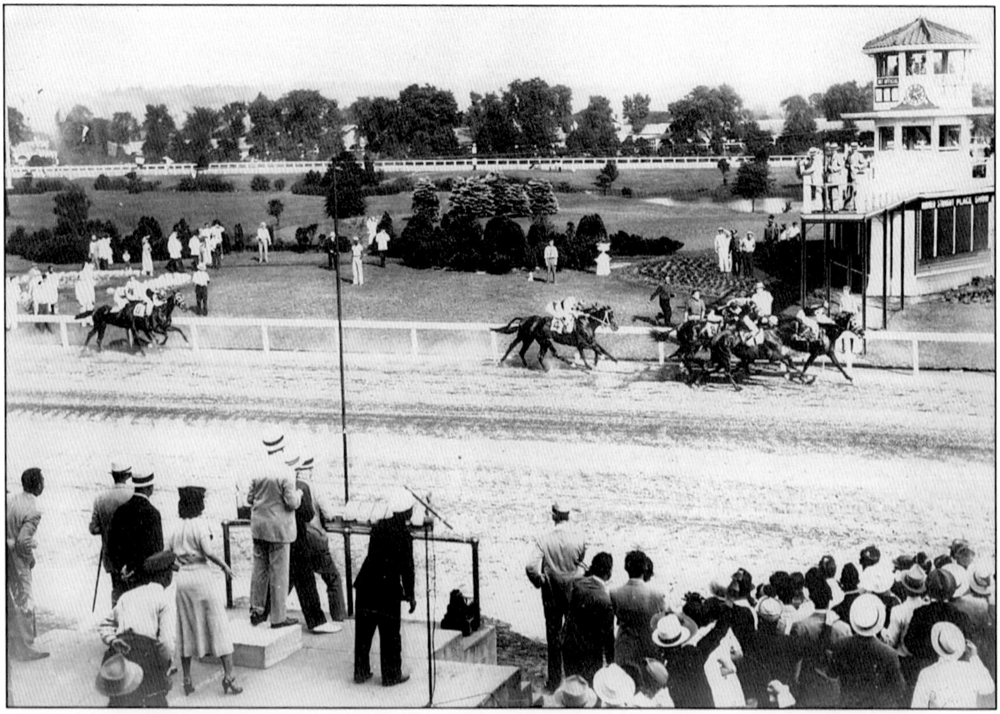

This close finish held the attention of onlookers in 1937.

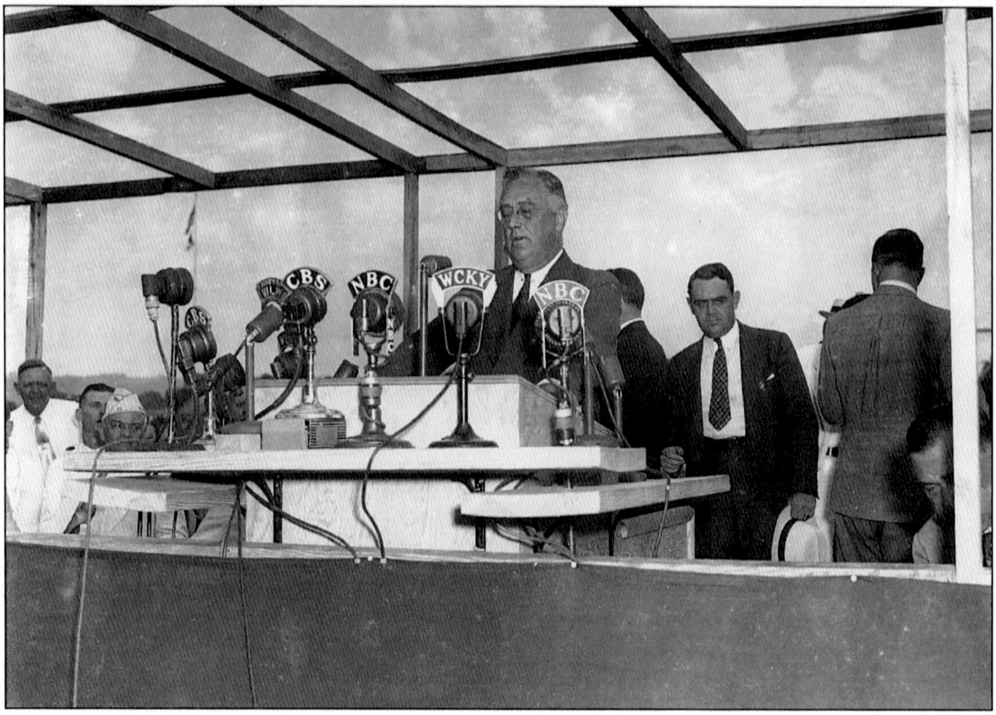

President Franklin D. Roosevelt appeared at the Latonia Race Track on July 8, 1938. He was campaigning in support of Alben W. Barkley, a Democratic candidate for the United States Senate.

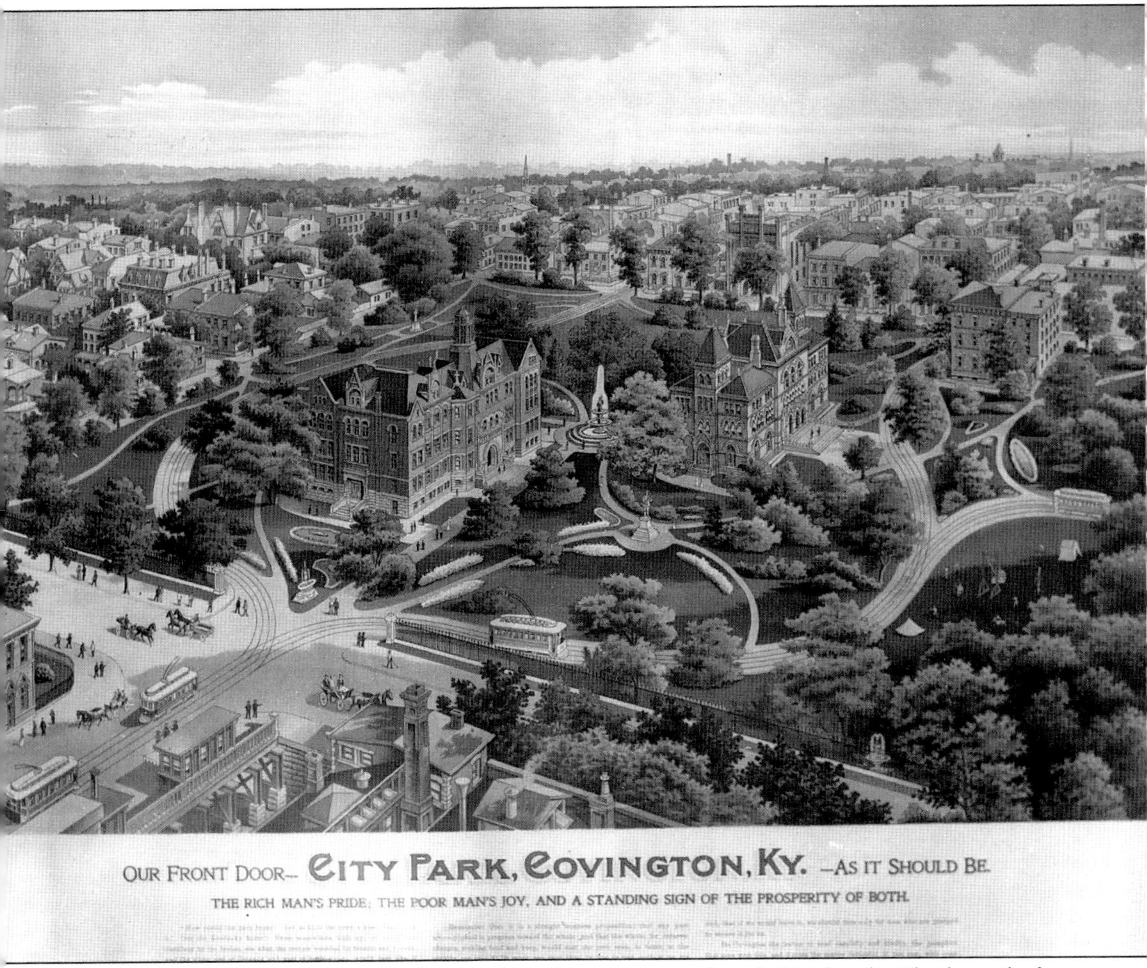

In 1903, supporters of a proposed urban park in downtown produced this sketch. The legend of the sketch reads, "Our front door —City Park Covington, KY. —As it should be. The rich mans pride; the poor man's joy, and a standing sign of prosperity for both." The plan was never carried out. In the center of the sketch can be seen Covington's old City Hall and Federal Building.

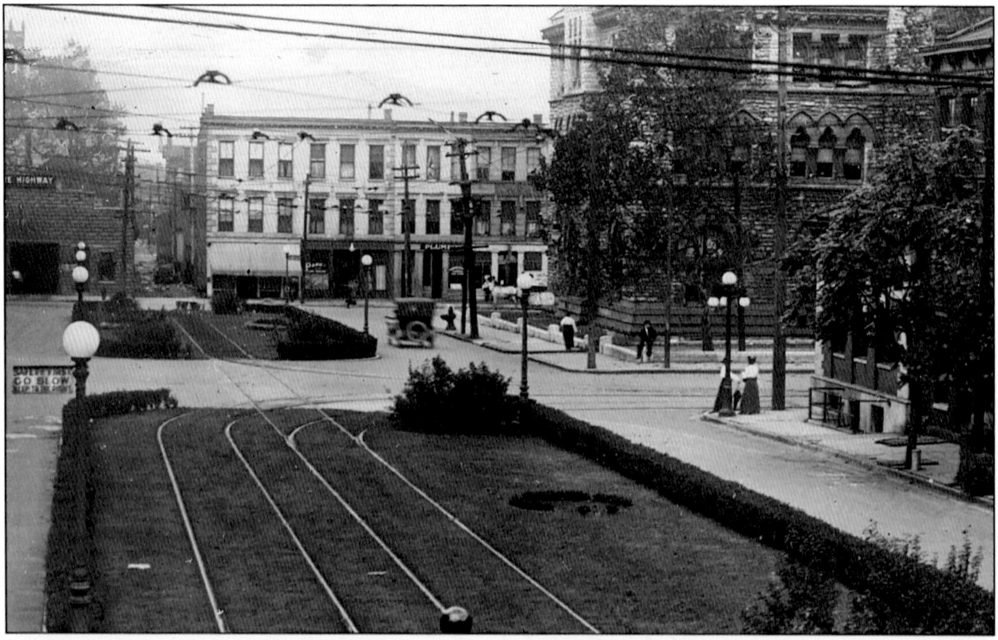

Withers Park was located at the corner of Court and Park Place. This small patch of grass was one of the few open spaces in downtown. The old Covington Federal Building can be seen on the right.

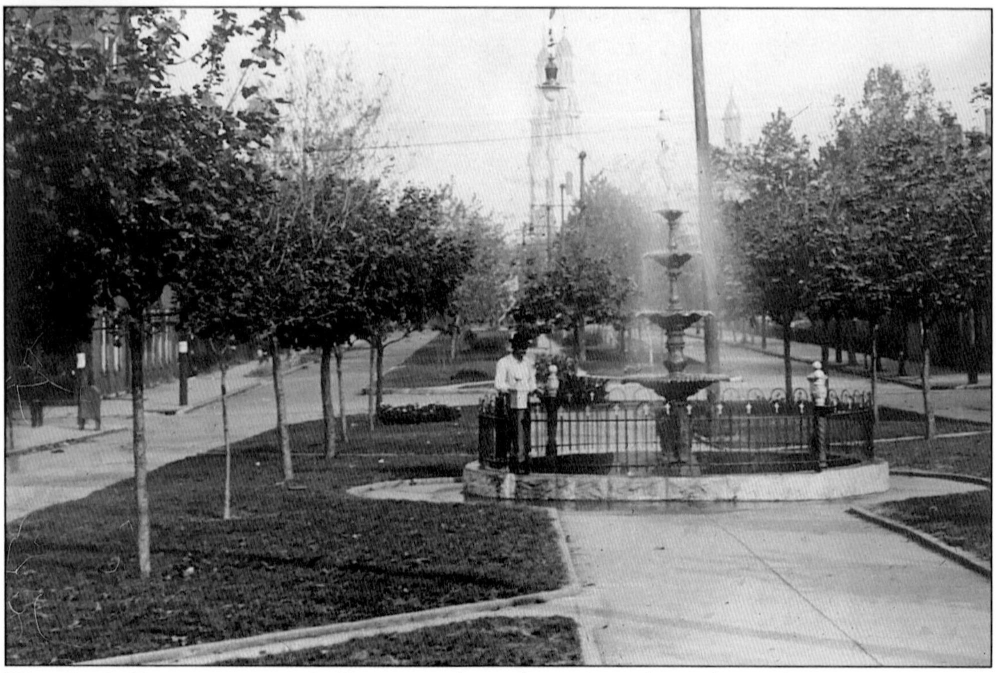

West Sixth Street once was the home to a large farmer's market. The market was constructed in 1861 and served the city's west end. By 1875, the market contained stalls for 16 butchers, 28 truck farmers, and 30 hucksters. In 1907, the market house was razed and the Covington Park Board landscaped the area and installed a cast-iron fountain. The Mother of God Church can be seen in the distance.

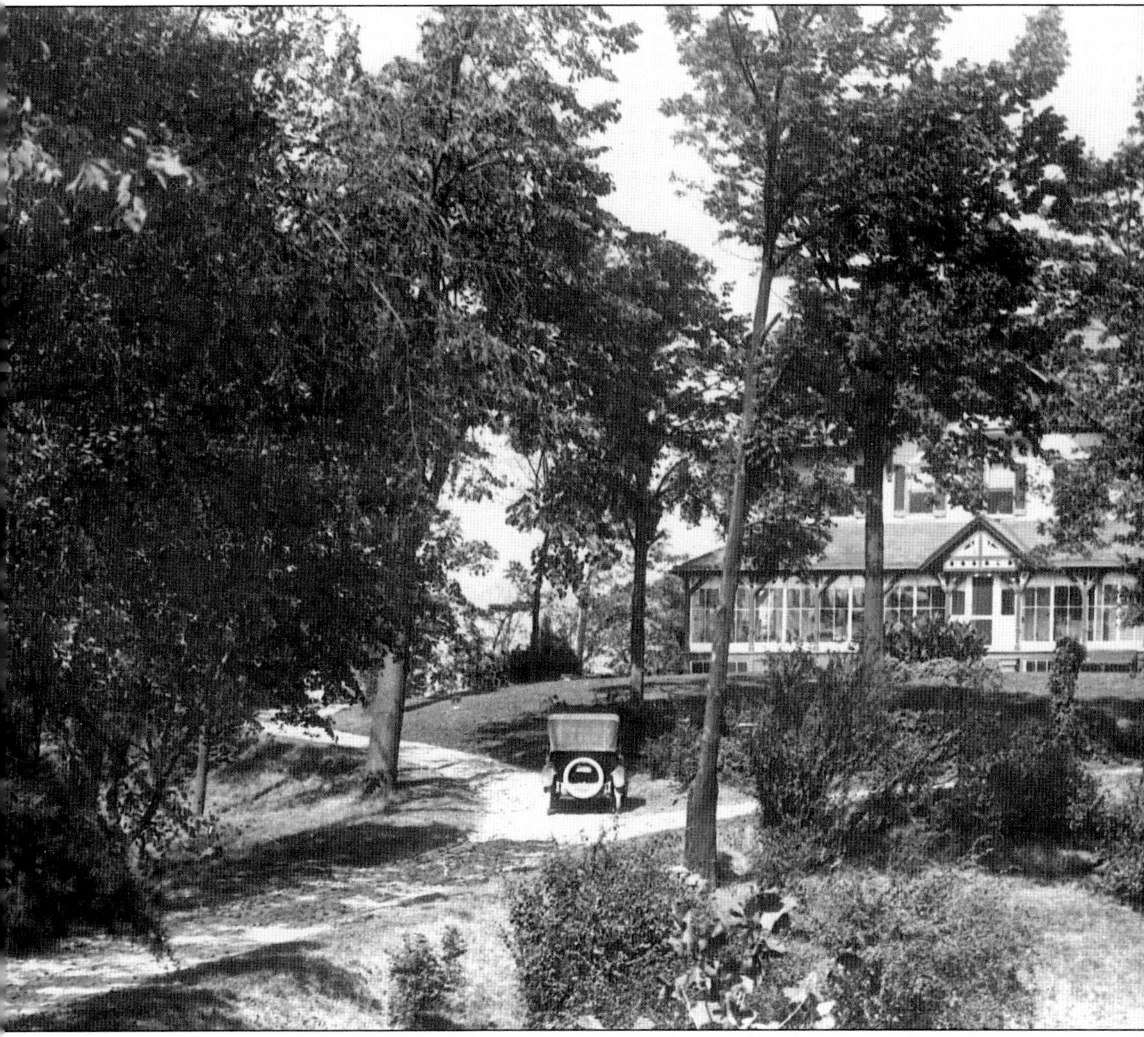

Covington's park system was greatly advanced in 1910 with the donation of a 500-acre parcel of land west of Western Avenue. The property was donated to the city by William P. and Charles P. Devou in memory of their parents. Covington voters passed a $100,000 bond issue that year to improve the grounds. In the photograph above, the Devou home is visible to the right.

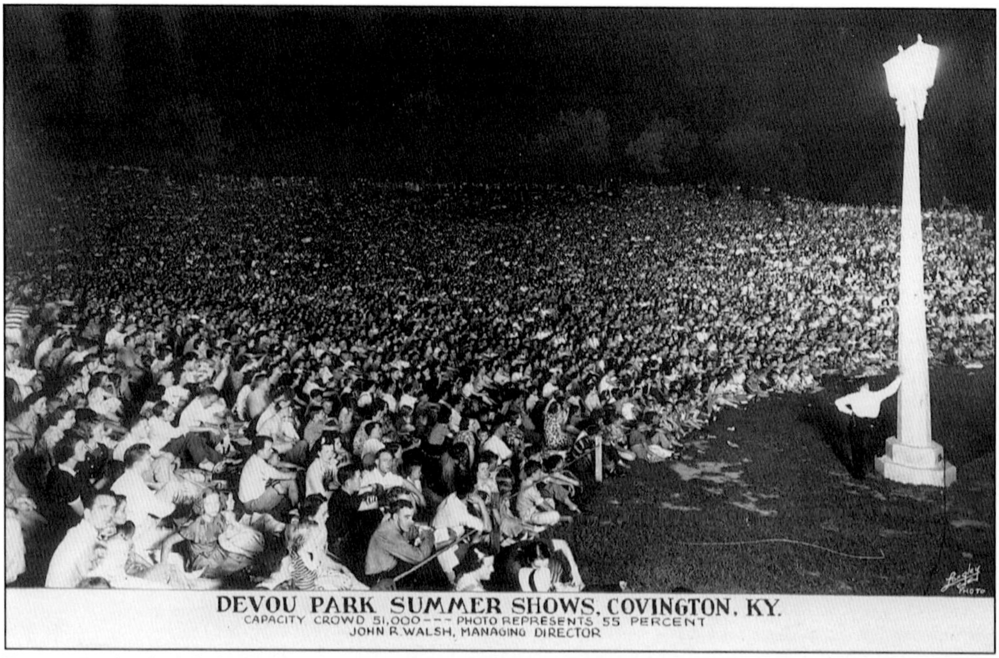

Devou Park's band shell was constructed in 1939 as a WPA project. The band shell was used during the summer months for concerts, theatrical performances, and variety shows. The photograph above shows a crowd of 51,000 who attended a concert on August 16, 1939. (Charles Longley, photographer.)

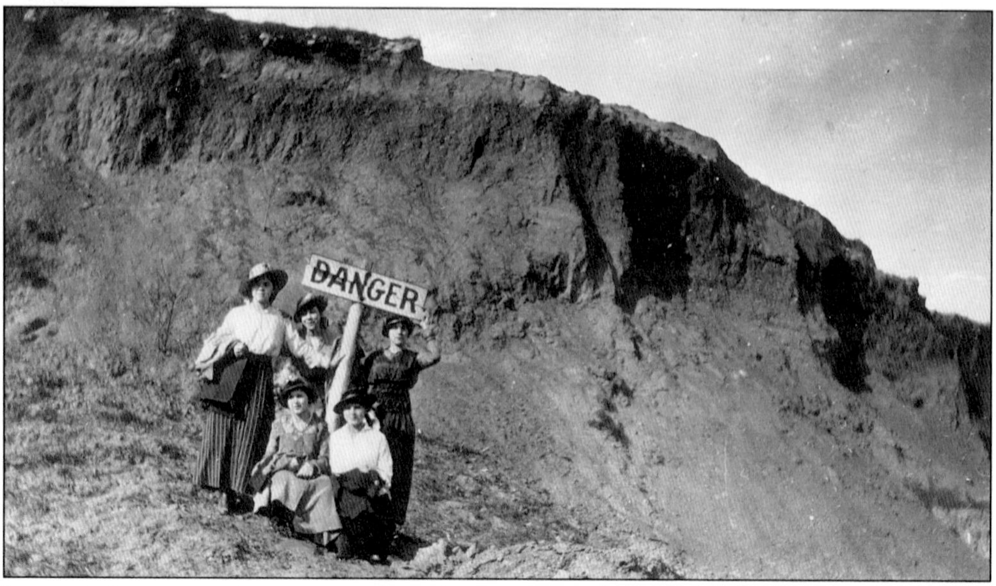

Devou Park was a work in progress from the time of its donation to the city. Here, a group of women pose in a barren portion of the park.

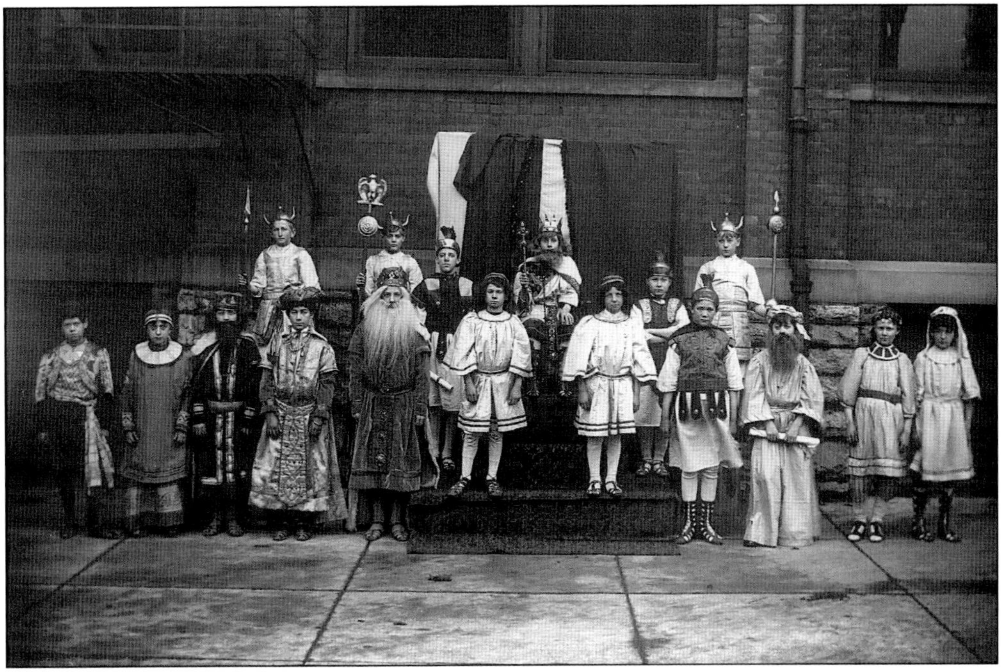

Theatrical productions were also very popular during the pre-World War I era. Above, the children of Mother of God School pulled out all the stops for their costumed extravaganza. (August Koenig, photographer.)

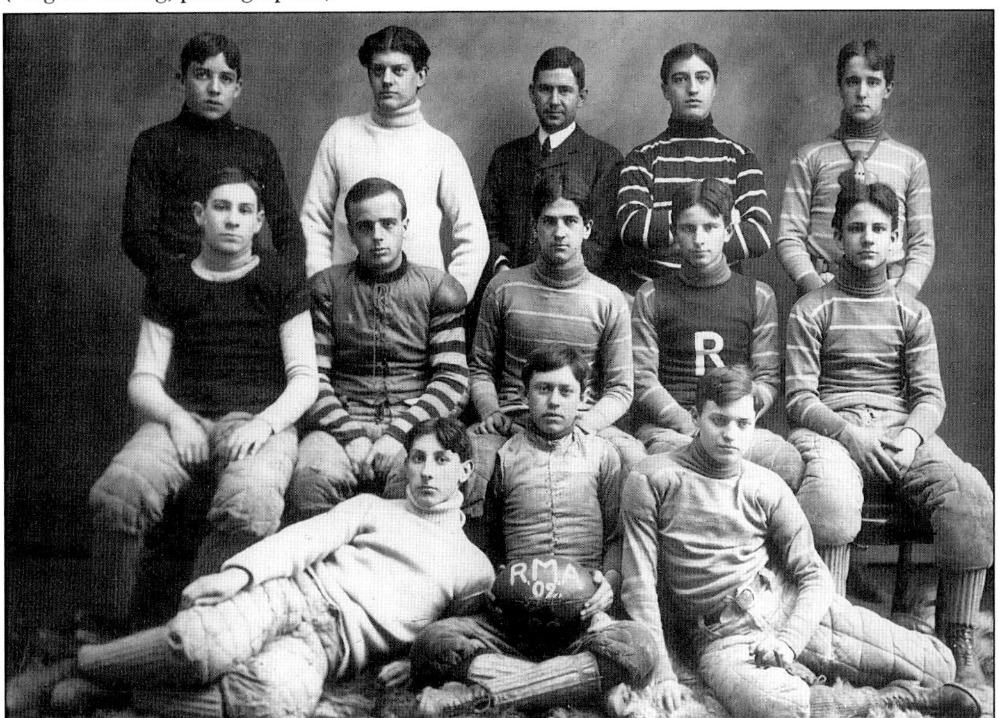

Covington's Rugby Military Academy on Sanford Street also fielded competitive sports teams. These young men posed for the camera in their primitive football gear in 1909.

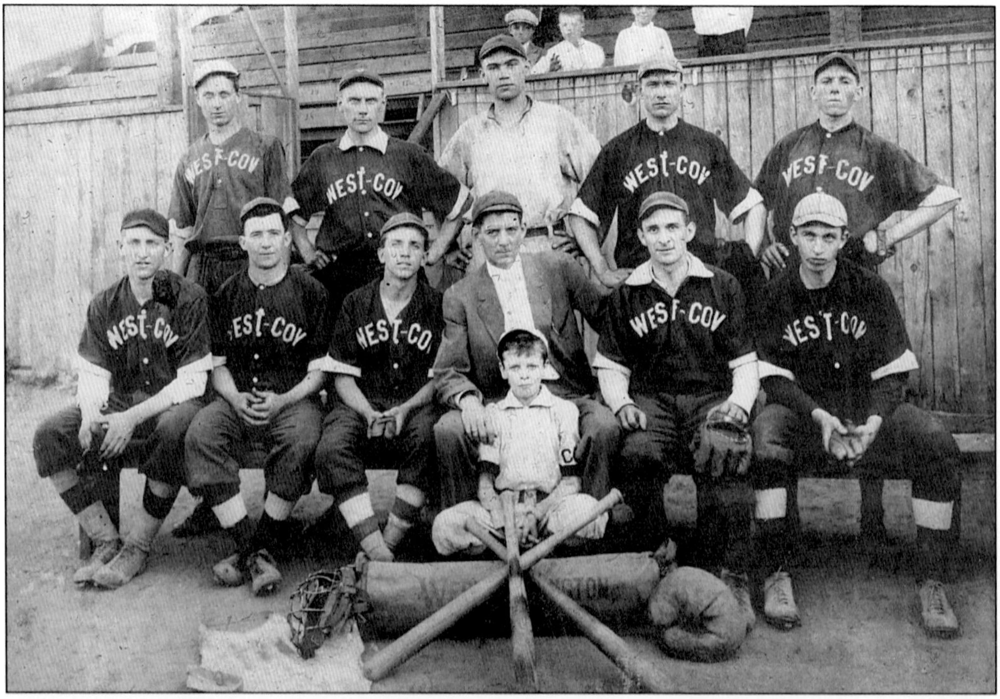

Baseball was an obsession for Northern Kentuckians at the turn of the century. One local team even challenged the Cincinnati Reds to a game! This photograph depicts the West Covington baseball team *c.* 1910.

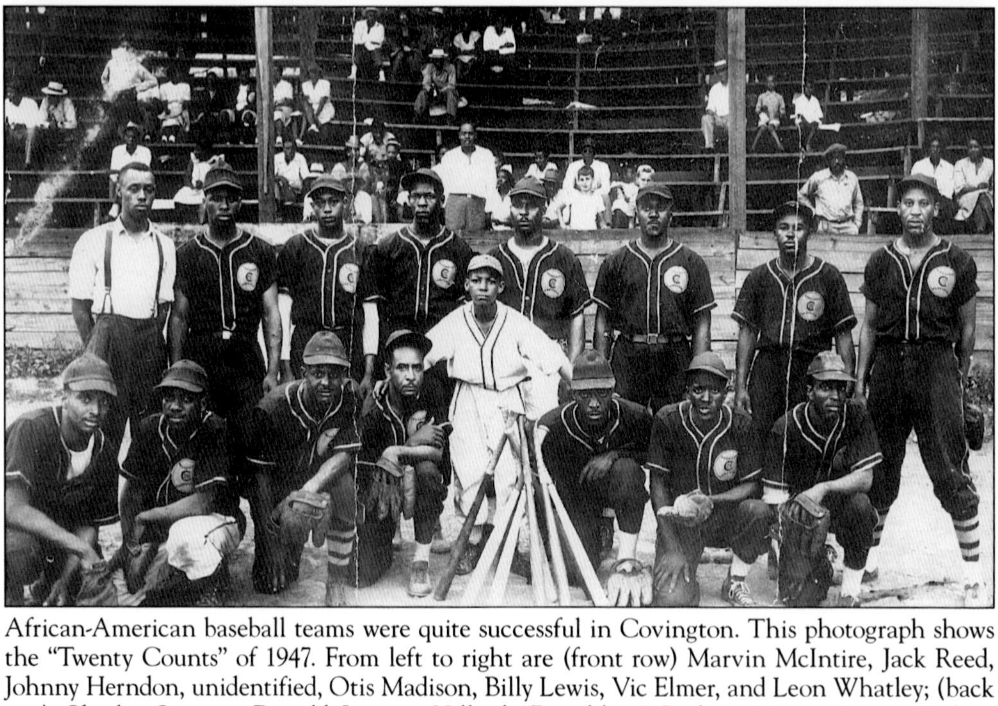

African-American baseball teams were quite successful in Covington. This photograph shows the "Twenty Counts" of 1947. From left to right are (front row) Marvin McIntire, Jack Reed, Johnny Herndon, unidentified, Otis Madison, Billy Lewis, Vic Elmer, and Leon Whatley; (back row) Charles Stewart, Donald Jonson, Hillard "Doughboy" Baskin, Vernon James, Robert Baughman, Raymond Gray, and "Cowboy" Gary.

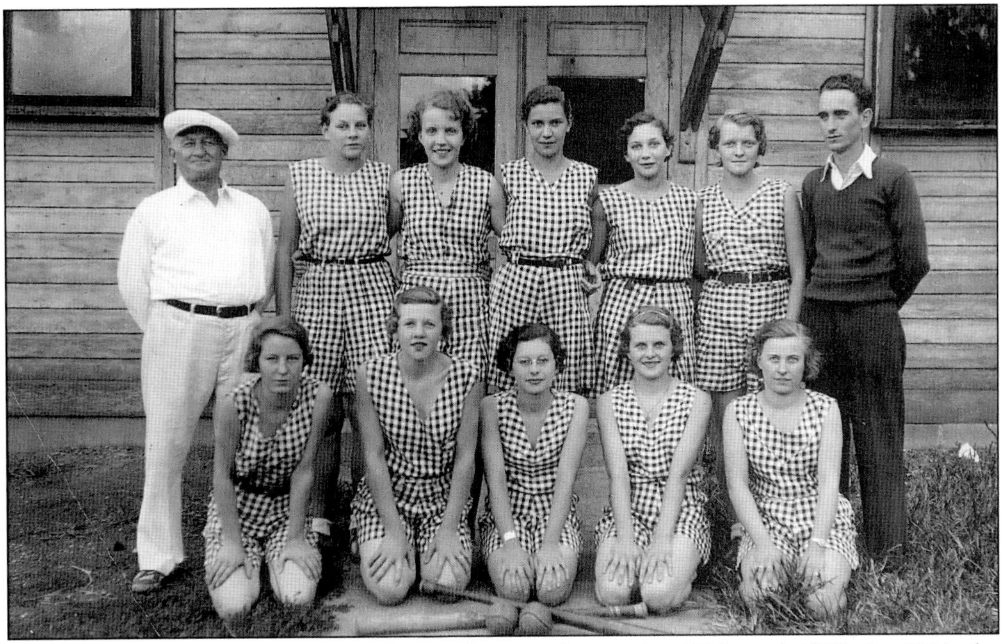

Women's sports became more popular in the area during the 1920s and 1930s. In 1934, the Klosterman Jailbirds competed in the Covington area softball league. From left to right are (back row) John Schroeder (president of the softball league), Rita Gausepohl, Delores Dickman, Florence Walten, Marian Gausepohl, Ann Lehr, and Charlie Briener (coach); (front row) Esther Lamb, Clara Koehne, Estelle Due, Francis Emark, and Mary Lou Hafner.

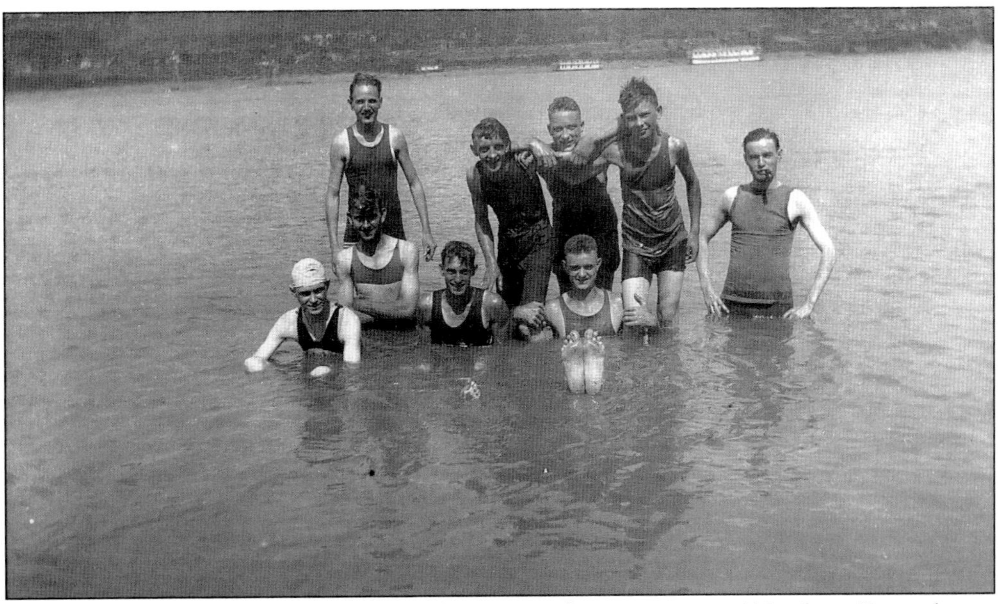

Swimming in the Ohio River was a popular activity for generations of Northern Kentuckians. These young men enjoyed a refreshing swim during the World War I era.

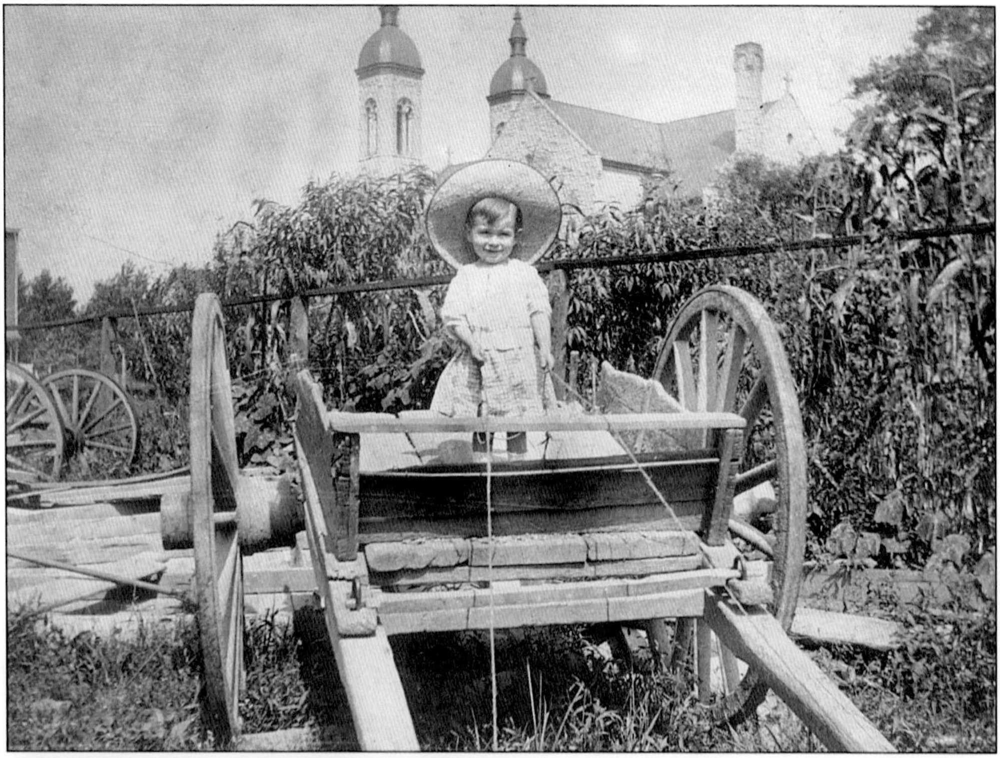

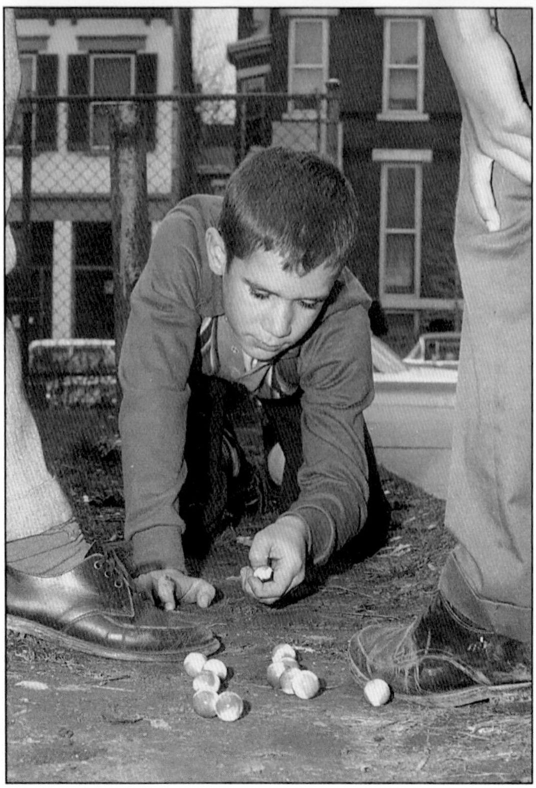

Recreation didn't always mean a formal activity—little Mark Dehlinger found the family horse cart a thing of joy. Holy Cross Church towers can be seen in the background.

Robert Jones of Glenway Avenue enjoyed a game of marbles in the 1960s. Shooting marbles had become a popular activity in the area during the 1920s.

Eight

CHURCHES AND SCHOOLS

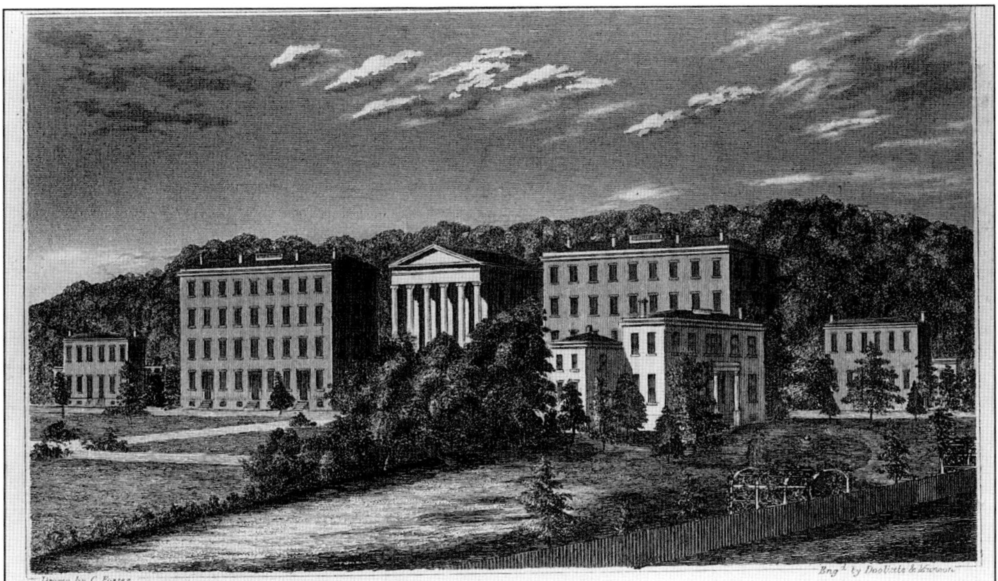

The need for Baptist ministers on the western frontier resulted in the establishment of the Western Baptist Education Society in the 1830s. The society purchased 350 acres of land south of Covington in 1835 with plans for classroom and dormitory buildings surrounded by spacious lawns. College Square was located between Madison and Russell Streets, north of Eleventh Street. The first classes were held in 1845 but the school's success was hampered by the national debate on slavery and the divisiveness of the school board. It closed in 1853 and all of the assets were equally divided between Northern and Southern seminaries. The main building was then used as a private female academy, and during the Civil War as a military hospital. In 1867 the Sisters of the Poor of St. Francis purchased the building for their fledgling St. Elizabeth Hospital. The building was later razed and replaced by the Wadsworth Electric building.

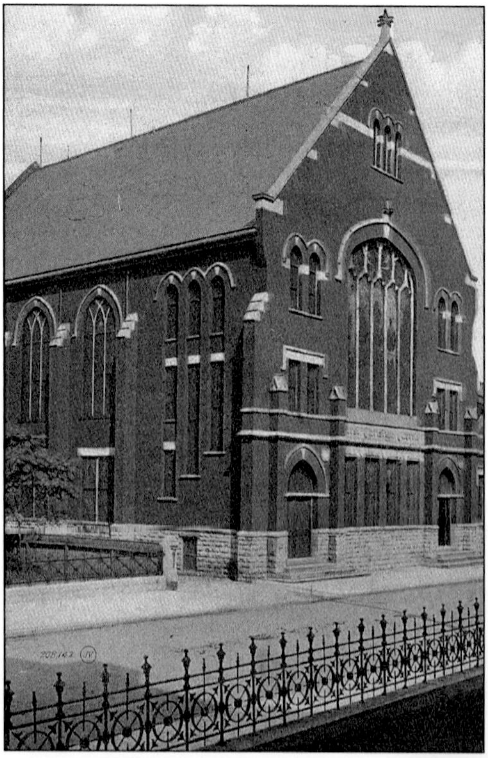

The history of the First Christian Church (Disciples in Christ) can be traced back to the year 1827. The current Gothic Revival edifice on West Fifth Street was designed by the architectural firm of Dittoe and Wisenall and was dedicated in 1894.

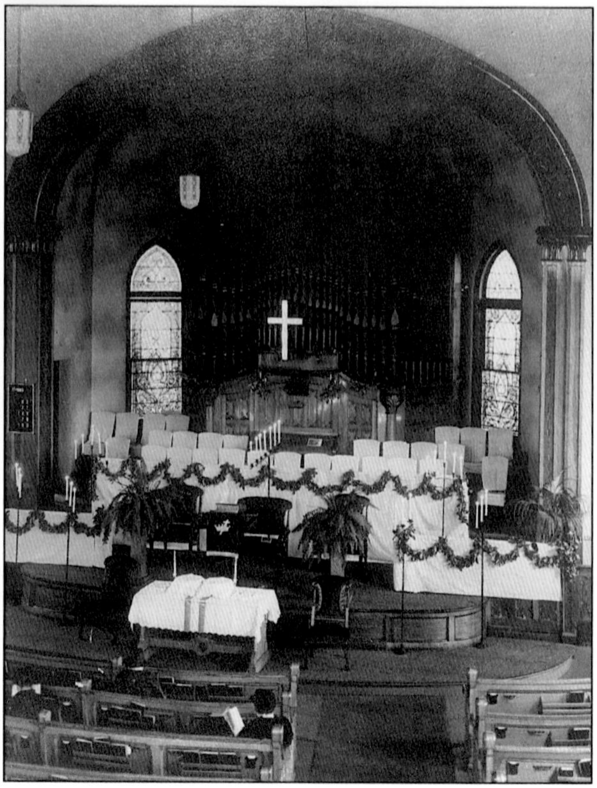

This photograph shows the beautiful Gothic Revival interior of the First Christian Church as it appeared in the early 20th century.

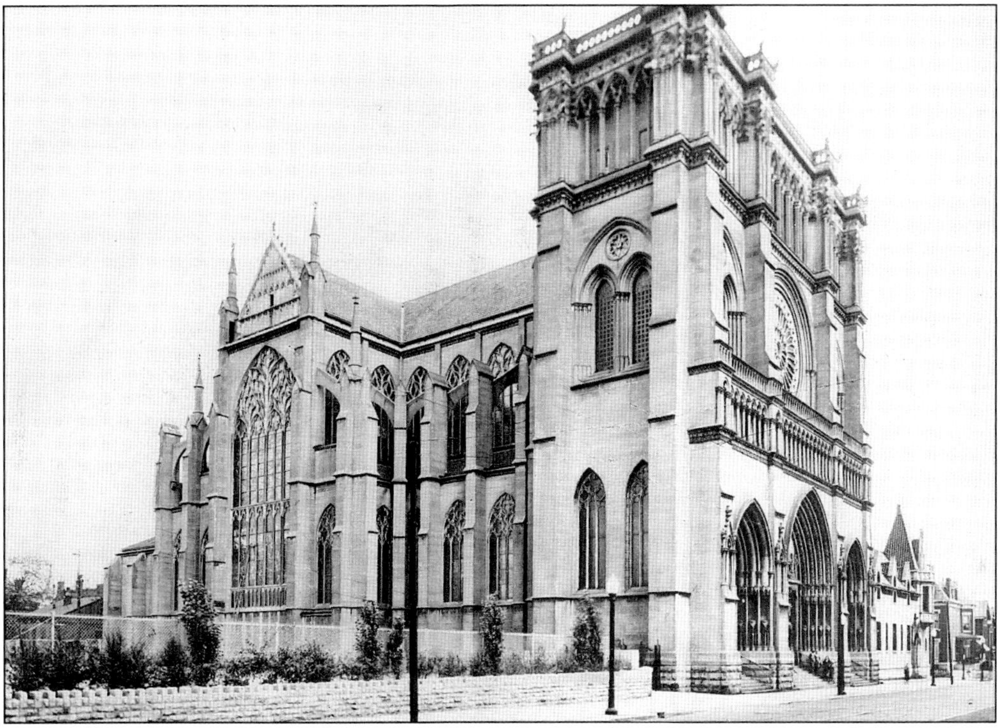

The congregation that was to become the Cathedral Basilica of the Assumption began in 1834 as St. Mary Parish on West Fifth Street. When the Diocese of Covington was established, St. Mary's was named the diocesan cathedral. A new cathedral was built on Eighth Street in 1854, but by 1894, the need for a larger cathedral building became apparent. The cornerstone of the current cathedral was set into place on September 8, 1895 by Bishop Camillus P. Maes. (Courtesy Diocese of Covington.)

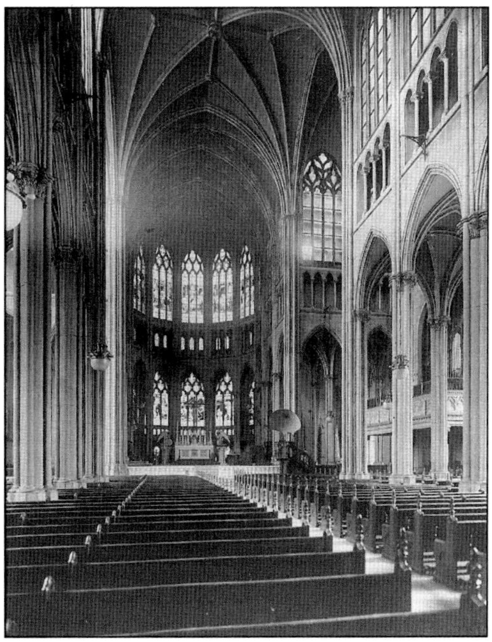

While the facade was patterned after Notre Dame Cathedral in Paris, the nave was copied from the church of St. Denis. The church contains stained glass windows imported from Munich, Germany, including one of the largest such windows in the world (67' x 24'). (Courtesy Diocese of Covington.)

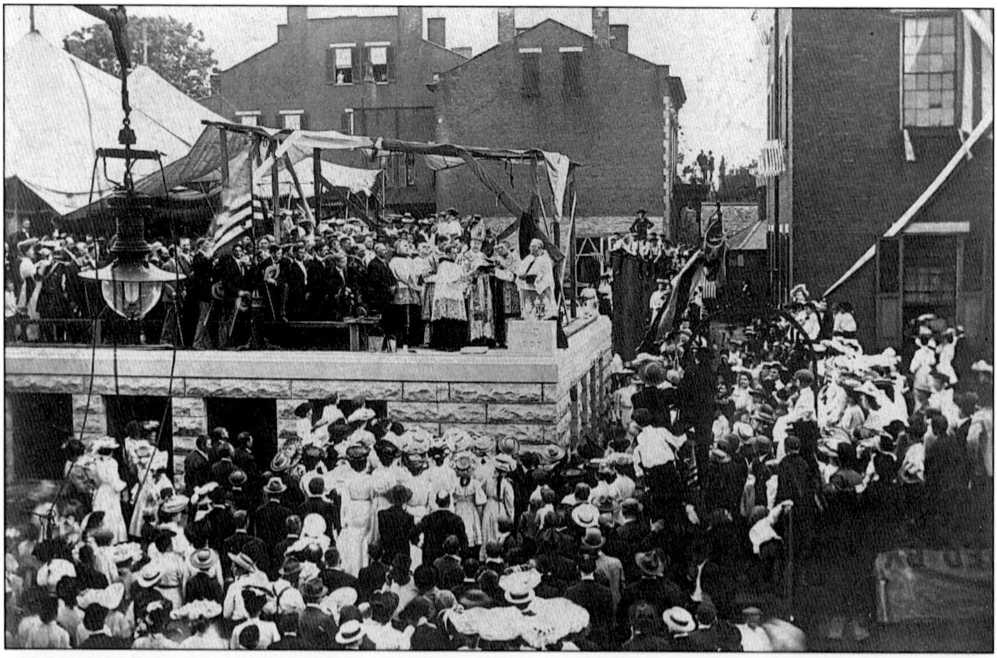

Mother of God Parish constructed a grand new elementary school on West Sixth Street in 1905. Bishop Camillus P. Maes set the cornerstone of the new school into place on August 13, 1905. The building (below) housed Mother of God Elementary School (1906–1962), Covington Latin School (1925–1926), Covington Catholic High School (1925–1955), Villa Madonna College (1957–1967), and Good Counsel School (1962–1971). The building was demolished in 1971. (August Koenig, photographer.)

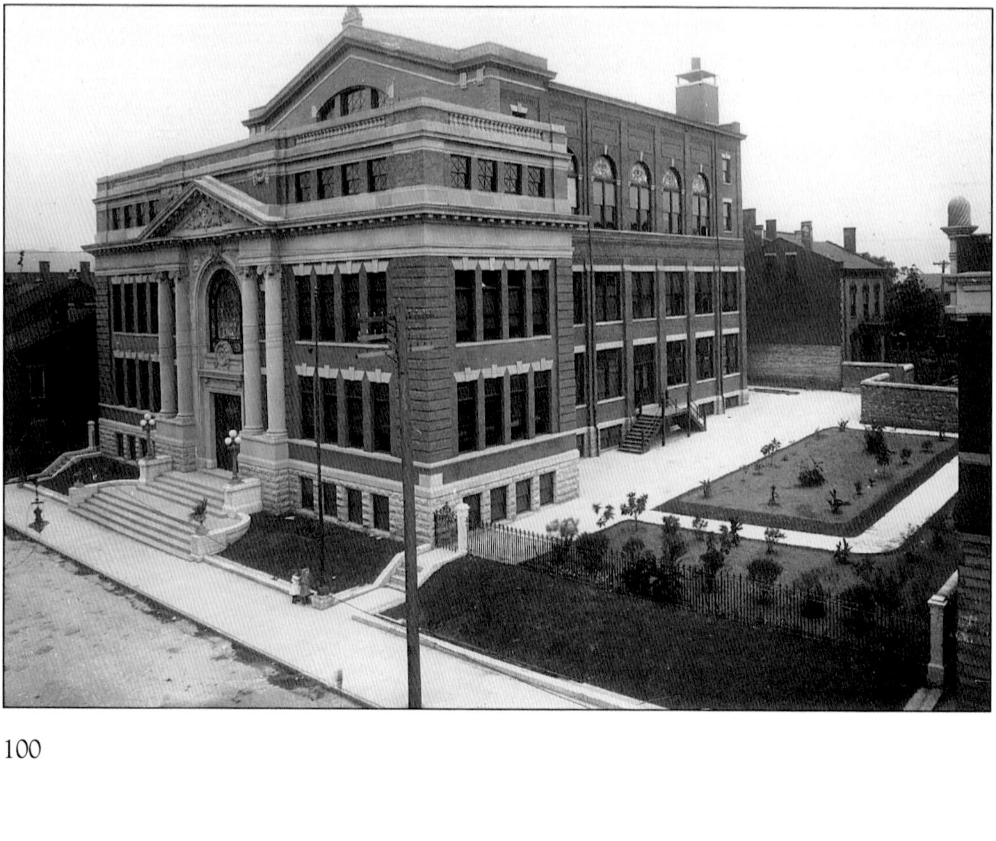

German Catholics established Mother of God Parish in 1842 under the guidance of Father Ferdinand Kuhr. The current Italian Renaissance Revival Style church was designed by the Cincinnati architectural firm of Walter and Stewart. The edifice was dedicated on September 10, 1871 and includes hand-carved wooden altars, imported stained glass, and mosaic tile floors.

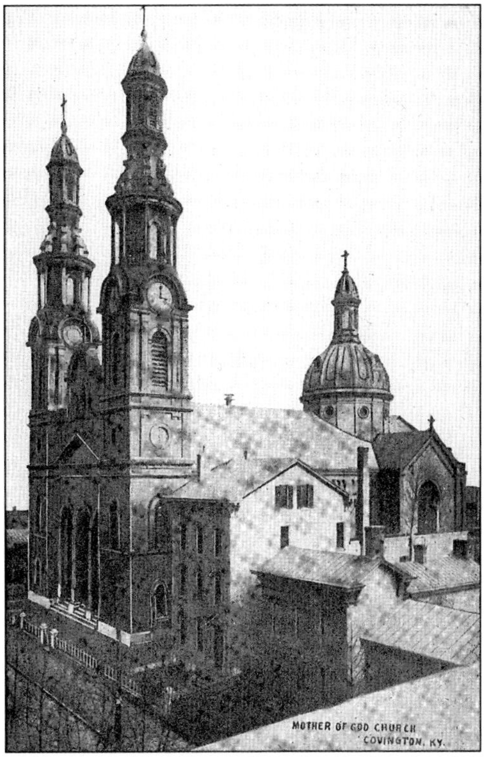

This portrait is of the first Confirmation class of St. Mark Evangelical Church in Latonia, c. 1910. From left to right are (seated) two unidentified, Fern Smith Gillham, unidentified, Rev.William Echelmeier, unidentified, Josie Huber Oelsner, Mamie Huber, and Catherine (Babe) Young Frank; (standing) unidentified, George Smith, two unidentified, Ethel Luzador, unidentified, Florence Fisk, and unidentified. (Courtesy Lisa Gillham.)

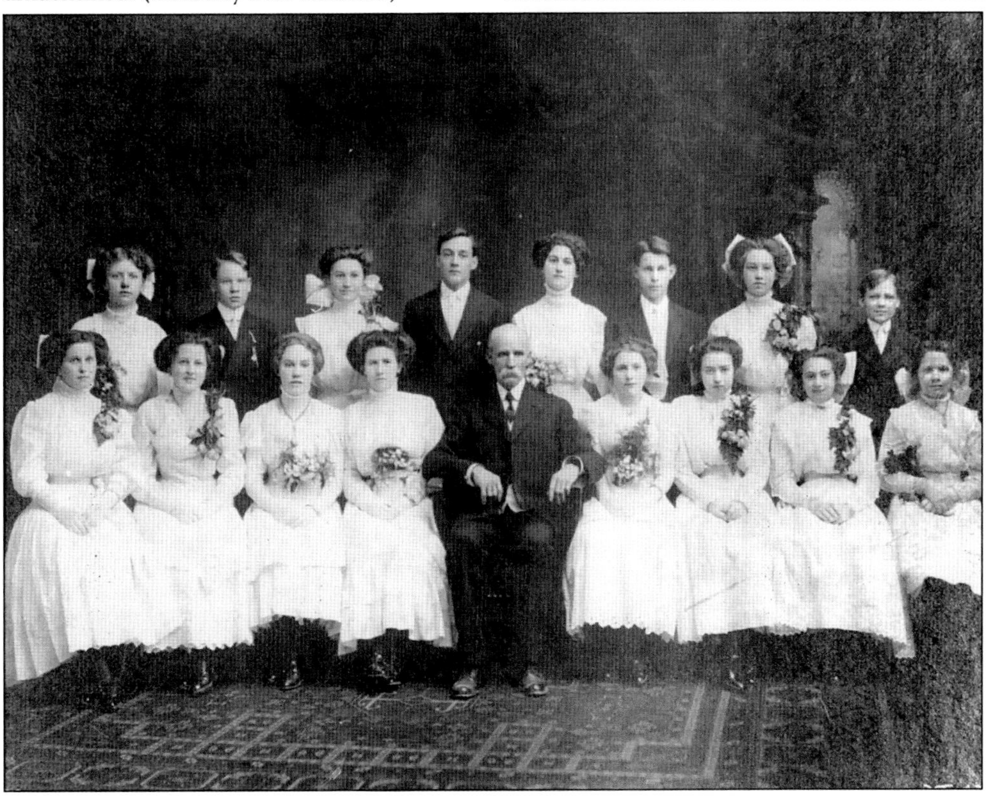

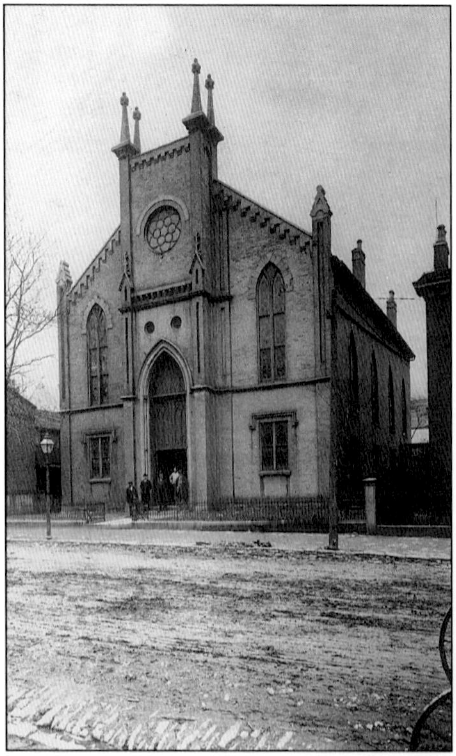

The members of the Scott Street Methodist Episcopal Church South built this beautiful building in 1843 on the eastside of Scott Street between Fifth and Sixth Streets. The building was later demolished in 1895 to make way for a new church building.

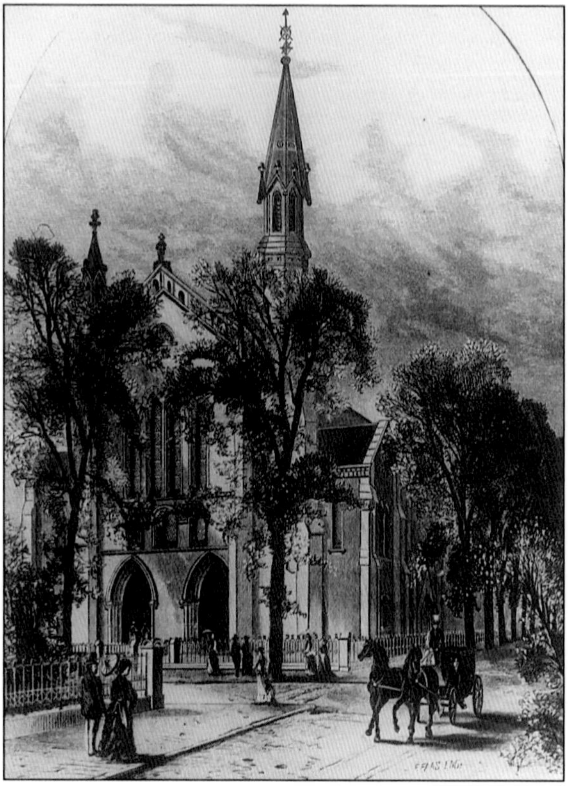

Covington's First Methodist Church was established in 1846, when 27 members of the Scott Street Methodist Episcopal Church South withdrew from the congregation over the issue of slavery. The dissenting members established a new congregation in a building at the southeast corner of Third and Scott Streets. This more handsome Gothic Revival structure was dedicated at the southwest corner of Greenup and Fifth Streets on July 14, 1867.

The German Methodists of the city's west side established Immanuel Church in 1847. The congregation built a new church at the corner of Tenth and Russell Streets in 1869. During the post-World War II era, many of the parishioners had moved to the suburbs and a new Immanuel Methodist Church was built in the City of Lakeside Park in 1950. The old church still stands and is used for commercial purposes.

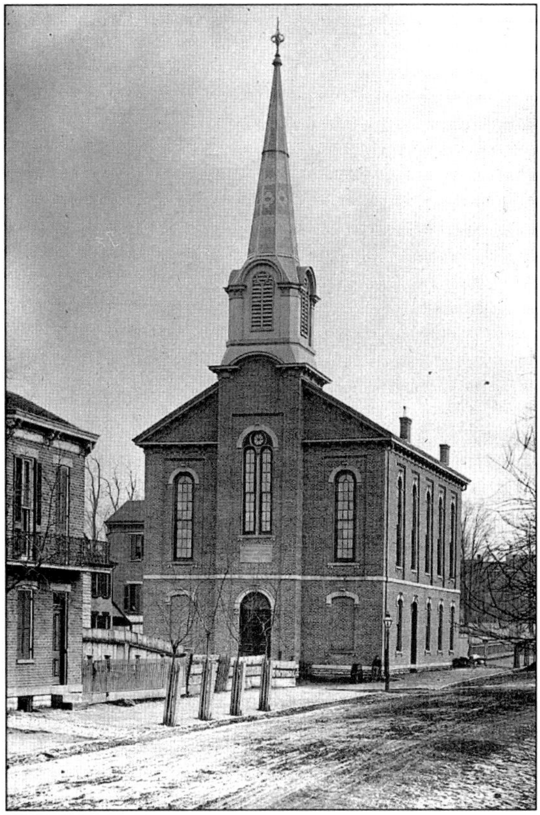

The Madison Avenue Presbyterian Church was organized 1855. The congregation commissioned the architectural firm of Crapsey and Brown to design a Gothic Revival Structure on the Madison Avenue property. The first services were conducted in the building on November 21, 1886. The church was demolished c. 1960, when the congregation moved to the suburbs.

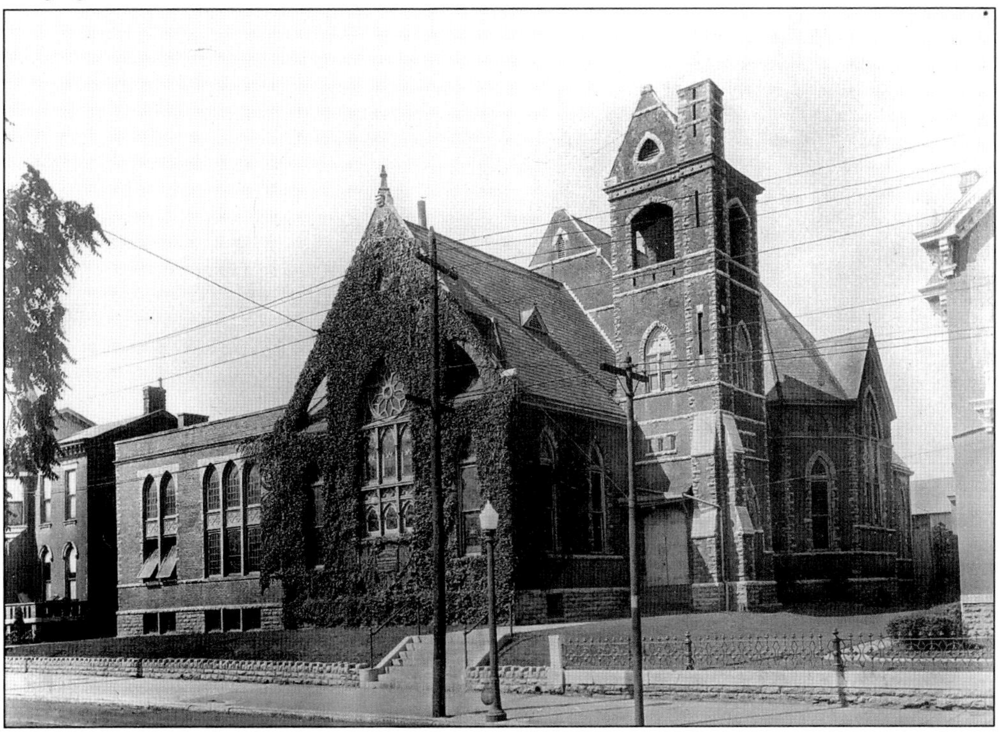

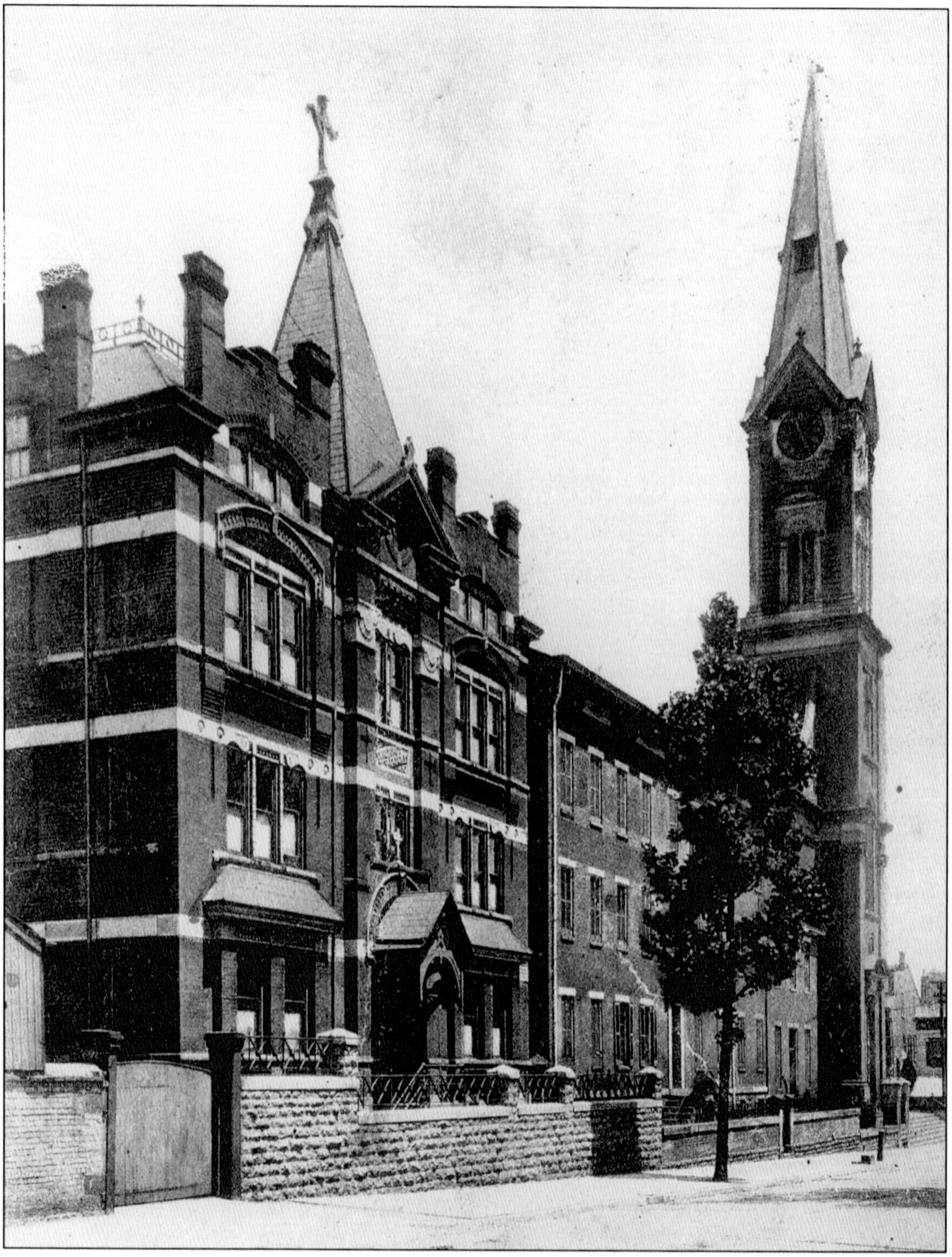

In 1853, the German Catholic residents living on the eastside purchased a lot at the northwest corner of Twelfth and Greenup Streets and established St. Joseph Church and School. St. Joseph Church was dedicated in 1859. As the Sisters of St. Benedict established their presence in the city they built St. Walburg Monastery (the simple brick building in the middle of the photograph) in 1860 and St. Walburg Academy (the Victorian structure to the left) in 1890. St. Walburg Academy closed in 1931 to become Villa Madonna College. The college remained in this building until the present campus was completed in Crestview Hills in 1968. None of these buildings remains today.

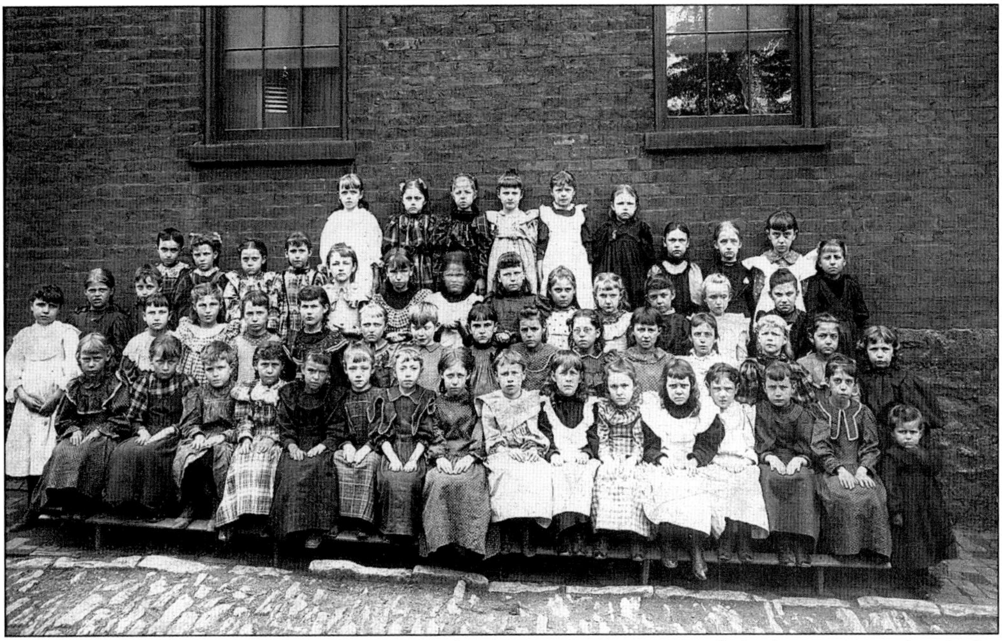

For many years, the larger Catholic parishes in Covington provided elementary schools for both boys and girls. St. Joseph Parish at Twelfth and Greenup Streets maintained a girl's school taught by the Sisters of St. Benedict and a boy's school taught by the Brothers of Mary. Above, a group of female students pose in front of their school building. Below, an orderly class of boys shows off their knickers and jackets. Both photos were taken c. 1895.

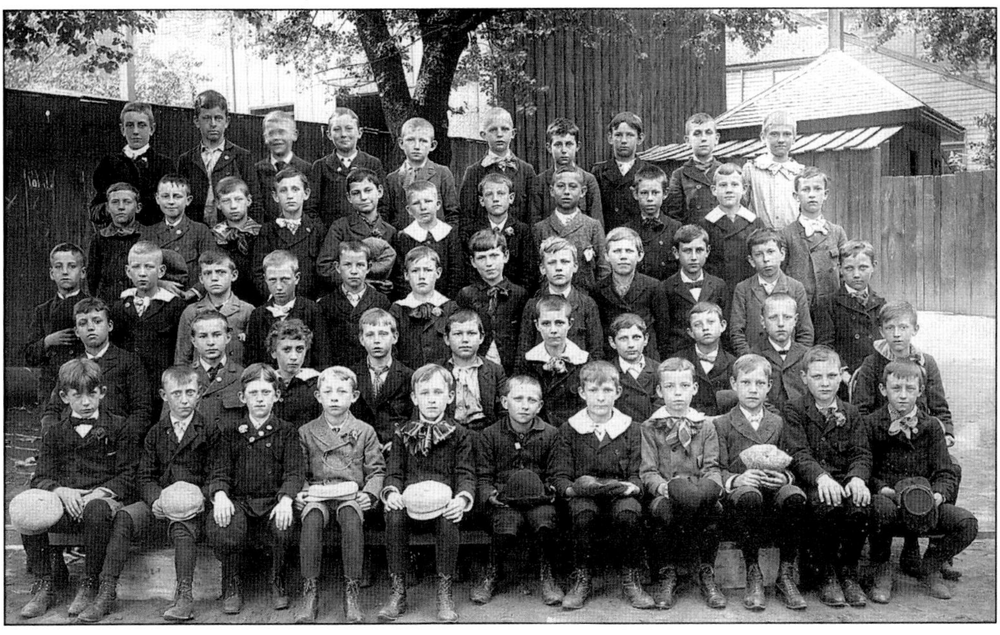

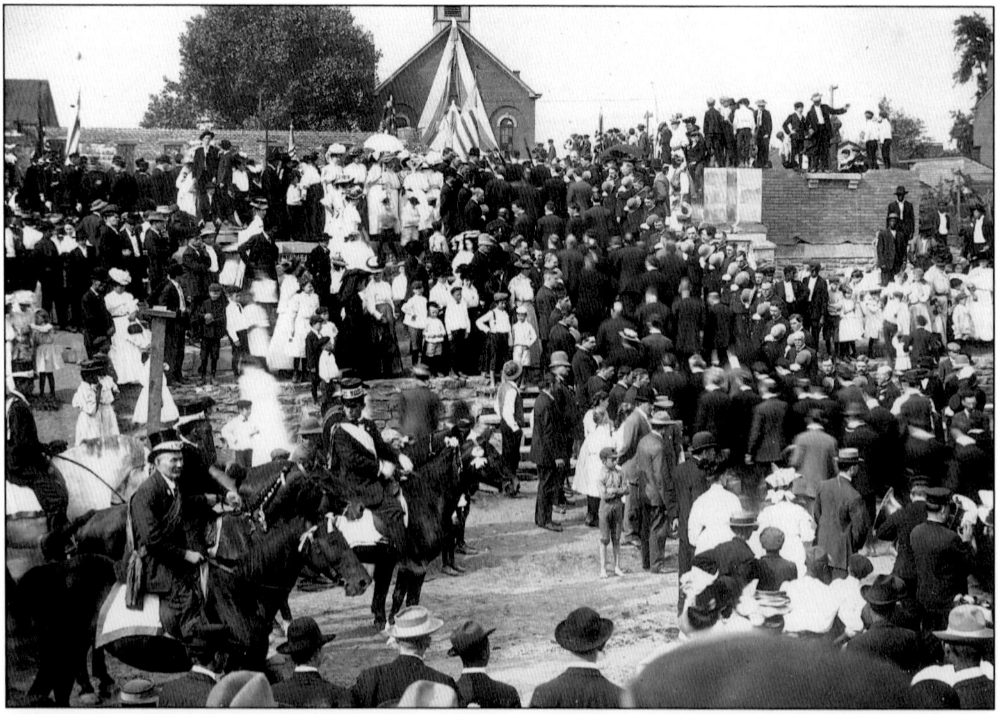

The German Catholics living in the Austinburg neighborhood established St. Benedict Parish in 1885. This photograph depicts the cornerstone laying ceremonies for the present church on September 22, 1907. The old combination church and school building on East Sixteenth Street can been seen in the background. (August Koenig, photographer.)

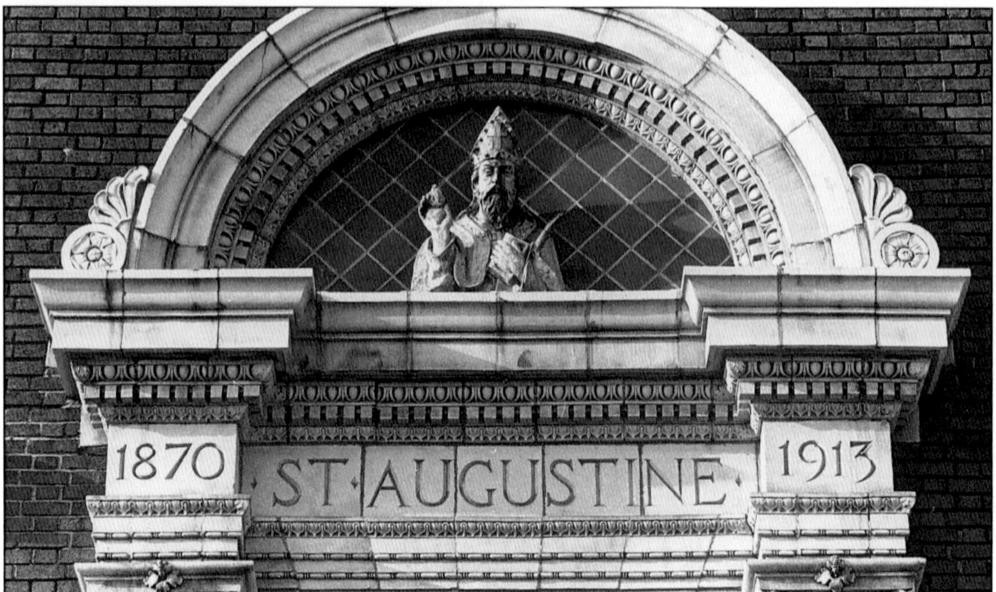

St. Augustine Parish was established in 1870 in what was then the city of Central Covington. A new church designed by architect David Davis of Newport, was constructed in 1913 on West Nineteenth Street. A new parochial school was built soon after.

The German Catholics of the west end established St. Aloysius Parish and School in 1865. In 1866, the congregation commissioned local architect Louis Pickett to design a permanent church to be located at the southeast corner of Seventh and Bakewell Streets. The new edifice was dedicated in 1867. On May 16, 1985, the building was struck by lightning resulting in the complete destruction of the beautiful church.

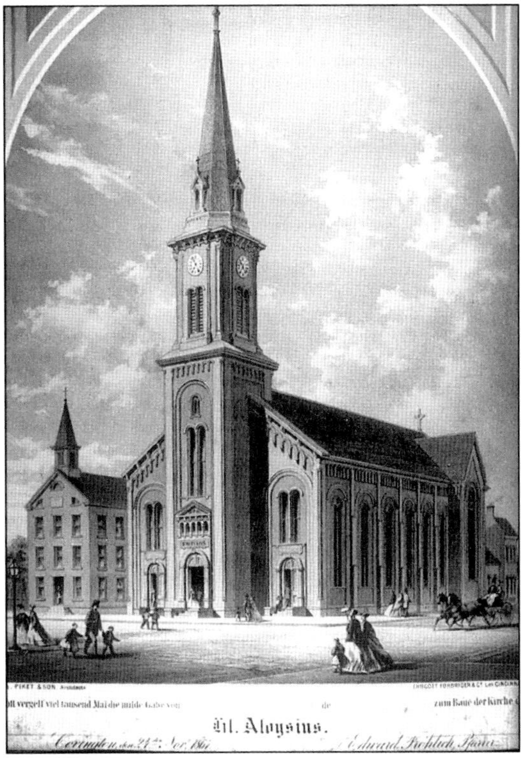

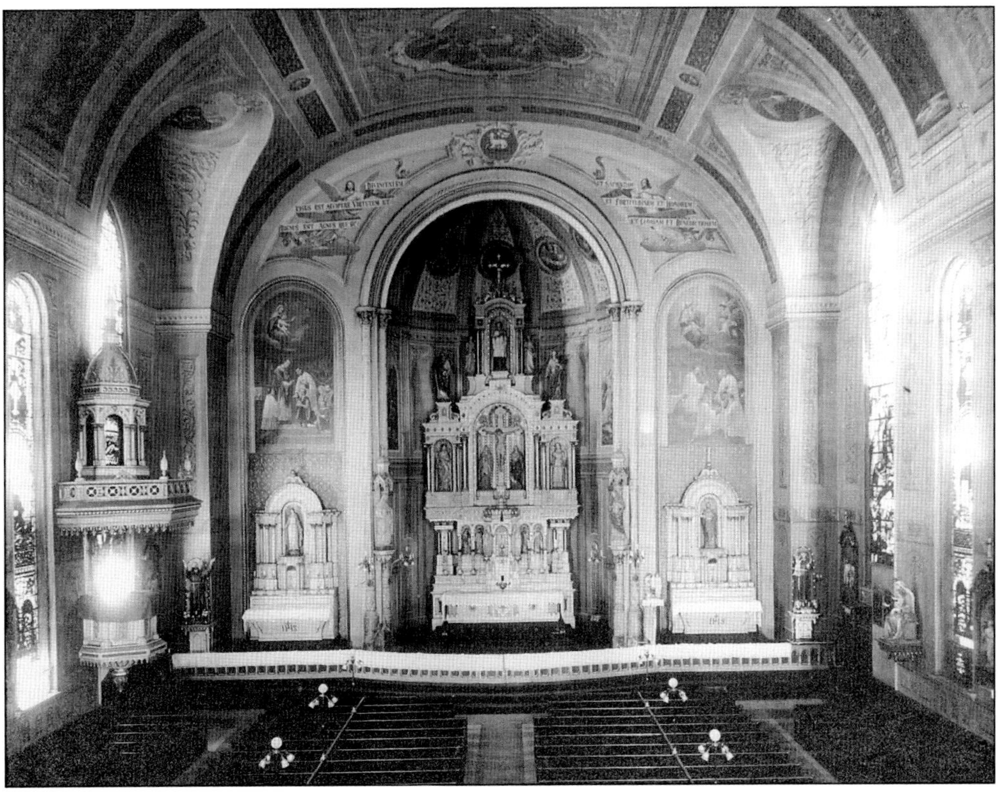

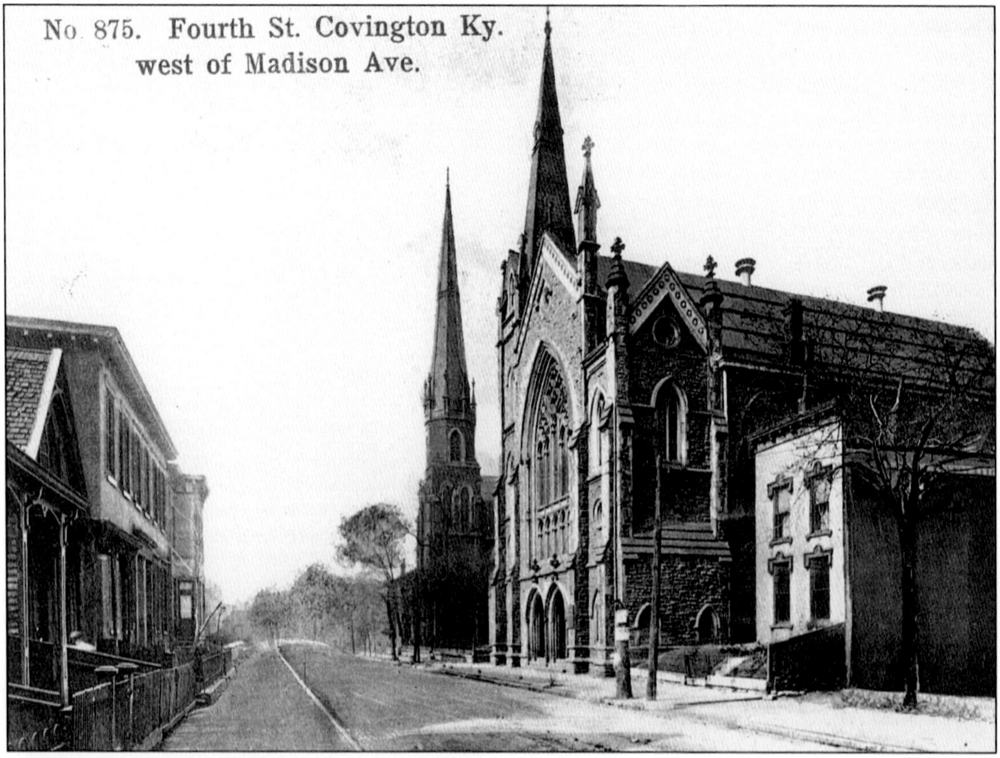

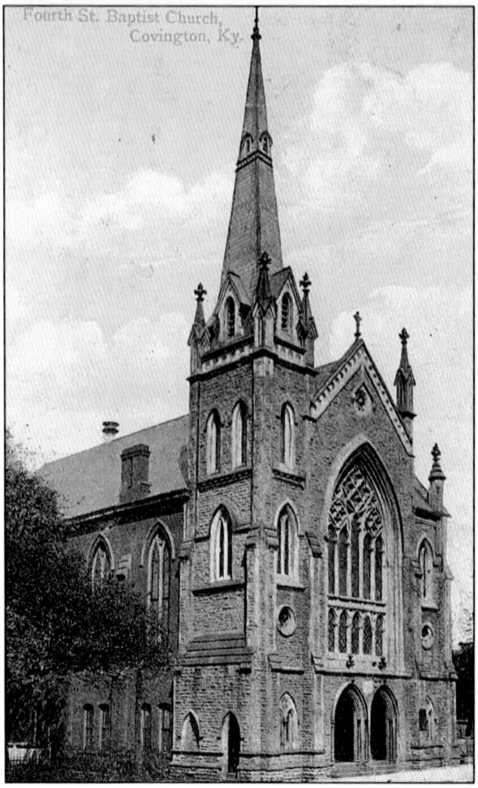

West Fourth Street was for many years graced by two of Covington's most beautiful churches. The First Baptist Church (foreground and on left) and the First Presbyterian Church (background) were both designed by the prominent architectural firm of Walter and Stewart. Both edifices were dedicated in 1873. In 1963, the First Presbyterian Church was demolished to make way for the new Internal Revenue Service building. The First Baptist Church is today an integral part of the downtown neighborhood. Its façade is built of native limestone.

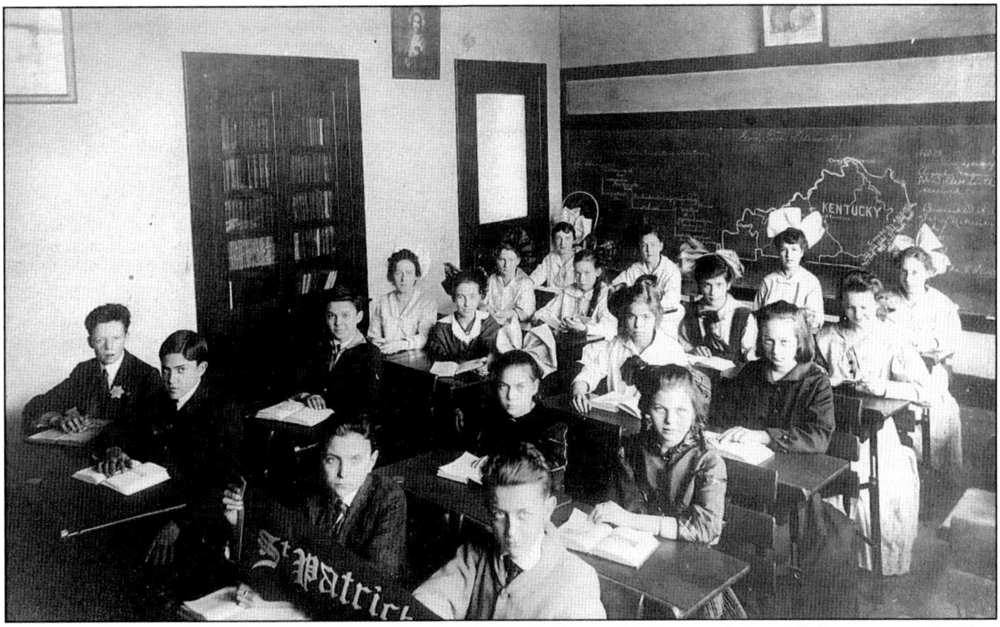

St. Patrick Parish, established in 1870, served the Irish Catholic residents of the west end. The parish church and school were located at the corner of Philadelphia and Elm Streets. The Sisters of Charity of Nazareth taught in the parish school. Above, this group of attentive St. Patrick students studied Kentucky history during the World War I era. The photograph below shows the interior of the church in the 1960s.

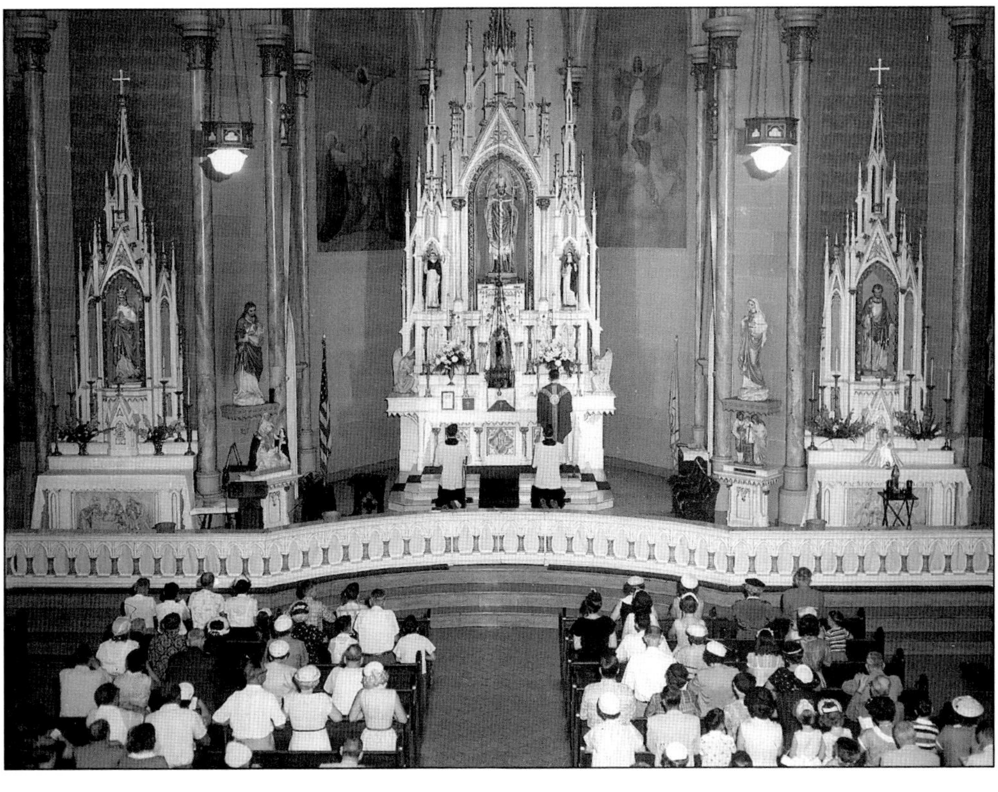

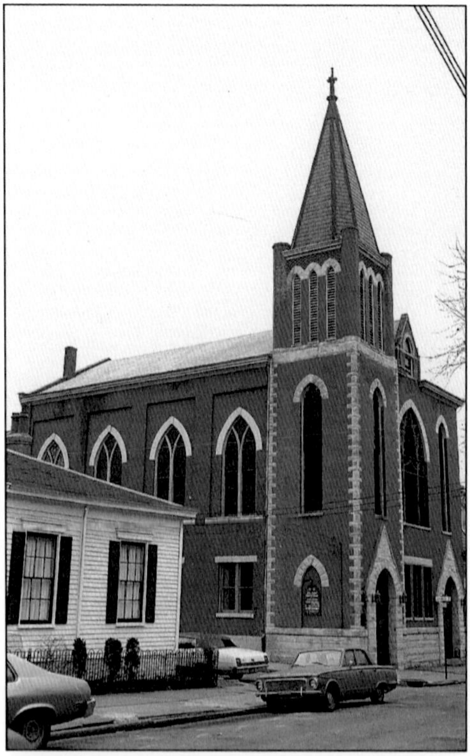

German Protestants established the Evangelical Reformed Church at the corner of Willard and Lockwood Streets in 1862. That same year, the congregation completed a Gothic Revival church building. A Victorian Gothic façade was added in 1895. During the anti-German hysteria of World War I, the congregation changed its name to Grace Reformed Church; that congregation dissolved in 1995. (Raymond E. Hadorn, photographer.)

The Jewish residents of the city established Temple Israel in 1911, in rented quarters on Madison Avenue. The Classical Revival style synagogue above was located on East Seventh Street near Greenup Street and was ready for occupancy in 1916. Temple Israel was demolished in 1938 to make way for a new post office. The congregation constructed a new synagogue at 1040 Scott Street *c.* 1939. That building was sold to a Protestant congregation in 1973. (Courtesy American Jewish Archives.)

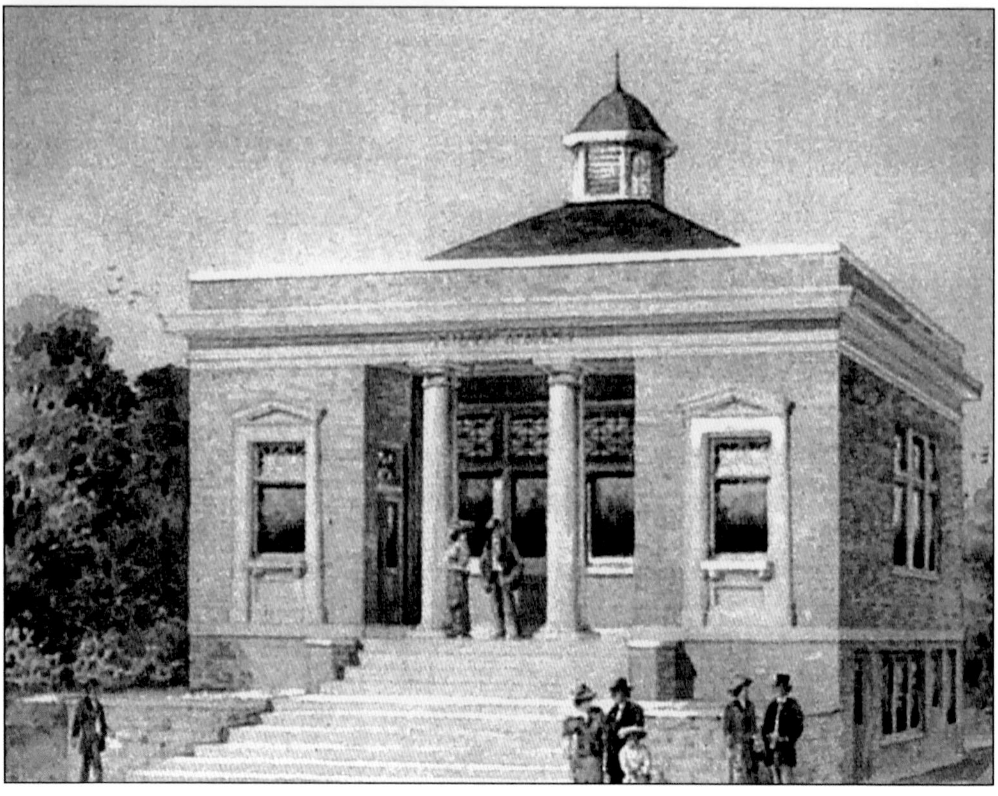

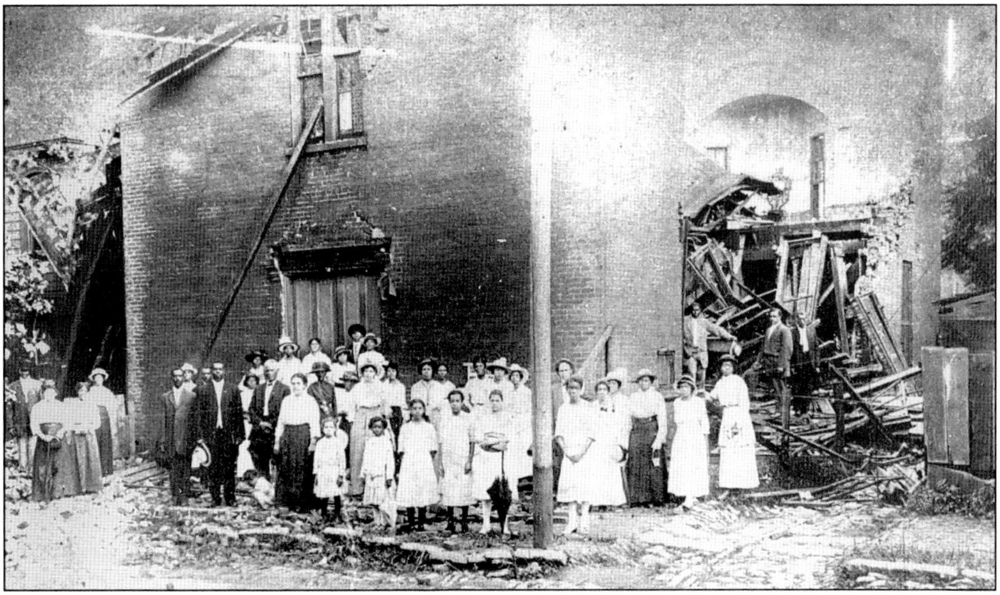

The African Americans of Covington established First Baptist Church in 1864 on Bremen Street (now Pershing). During the early days, the congregation moved many times. In 1877, a new building was constructed at the corner of Thirteenth and Spring Streets. This structure was completely destroyed by the 1915 tornado. Above, members of the congregation stand in front of their once beautiful house of worship. A new First Baptist Church was eventually constructed at 120 East Ninth Street.

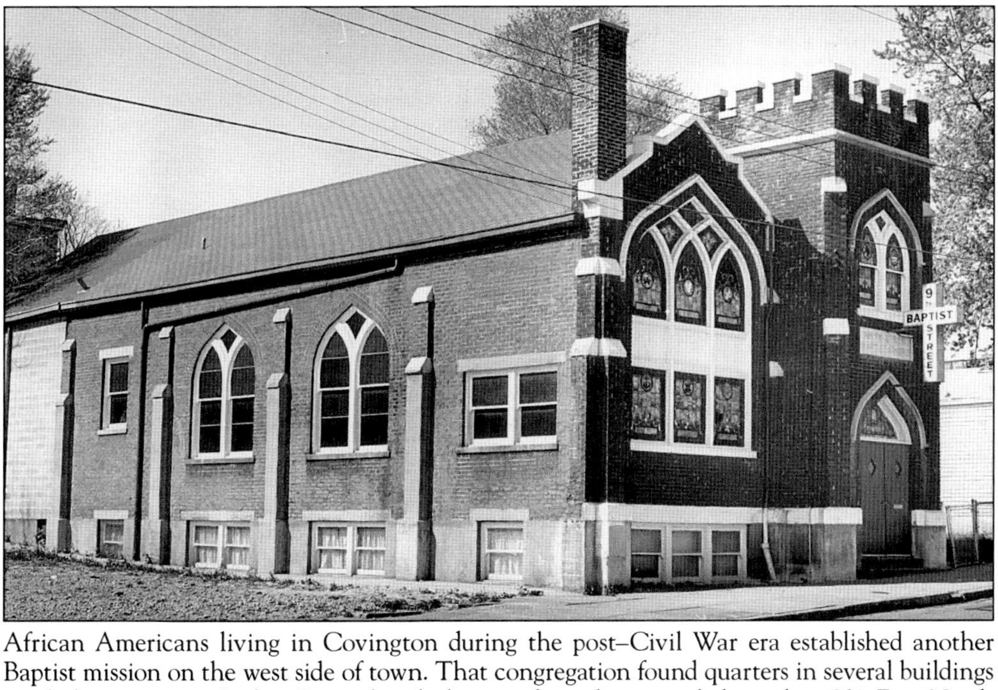

African Americans living in Covington during the post–Civil War era established another Baptist mission on the west side of town. That congregation found quarters in several buildings until their current Gothic Revival style house of worship was dedicated at 231 East Ninth Street in 1921. At that time, the congregation became officially known as the Ninth Street Baptist Church.

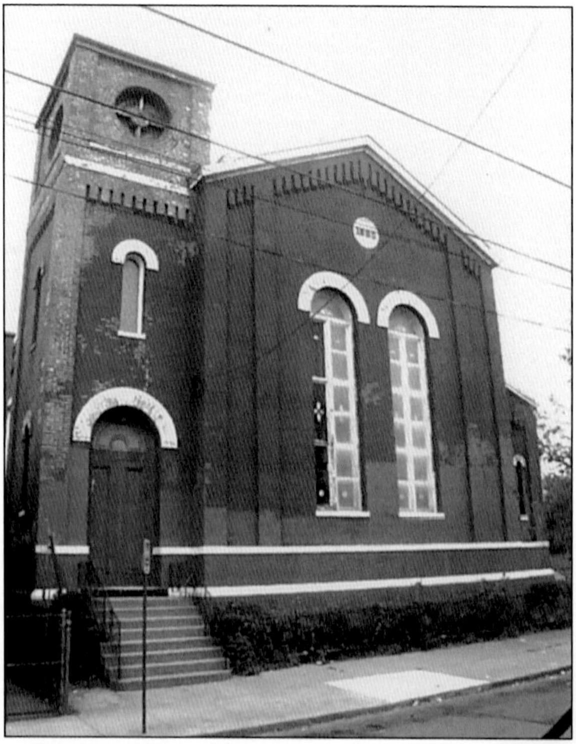

Big Ninth, as the Ninth Street United Methodist Church has been affectionately called, was built in 1860 as the Second Presbyterian Church. The building was designed by Cincinnati architect James W. McLaughlin. In 1881, with the aid of philanthropist Amos Shinkle, the church was sold to an African-American Methodist Episcopal congregation. That congregation still occupies the church today. Haven Gillespie, composer, was also a member of this church. (Historic photograph not available.)

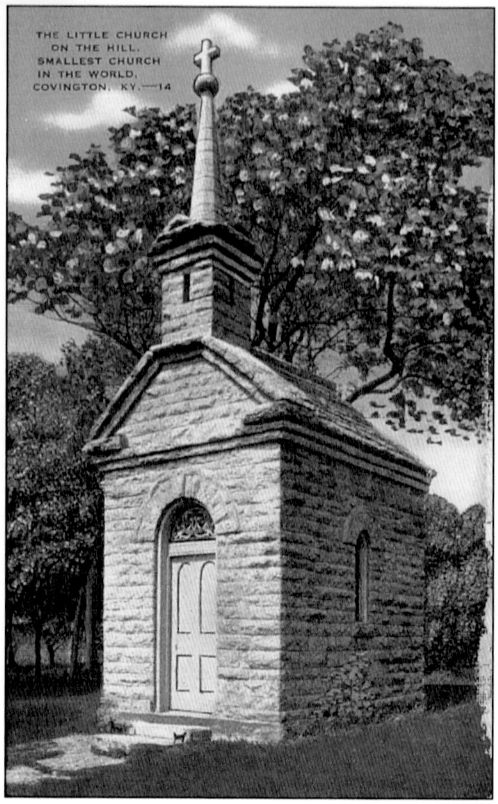

The Benedictines of St. Vincent Abbey in Pennsylvania established Monte Casino Monastery and Winery in the Peaselburg area of Covington in 1877. The Benedictine Brothers tended the vineyards and produced both altar and table wine at the location. In the early 1900s, Brother Albert Soltis constructed a small fieldstone chapel dedicated to the Sorrowful Mother. The structure was once featured in *Ripley's Believe it or Not* newspaper column as the smallest church in the world. In the 1960s, the chapel was moved to the campus of Thomas More College in nearby Crestview Hills, Kentucky.

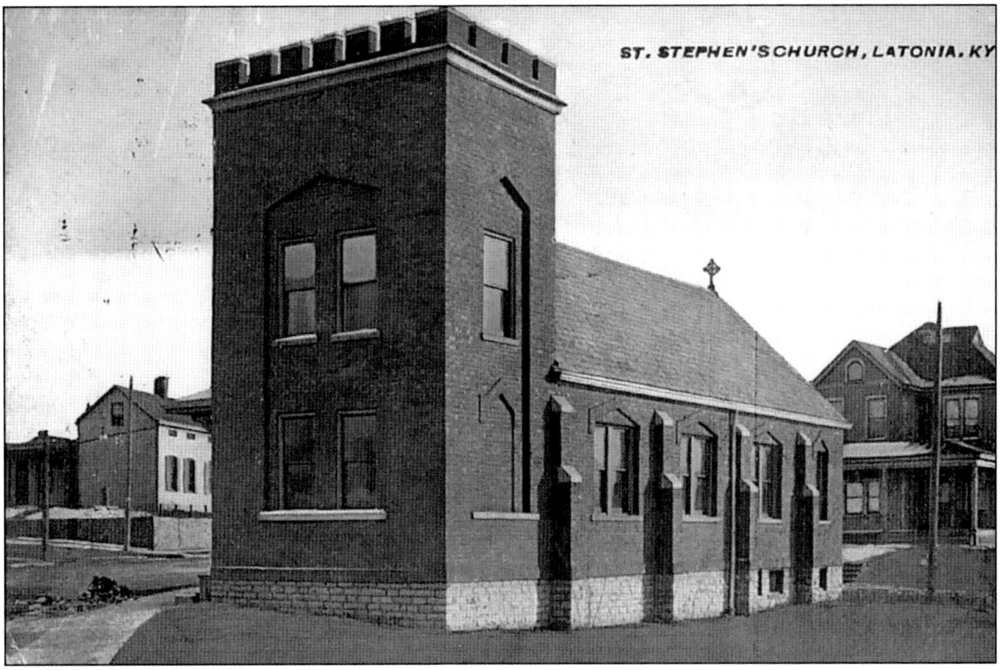

In 1910, the Episcopalians living in Latonia established St. Stephen Mission. The congregation financed the construction of this unusual building that same year. The church is located on an irregular lot at the intersection of Decoursey Pike, Thirty-ninth Street and Lincoln Avenue.

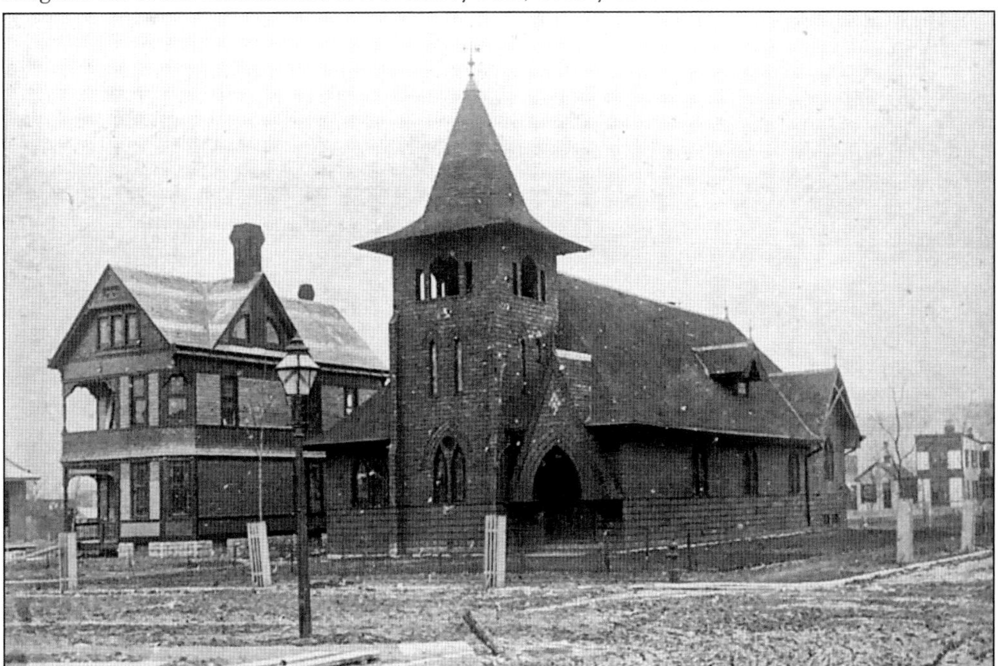

St. John Episcopal Church was established as a mission of Trinity Episcopal in 1890. The congregation built this handsome church and rectory at the northeast corner of Eighteenth and Scott Streets. It is now the St. Luke Methodist Church.

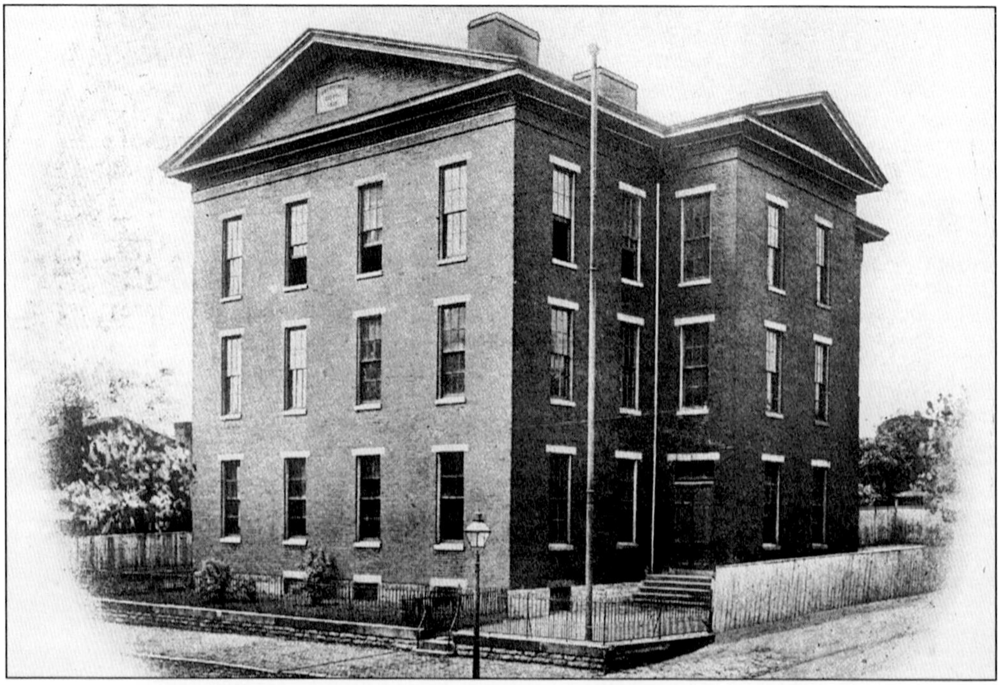

First District School was established in Covington in 1842 on the west side of Scott Street between Fifth and Sixth Streets. In 1864, the original building was replaced by a more modern brick structure (see above). This building contained 12 classrooms each with 56 desks. During the Depression era the Covington School Board replaced a number of their buildings using WPA funds. Construction on the current building began in 1937 with completion in the following year (see below). Today, the building is still used by the system and is known as the Two Rivers Middle School.

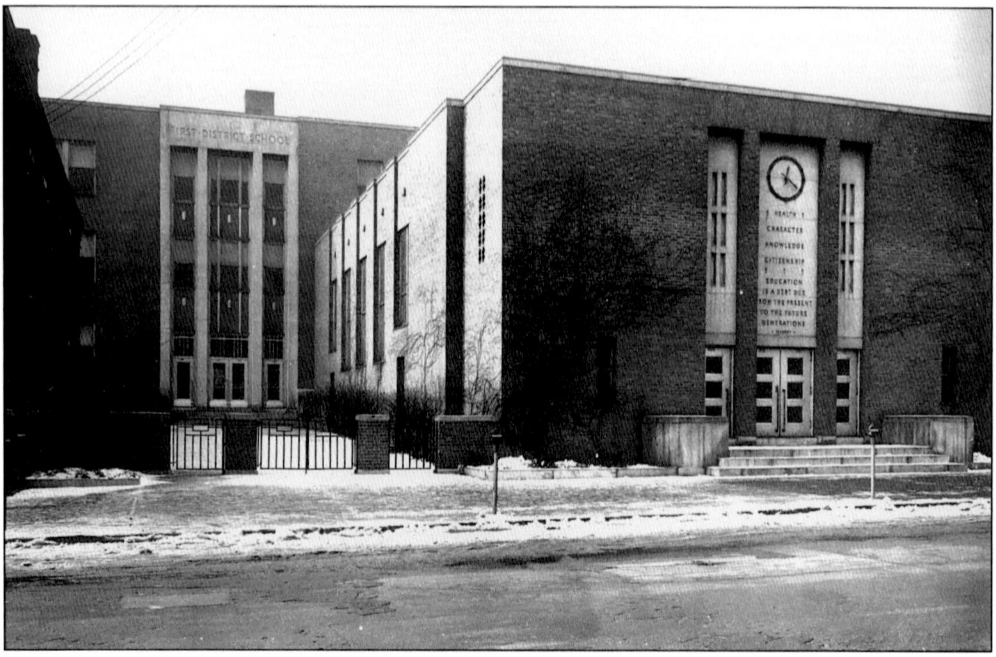

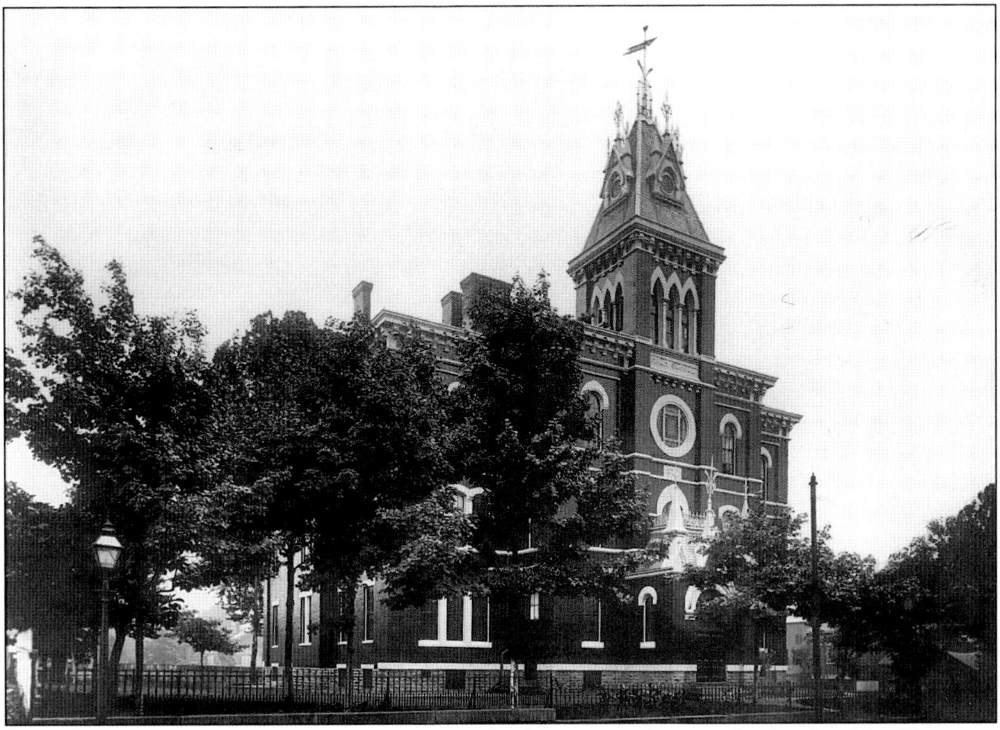

The first Covington High School was established in 1853. This new high school building was constructed at the corner of Russell and Twelfth Streets in 1872 and was turned over to the students of John G. Carlisle Junior High School when the new Covington Holmes High School was built in 1919.

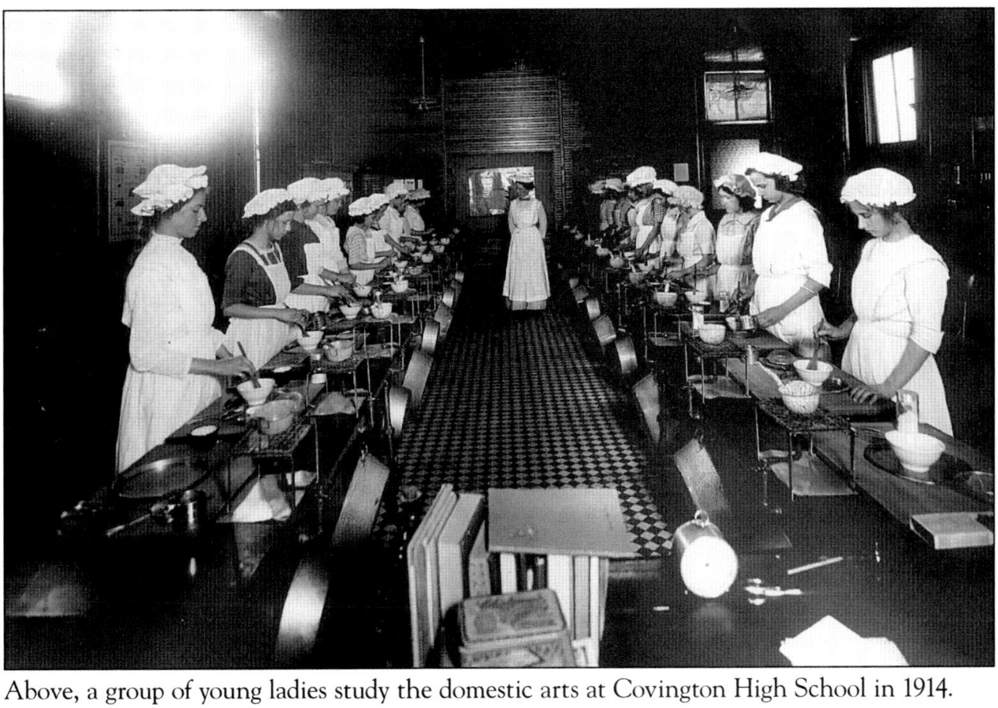

Above, a group of young ladies study the domestic arts at Covington High School in 1914.

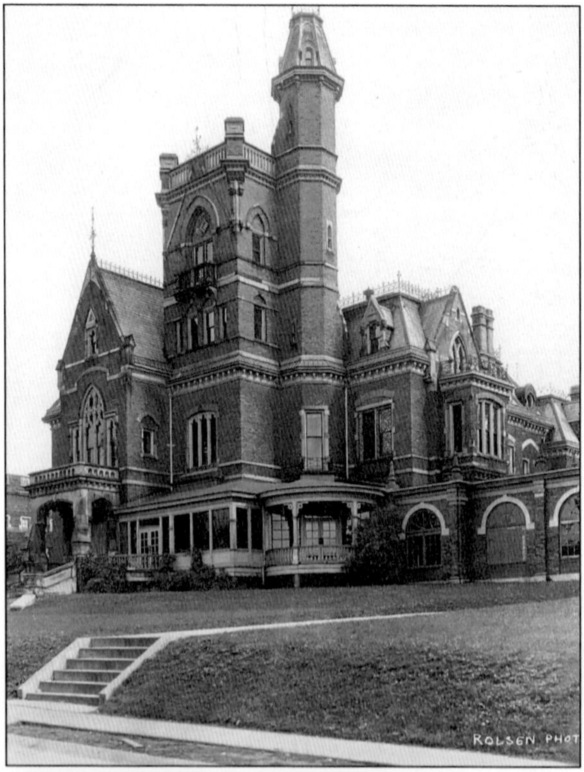

Daniel Henry Holmes, a wealthy department store owner, built his Gothic Revival home named Holmesdale in the Buena Vista neighborhood south of Covington in 1866. The 32-room palatial mansion sat on 17 manicured acres. In 1919, the Holmes family sold the property to the Covington School Board for $50,000 as a site for a new high school. The Holmes High School was then built on the property. For a number of years, the old Holmes mansion was used as a cafeteria by the school. In 1936, the house was demolished to make way for a new administration building.

This is Holmes High School as it appeared *c.* 1941.

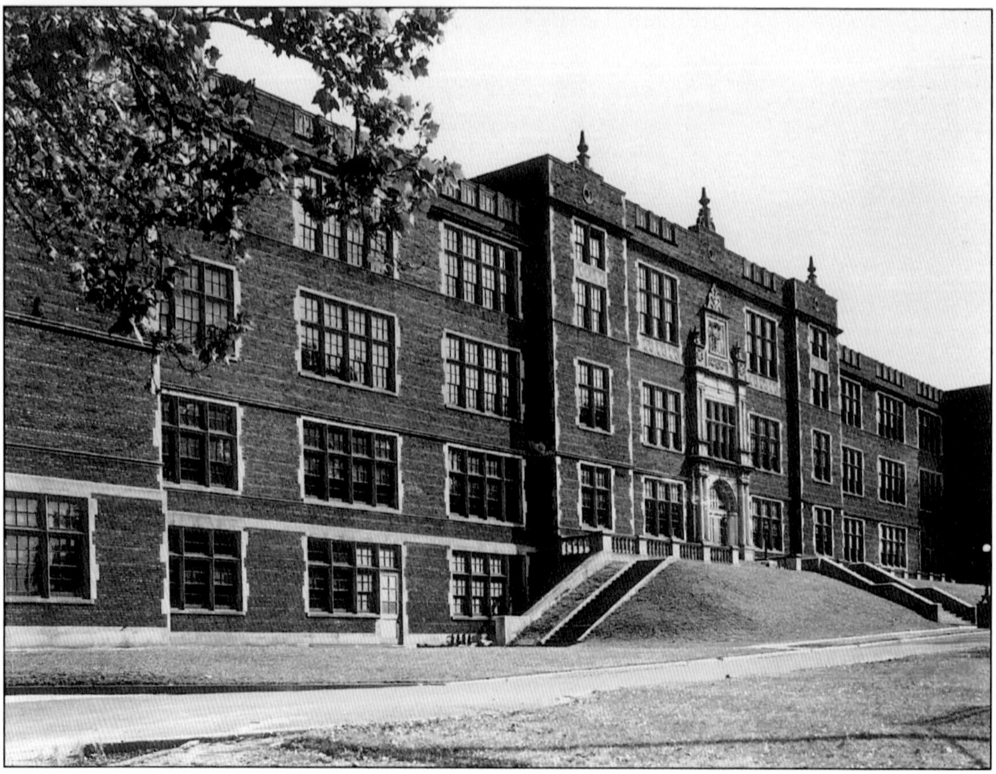

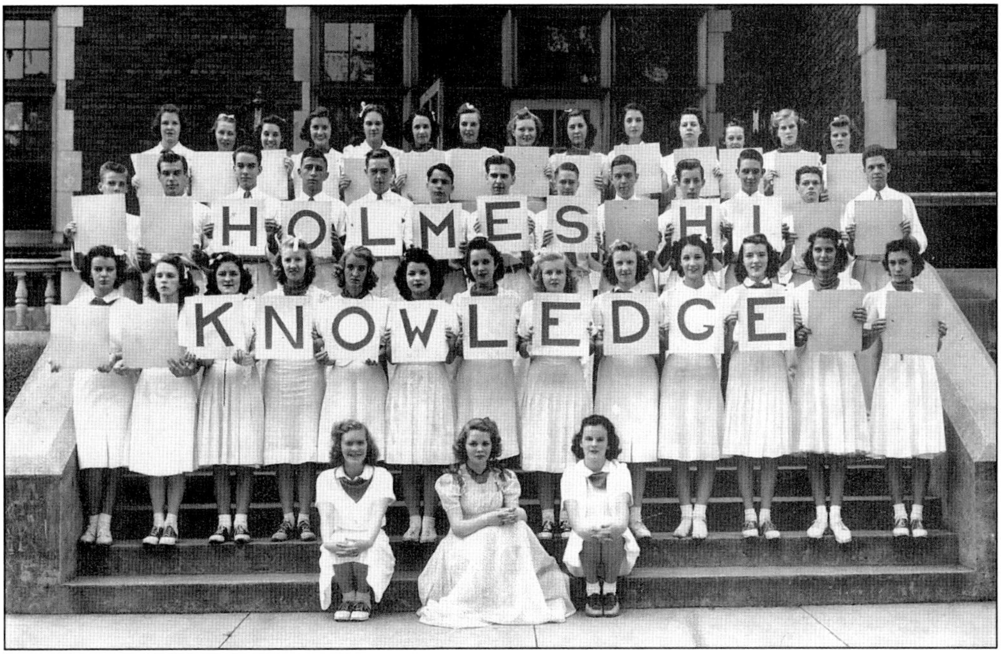

A group of Holmes High School students pose on the school's steps *c.* 1940.

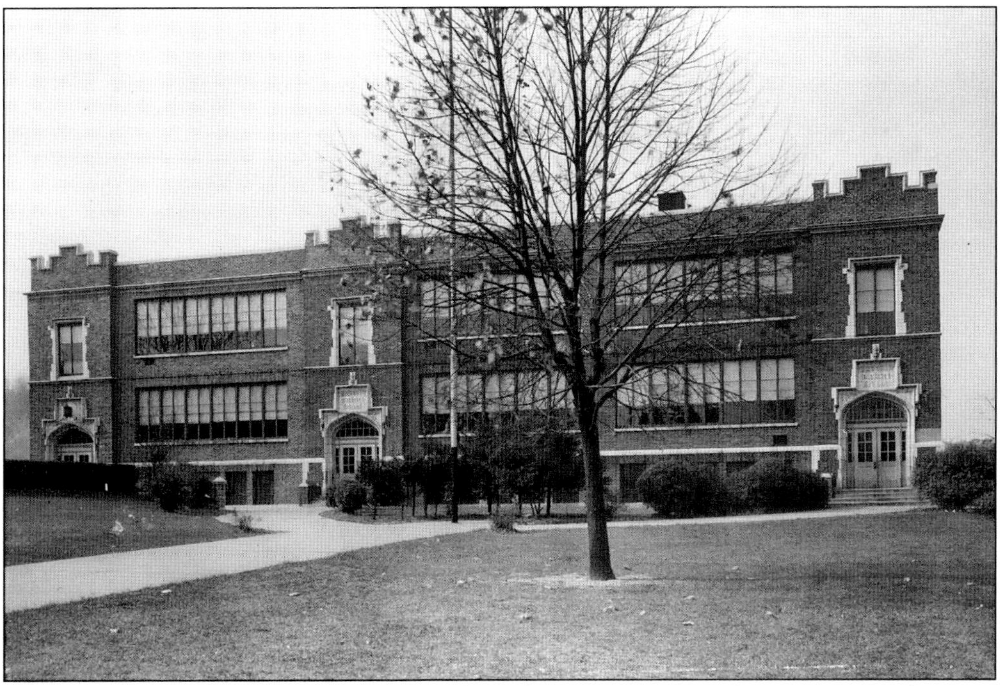

West Covington was established as an independent city in 1858. That same year, the town officials financed the construction of a public school on Main Street (present Parkway Avenue). West Covington was annexed by the City of Covington in 1916, and at that time the West Covington School was renamed Eleventh District School. A new Eleventh District School building (pictured above) was built on Parkway Avenue and dedicated in 1923. The school closed in 1979 and was converted into apartments.

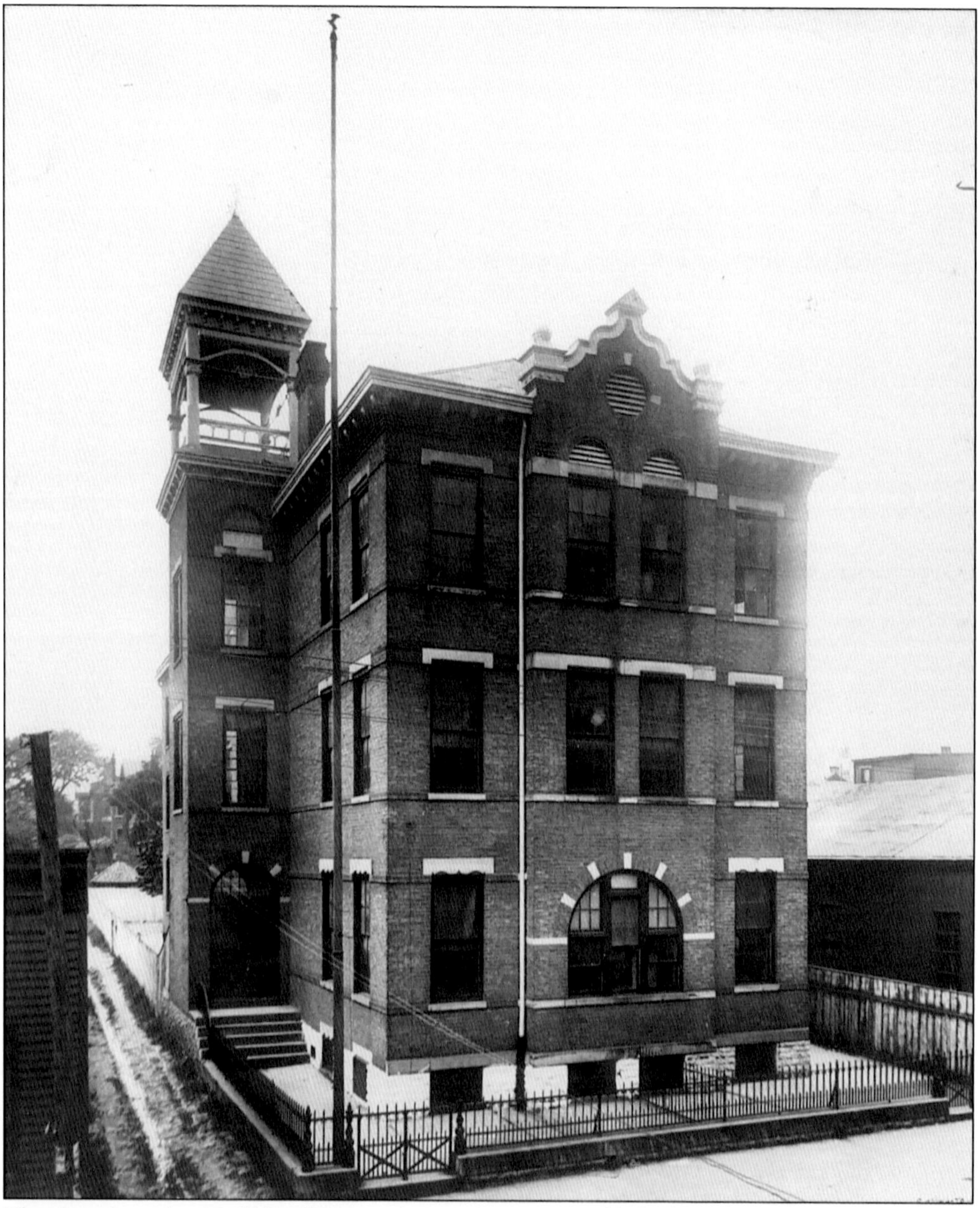

The first formal school for African Americans was established in Covington in the years following the Civil War. In 1890, the Covington School Board financed the construction of this commodious three-story brick building on Seventh Street for the African-American children of the city.

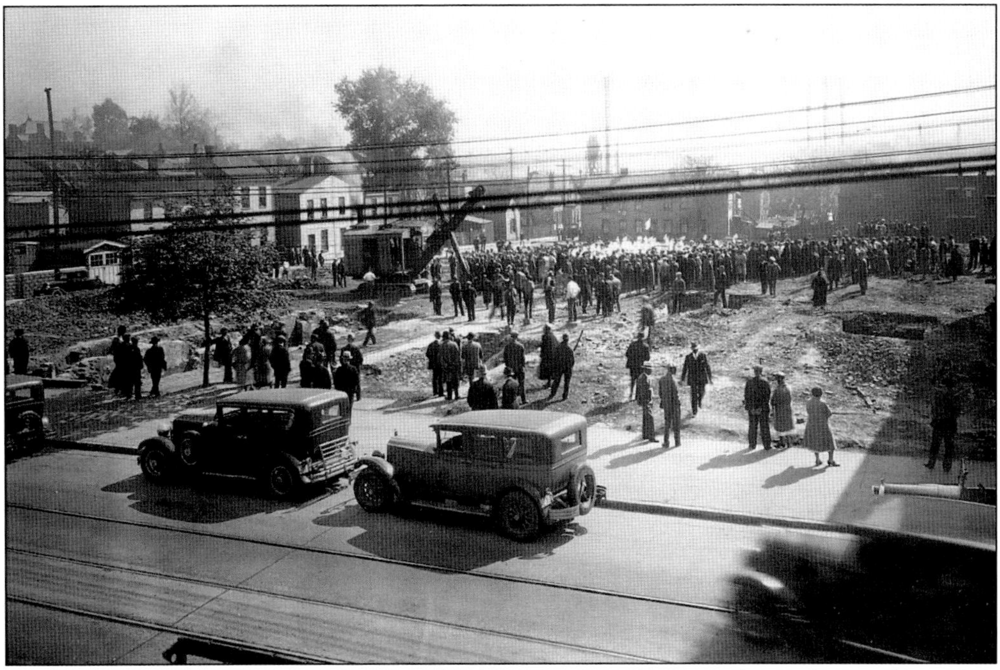

A new school for African Americans was built on Greenup Street in the city's eastside in 1932. The photo above shows the groundbreaking ceremonies for the new Lincoln Grant School. Below is an image of the completed building. Following the desegregation of the Covington schools, the old Lincoln Grant building became the home of the Northern Kentucky Community Center.

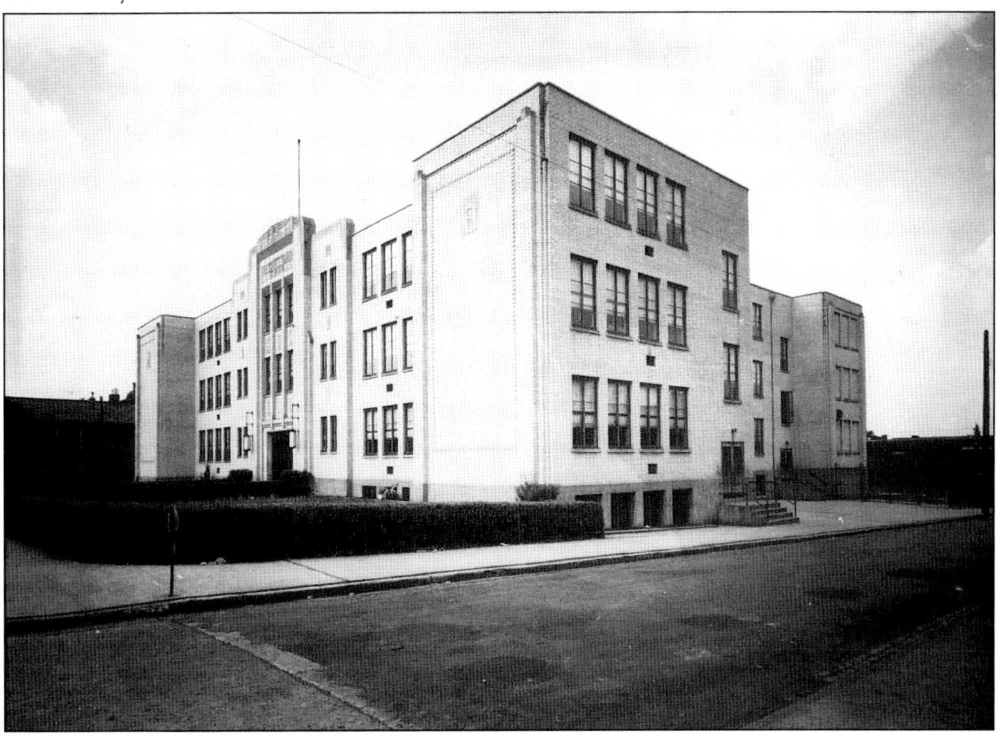

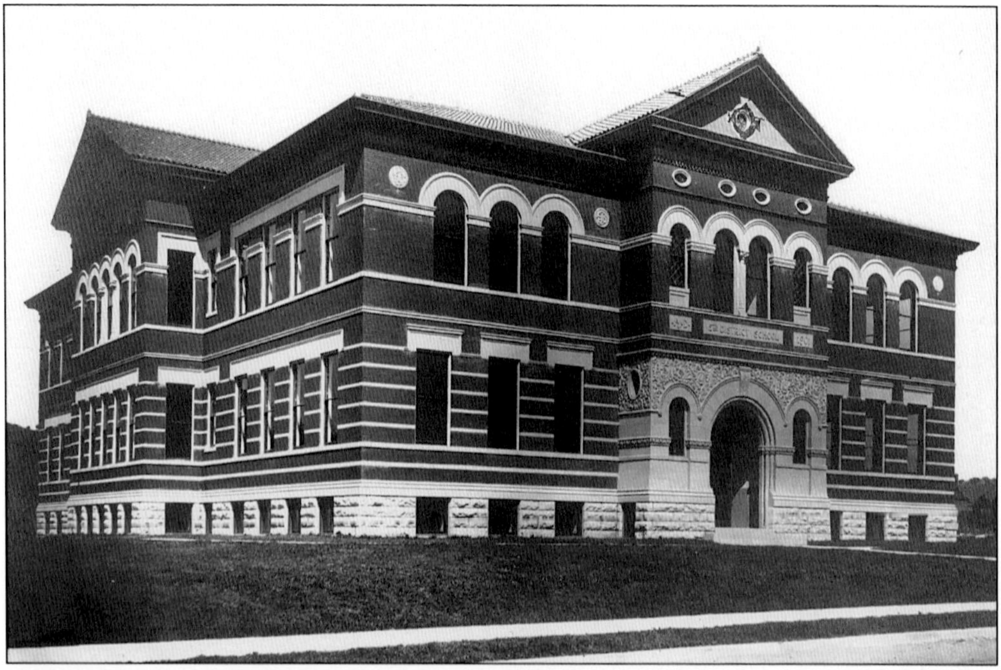

The new handsome Fifth District School, completed in 1902, was located at the corner of West Eighteenth and Holman Streets. At the time of construction, local newspapers hailed its modern conveniences, including cloakrooms, indoor restroom facilities, and water fountains.

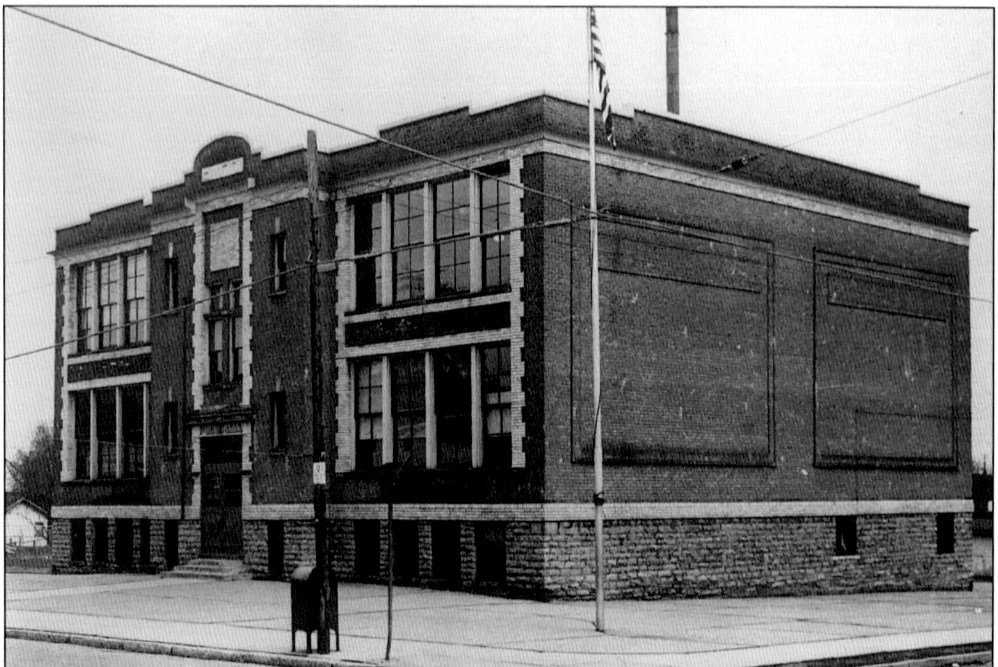

The Covington School Board financed the construction of what was then Seventh District School in 1910. Located at Twenty-third and Howell Streets, the building served the Peaselburg neighborhood.

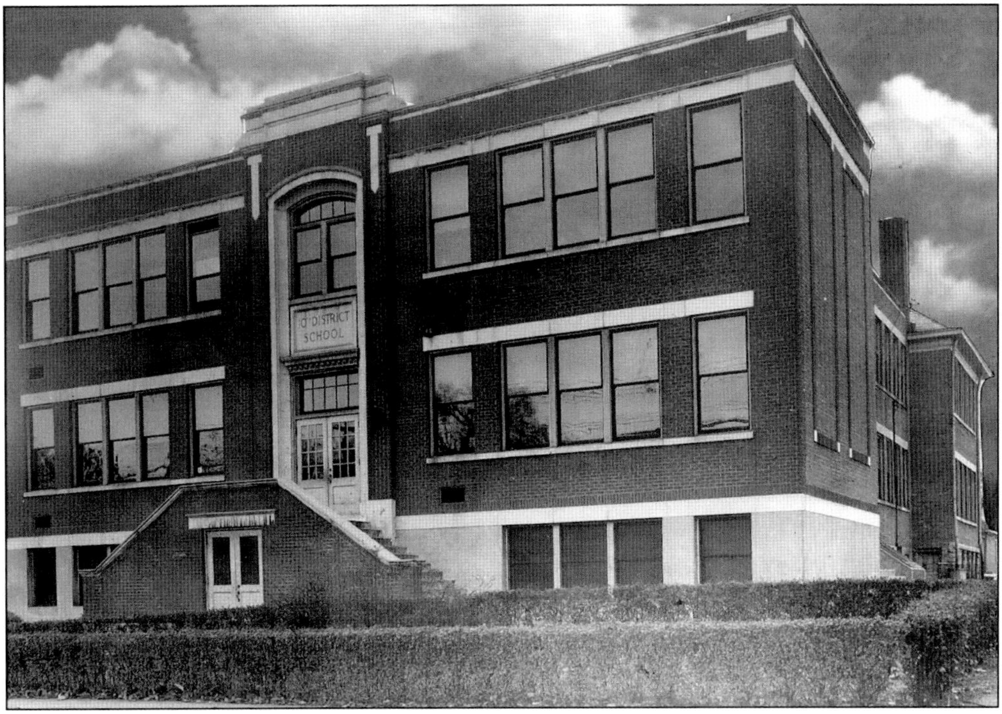

Three public schools served the children of the former City of Latonia. Among these was the Clifford Avenue School. Following the annexation of Latonia by Covington in 1909, the Clifford Avenue school was renamed Tenth District School. This photograph shows the school in 1940.

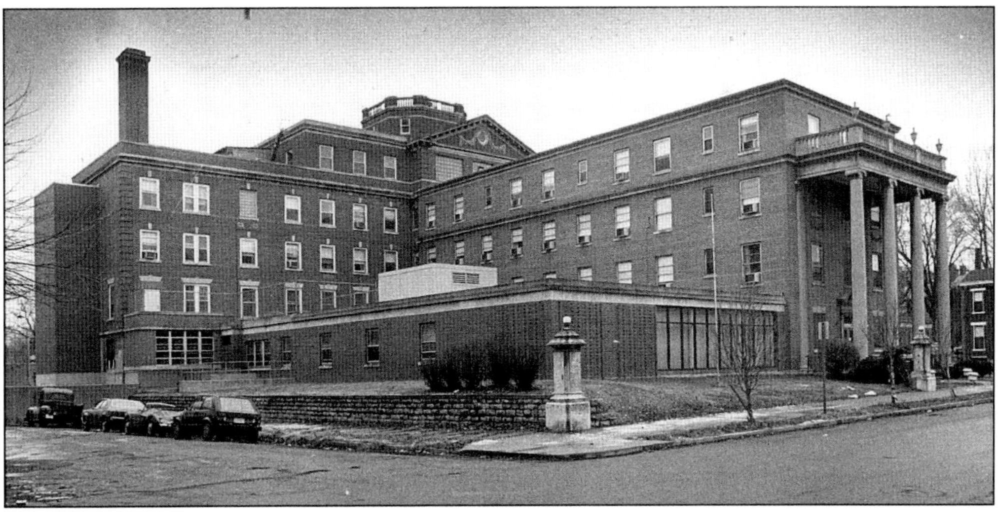

The Salvation Army established Booth Memorial Hospital in 1914 in the old Shinkle Mansion at 323 East Second Street. During the 1920s, the mansion was demolished and replaced with a new modern facility. During the Great Depression, the hospital closed its doors, but reopened in 1937 and faithfully served the people of Covington until 1979. At that time, a new Booth Memorial Hospital was established in Boone County. The former Covington facility has since been converted into a condominium complex called Governor's Point. (Terry Duennes, photographer.)

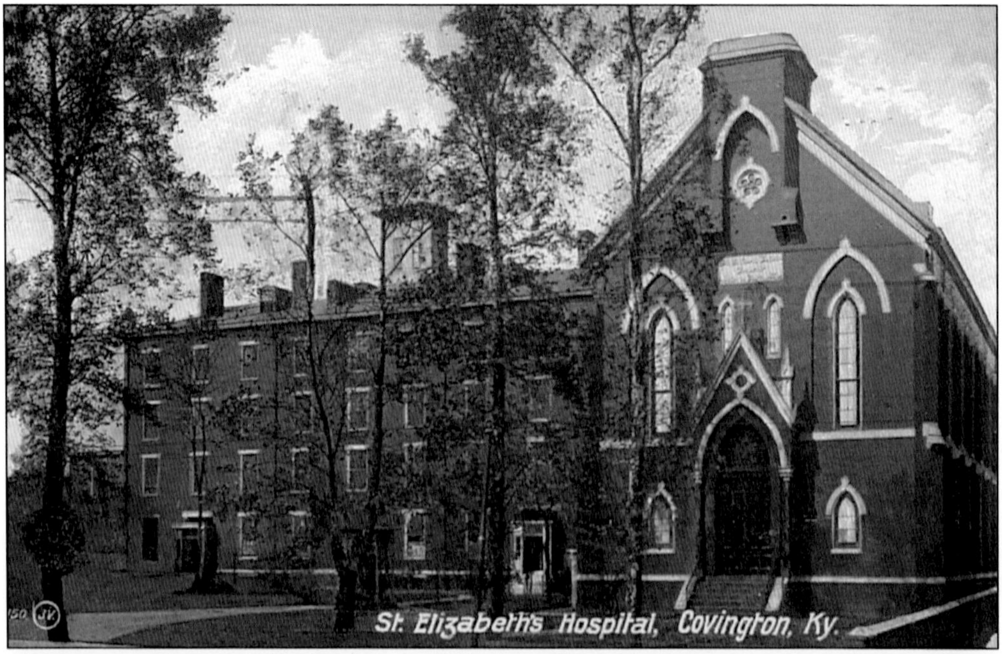

The Sisters of the Poor of St. Francis established St. Elizabeth Hospital in Covington in 1861 in an old grocery store on East Seventh Street. The hospital grew quickly, and in 1867, the Sisters purchased part of the former Western Baptist Theological Institute on West Eleventh Street and remodeled the building for hospital purposes. A Gothic Revival Chapel was constructed on the eastside of the building in 1871. The new St. Elizabeth Hospital on East Twentieth Street, shown below, was dedicated in 1914.

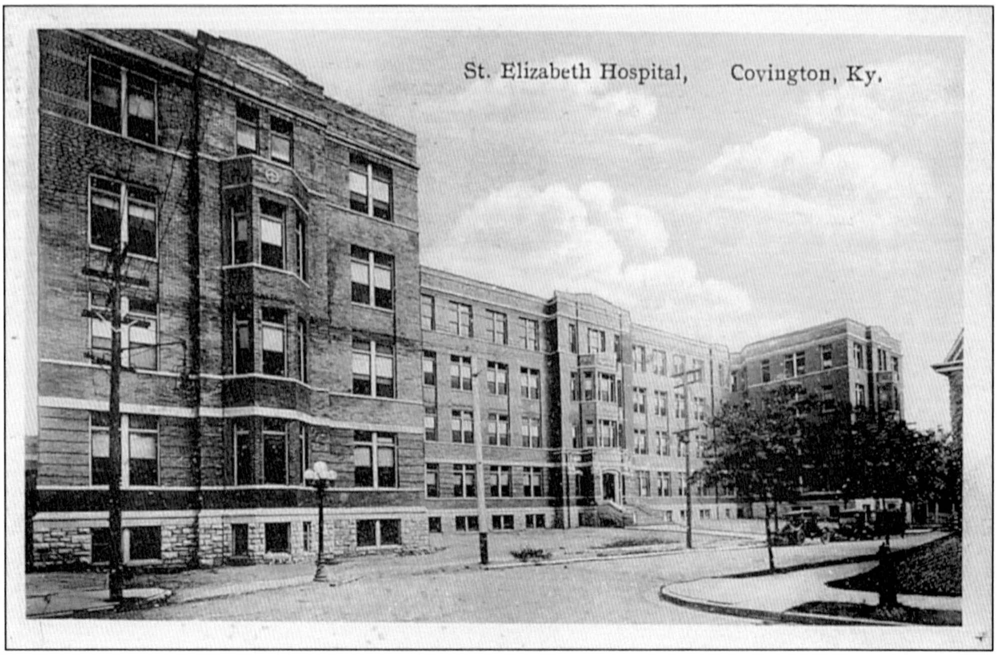

Nine

COVINGTON READS

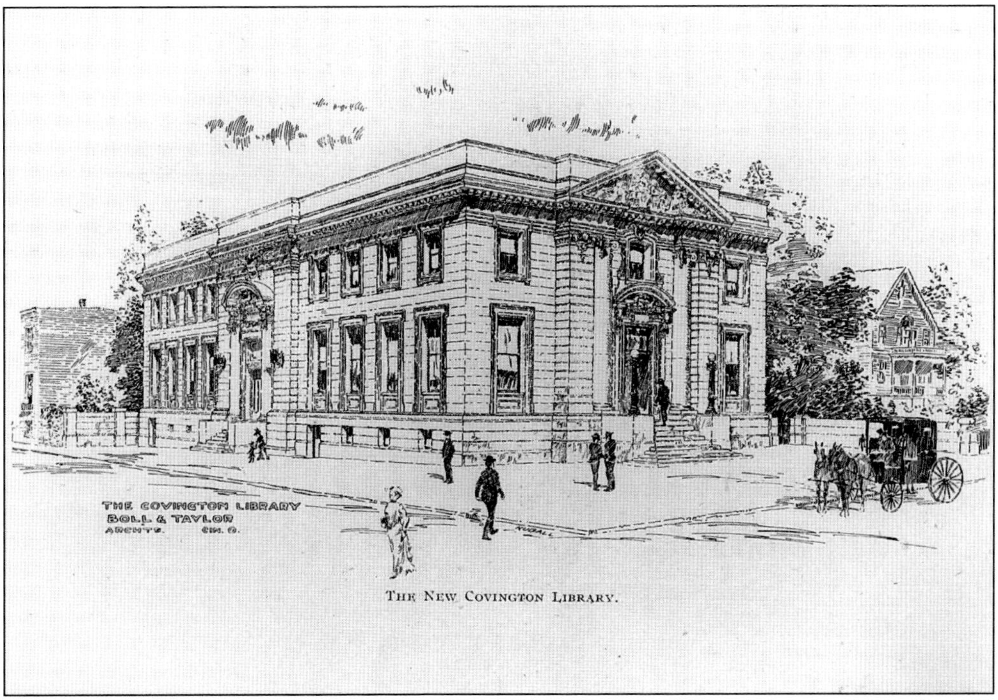

This architect's rendering of Covington's first public library building shows the design by Boll and Taylor Architects of Cincinnati, Ohio. The structure was designed in the Neo-Classical style of the French Renaissance Revival. The library was funded with money from Andrew Carnegie, the steel magnate and philanthropist who personally gave away some $40 million to cities for construction of libraries between 1886 and 1911; $40,000 was donated to Covington and the new Covington Library opened in 1904.

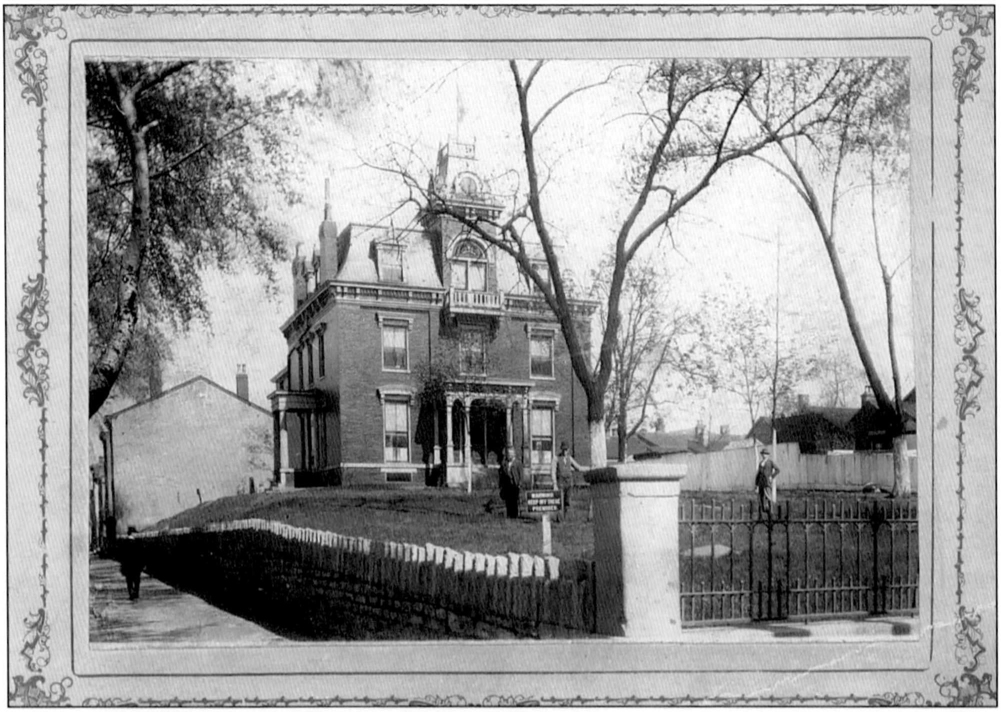

The Nimrod H. Sinclair house was located on the southeast corner of Scott and East Robbins Streets, *c.* 1845 (photo *c.* 1890). Sinclair was a wholesale grocer who lived here until his death in 1881. After that it was the home of Llewellyn N. Crigler, of Crigler and Crigler Distillers. Crigler remained there until he sold the house to the Covington School Board in *c.* 1898. It was used as the Fifth District School, or the "New School," until *c.* 1902 when it was demolished for the construction of the new Covington Library.

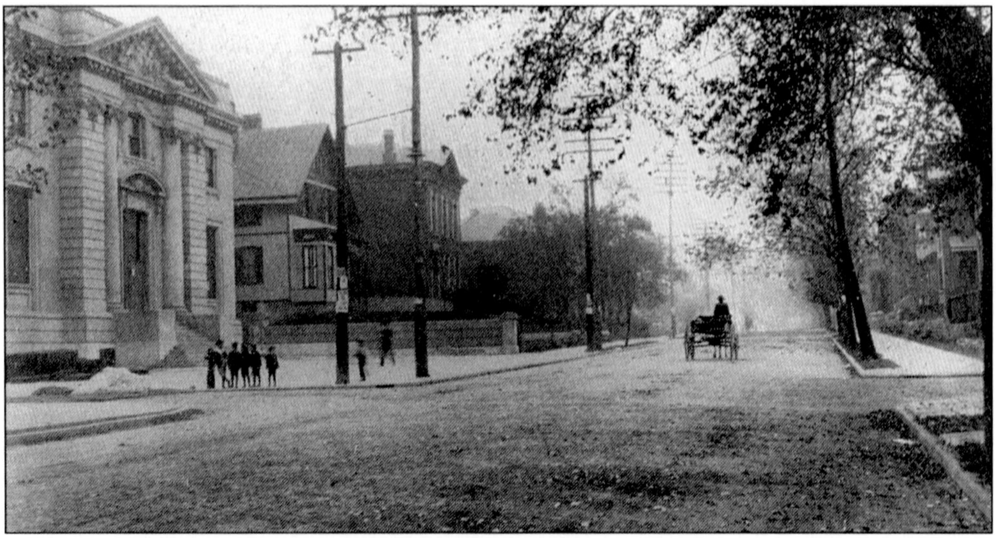

This photograph shows the completed Covington Library, *c.* 1905. The Covington Library was one of the first libraries in the segregated South to provide racially-integrated service in 1901. The Covington Library remained in this building until 1974. It has since become the Carnegie Arts Center.

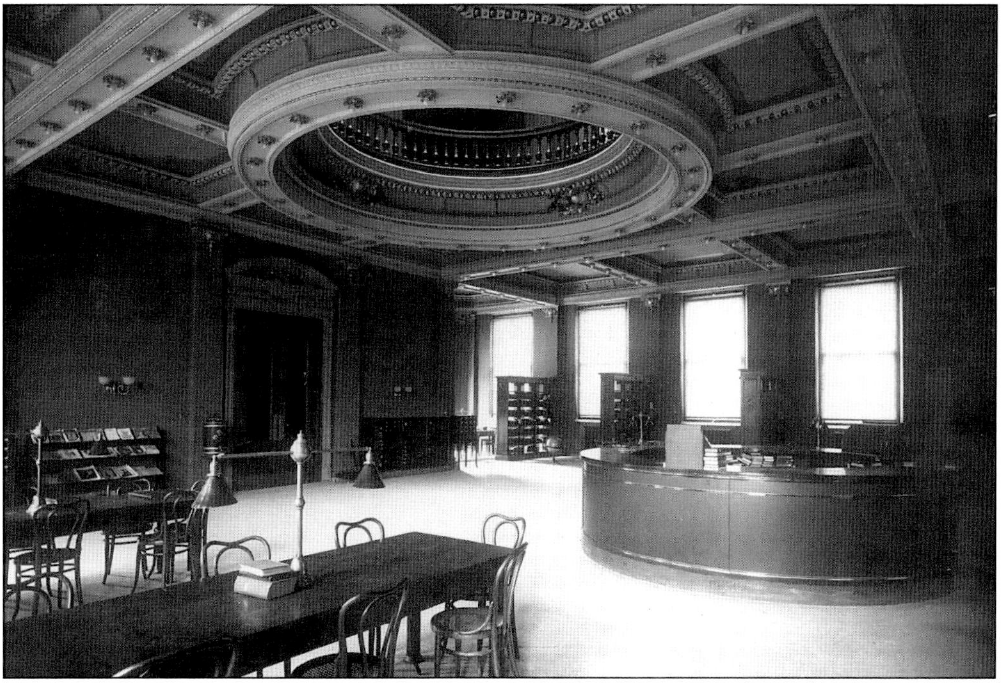

This is Covington Carnegie Library's Main Reading Room, c. 1904. Note the exquisitely detailed coffered ceiling with miniature rosettes. Several of the library tables and shelves are still in use today in the local history section of the Mary Ann Mongan Library on Scott Boulevard.

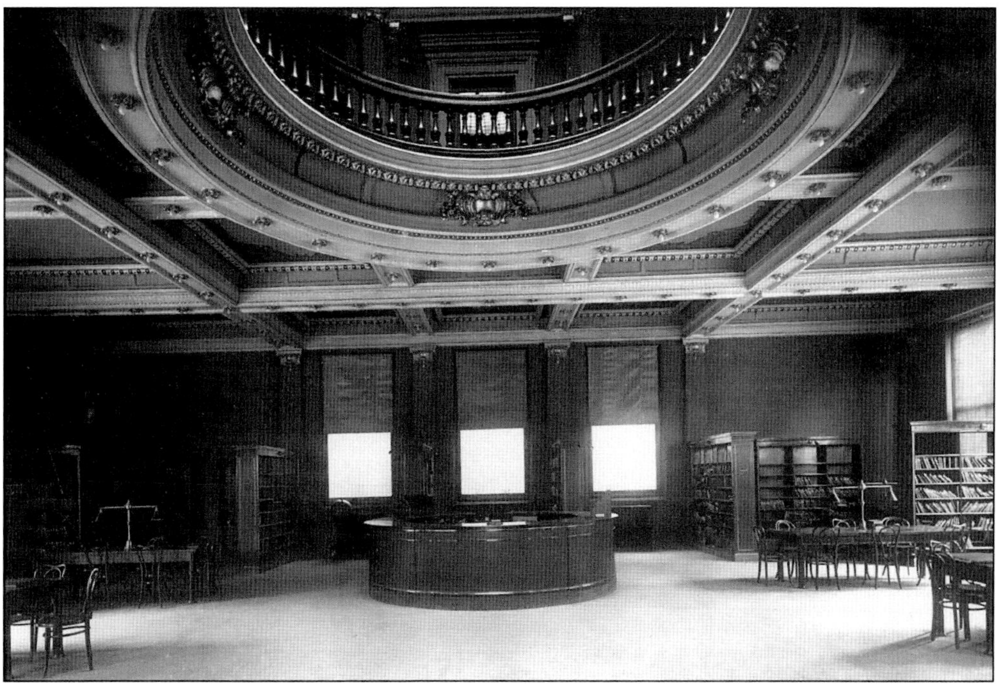

Here is another view of the Covington Carnegie Library's Main Reading Room. The mezzanine railing is visible in this c. 1904 photo.

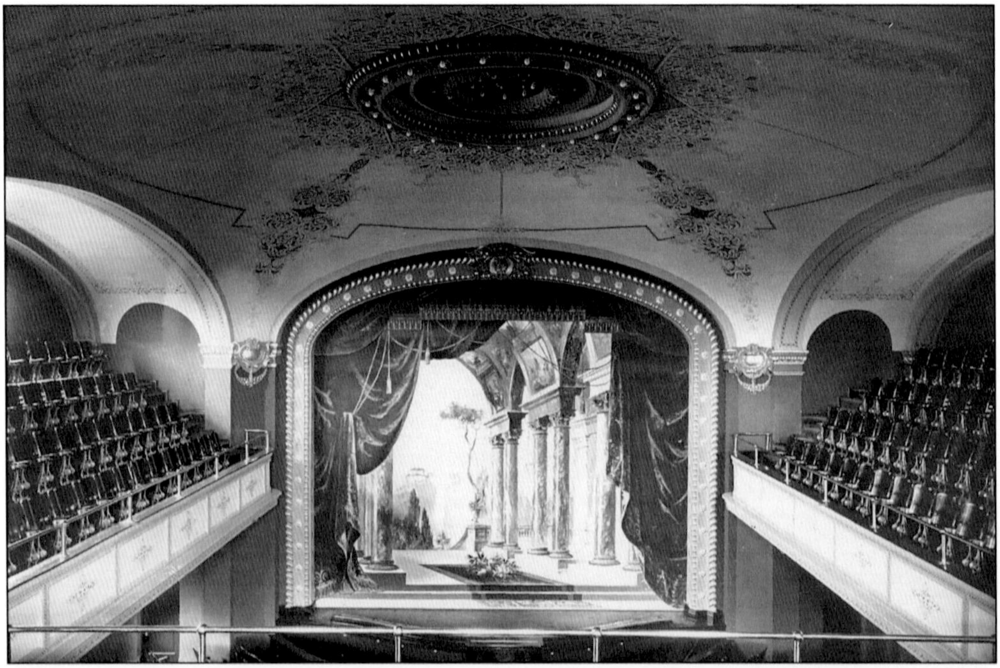

This is a view of the Carnegie Auditorium's stage, as seen from the balcony, *c.* 1910. Covington's Carnegie Library was one of only a handful in the country built with an attached auditorium/theater. The auditorium was remodeled shortly thereafter and a new proscenium was added. During the 1930s, as a WPA project, noted artist Harlan Hubbard painted a mural on the proscenium, which can still be seen today.

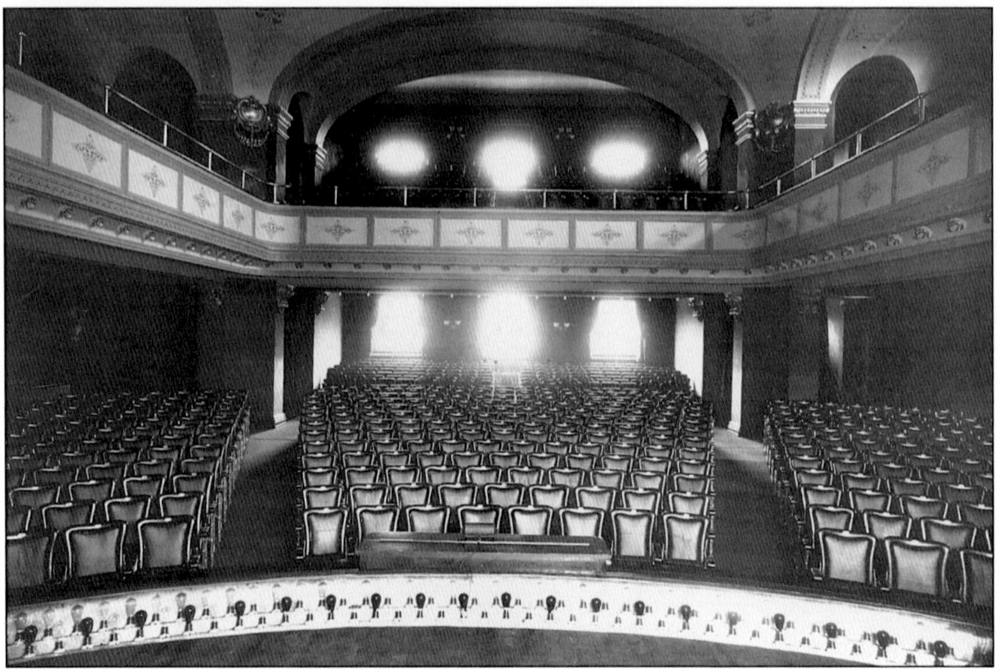

This is a view of the Carnegie Auditorium, as seen from the stage, *c.* 1904. Note the decorative detailing on the balcony and in the frieze below the balcony and the leather seats.

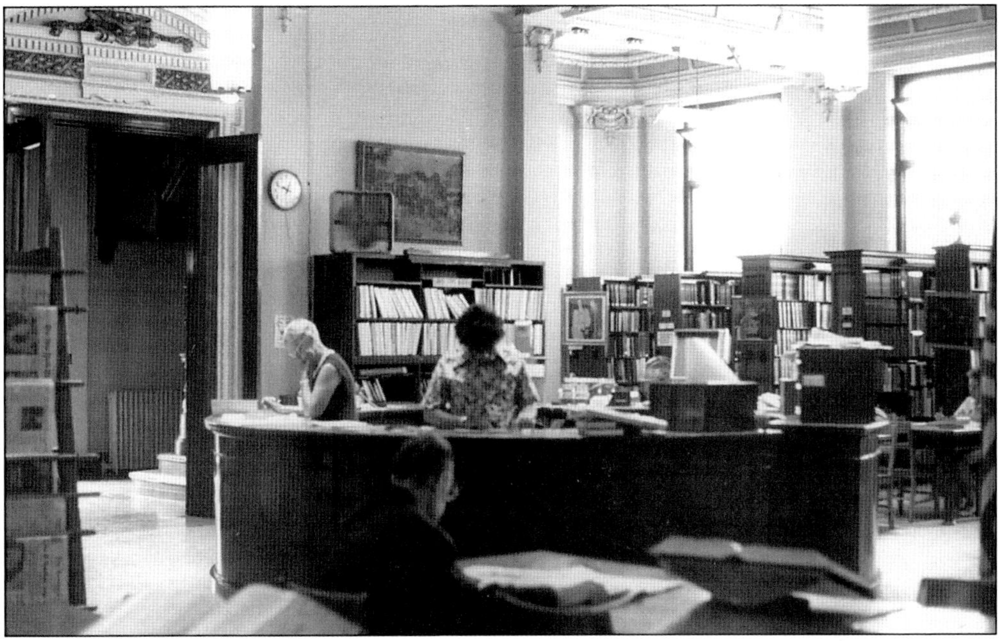

Librarians are at work at the Covington Public Library in 1973. The Carnegie Library building closed the next year and the public library moved to its new location at 502 Scott Boulevard.

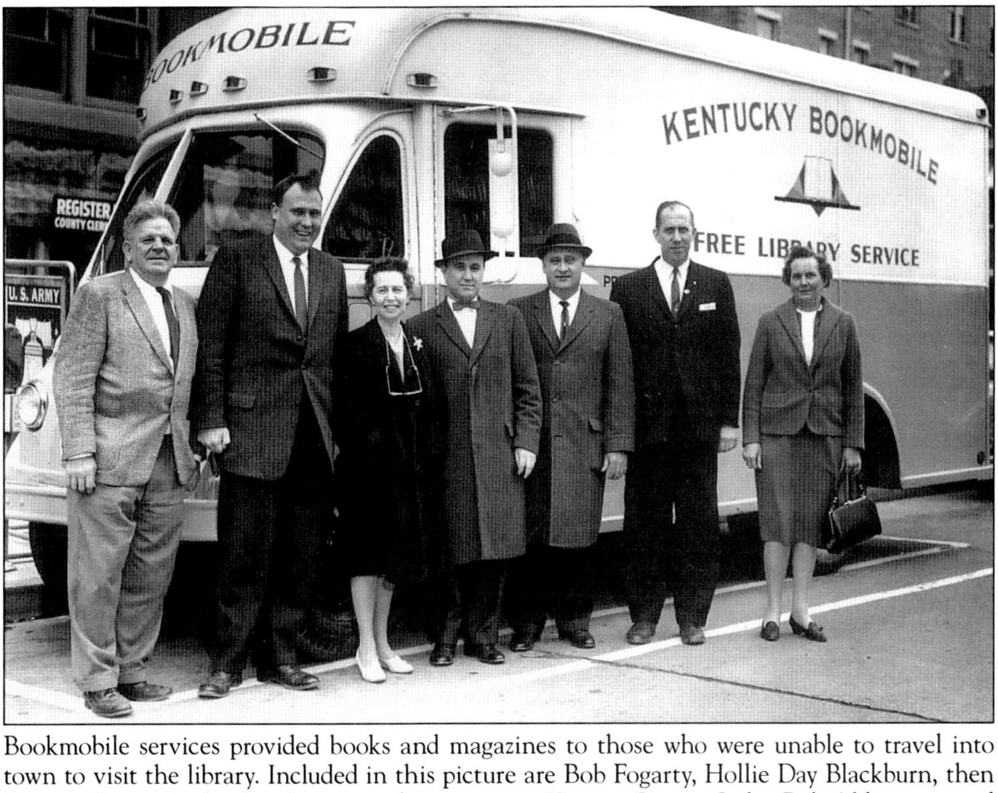

Bookmobile services provided books and magazines to those who were unable to travel into town to visit the library. Included in this picture are Bob Fogarty, Hollie Day Blackburn, then Kenton County Judge Jim Dressman, his successor, Kenton County Judge Bob Aldemeyer, and Miss Bender, the Bookmobile driver, *c.* 1964. (Russell Manuel, photographer.)

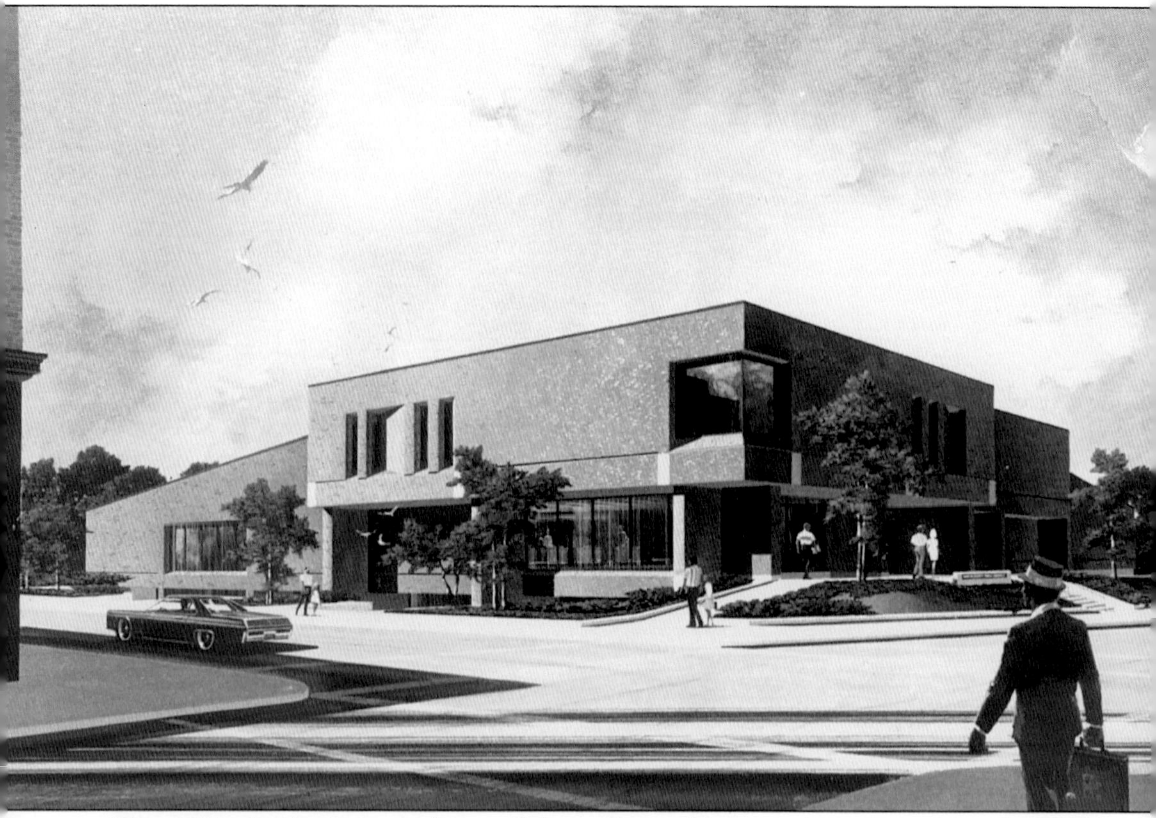

This 1974 sketch shows architect Robert Ehmet Hayes and Associates' rendering of the new library at 502 Scott Boulevard. In 1967 the library began a campaign to form a county-wide library district. The district was approved that same year, allowing for the financing of new library buildings throughout the county. Construction of the new Kenton County Public Library in Covington began in 1971 and it opened in 1974. The current library was named in honor of Mary Ann Mongan, a longtime library director, in 1999. There are two branches of the Kenton County library system, located in Erlanger and Independence. The Kenton County Public Library has consistently been rated as one of the best in the Commonwealth of Kentucky.